WITHDRAWN

Cultures of Shame

Also by David Nash

HISTORIES OF CRIME: Britain 1600–2000 (*Co-authored with Anne-Marie Kilday*)
BLASPHEMY IN THE CHRISTIAN WORLD
BLASPHEMY IN MODERN BRITAIN 1789–PRESENT

Also by Anne-Marie Kilday

WOMEN AND VIOLENT CRIME IN ENLIGHTENMENT SCOTLAND

Cultures of Shame

Exploring Crime and Morality in Britain 1600–1900

David Nash
Professor of History, Department of History, Oxford Brookes University

Anne-Marie Kilday
Assistant Dean (Teaching and Learning) and Principal Lecturer in History, Oxford Brookes University

First published 2010 by
PALGRAVE MACMILLAN

Palgrave Macmillan in the UK is an imprint of Macmillan Publishers Limited, registered in England, company number 785998, of Houndmills, Basingstoke, Hampshire RG21 6XS.

Palgrave Macmillan in the US is a division of St Martin's Press LLC, 175 Fifth Avenue, New York, NY 10010.

Palgrave Macmillan is the global academic imprint of the above companies and has companies and representatives throughout the world.

Palgrave® and Macmillan® are registered trademarks in the United States, the United Kingdom, Europe and other countries

ISBN 978-0-230-52570-2 hardback

This book is printed on paper suitable for recycling and made from fully managed and sustained forest sources. Logging, pulping and manufacturing processes are expected to conform to the environmental regulations of the country of origin.

A catalogue record for this book is available from the British Library.

Library of Congress Cataloging-in-Publication Data
    Nash, David (David S.)
    Cultures of shame : exploring crime and morality in Britain 1600–1900 / David Nash and Anne-Marie Kilday.
       p. cm.
    ISBN 978-0-230-52570-2 (hardback)
      1. Great Britain–Moral conditions–History. 2. Shame–Great Britain–History. 3. Punishment–Great Britain–History. 4. Conduct of life–History. I. Kilday, Anne-Marie. II. Title.
    HN400.M6N37 2010
    302.5′4–dc22   2010027544

10   9   8   7   6   5   4   3   2   1
19   18   17   16   15   14   13   12   11   10

Printed and bound in Great Britain by
CPI Antony Rowe, Chippenham and Eastbourne

To our Parents

Cecil and Katherine
John and Anne

Contents

List of Illustrations

Acknowledgements

The authors would like to thank the numerous people who have helped in the development and creation of this book. Firstly, we would like to express our thanks to staff at the National Archives, the National Archives of Scotland, the National Library of Scotland, the National Library of Wales, the Jersey Archive, the British Library, the National Newspaper Library (Colindale) and the Bodleian Library, Oxford for their patience and helpful advice. We would also like to thank audiences in Oxford, Exeter, Bath, Warwick, Lisbon, Sydney and St Petersburg. These have heard earlier unpolished versions of the stories and analyses contained in this book and cheerfully contributed insights that have helped with our understanding of them.

We would also like to thank those involved at Palgrave publishing in the production of this book from embryonic series of ideas to published work. Thanks go to our commissioning editor Michael Strang and to our editorial contact Ruth Ireland. We would also like to thank our anonymous reviewers for their insightful, positive and important contributions.

Finally we would also like to thank family, friends, and colleagues for their advice and support for both of us during the writing of this book.

1
The History and Theory of Shame – Then and Now

> Shame is particularly challenging to study since it is situated betwixt and between – on the border between the personal and the social. Yet there is no rigid boundary between these two aspects of shame.[1]

> Shame is the primary social emotion.... If this line of thought is correct, shame would be the most frequent and possibly the most important of emotions, even though it is usually invisible.[2]

> Everywhere man blushes and conceals. Human life, under all conditions, seems to move within the frame of a fundamental pattern in which an attitude called shame may have a hidden place.[3]

When Joseph Arch sat down to write his autobiography in 1898, he clearly contemplated at great length the formative experiences that led him on his course from 'plough-tail to parliament' – his quest to become the first working-class M.P. A fundamentally important episode from his childhood stood out for him, and his very public examination of this should provide important insights for the historian of eighteenth and nineteenth century social relations and behaviour. Arch recalled how the rector's wife in his local village decreed that the labourers should sit separately from their wives during divine service in the local church. These women were also made to curtsey histrionically, and in Arch's words:

> You may be pretty certain that many of these women did not relish the curtsey-scraping and other humiliations they had to

put up with, but they were afraid to speak out. They had their families to think of, children to feed and clothe somehow.[4]

Arch manages to conjure up a degree of respect for these women since their compliance was born of the need to provide for their families and to 'store up' goodwill with the rector's wife, should they need to call upon her for alms. This burden could also be carried with resignation because it was in some sense communal, since the women and their husbands had to endure this ritual of subservience *en masse* and individuals were not singled out for especially harsh treatment. Yet something happened when Joseph Arch was seven years old which focussed the idea of shame for him, since it was aimed at a target considerably too close to home. It was customary for the young of the parish to be excluded from the church when the service reached the celebration of the Eucharist. Arch already felt this was concealing some dark secret, since one day he ventured to look through the keyhole of the church door to observe what transpired at the chancel. The illicit nature of his observation must have been a crucial element in Arch's reaction to an apparently dreadful shame concealed. The sight that greeted Arch 'caused a wound which has never been healed'. The sacrament was being dispensed to the community in strictly hierarchical order. Landowners and gentry went first, followed by a highly regulated and choreographed pecking order amongst the middling sort. Last, and most definitely least, were the humble agricultural labourers of the area of which Joseph Arch's father was one. Upon seeing this, Arch declared that 'the iron entered straight into my poor little heart and remained fast embedded there.'[5] Arch makes it clear that this was a considerable slight that he could not bear alone and felt compelled to communicate this to his mother. He, however, proceeds to analyse why his father continued to bear such behaviour speculating that his father had in some sense had been 'brought up to it'.

This particular incident suggests strongly to historians why shame is fundamentally important and worthy of study. It also suggests that the spectre of shame could emerge on a regular basis, and may even have been a comparatively routine occurrence in many areas of eighteenth and nineteenth century society. Whilst the behaviour of Arch's father demonstrates the power of shame to coerce and control at a rudimentary level, Joseph Arch and his mother clearly internalised their feelings about this ongoing slight. For them, its power never diminished over many long years in both of their minds, turning them eventually into religious dissenters. Throughout this story, shame and its machinery told individuals and groups their social place and indeed stigmatised it. Yet in some instances, this act had unforeseen consequences. Its reappearance decades later as a stark memory in Joseph Arch's autobiography, suggests that it had a singular effect upon Arch's self image, as well as a profound impact upon his sense of ambition. Arch felt he had risen through society in response to the slight he had felt many years ago as a child. It is in places like this that the historian readily, and keenly, feels the enduring power of shame as a social emotion. Moreover we also learn the potential for the episode of shame to go beyond the communally negotiated incident to become a part of the psychological makeup of the individual, ensuring its enduring impact.

Despite its power in the example outlined above, the emotion of shame has in part eluded historical investigation. As we begin to look closer at the phenomenon, this lacuna appears all the more perplexing and intriguing. Where it does appear in historical writing, it is viewed as a collective phenomenon. Nations, states, societies or groups of individuals are sometimes encouraged through historical writing to feel shame for their collective actions. Shame has been a tool used by historians to indict those involved in the holocaust, the treatment of slaves before emancipation as well as the extent of French collaboration with the Nazi occupation during the Second World War, and many more besides. Very rarely has the dimension of shame been explored in relation to the experiences and feelings of individuals. This gap is intriguing and seductive – especially if shame really is 'the social emotion'.

Definitions

Academics have episodically approached the subject of shame from the disciplines of anthropology, ethnography, psychology and sociology with somewhat mixed results. Some have struggled to define the term 'shame' whilst others have been unable to locate either its presence or its functions with any degree of precision. Those who have been bolder with their assertions have problematically produced generalised or 'ideal type' definitions of the phenomenon. This has led some to criticise such approaches as over theoretical and lacking the closely observed social dimension provided by nuanced individual examples. This in itself has been a creative spur to the current study. Thus we hope that detailed interrogation of real life examples, intended to show the phenomenon of shame in action, will uncover its history to note both continuities and changes over the period covered by this study.

The Oxford English Dictionary (OED) defines shame as both a noun and a verb and elements of both these definitions have shaped how society and scholars have generally conceived of shame. When defined as a noun, the OED sees it as:

> The painful emotion arising from the consciousness of something dishonouring, ridiculous, or indecorous in one's own conduct or circumstances (or in those of others whose honour or disgrace one regards as one's own), or of being in a situation which offends one's sense of modesty or decency.

When defined as a verb, the OED substantially demonstrates the scope of shame as an action. However, importantly it specifically distinguishes between the individual's ability to 'feel' shame, but also to actively 'conceive' of it at a distance. Whilst these definitions are helpful in establishing the parameters of the subject, they are limited and problematic. This book seeks to take our understanding of this concept beyond this ineffective and inaccurate definition to see shame in action in real circumstances. The existing definitions described above are inclined to see shame as static, simple, one-dimensional, instantaneous and isolated. One other, perhaps unforeseen quality of these definitions, which is especially unhelpful, is their capacity to root the definition solely within primitive societies, which modern and sophisticated 'guilt'-based cultures have transcended. This is evident in the phrase 'honour or disgrace one regards as one's own' which has self-consciously fed the idea of so-called shame societies. These are conceived of as wholly family and kin orientated, whilst the phenomena of shame and shaming too readily appears to be a localised small-scale species of discipline carried out solely within the local community. In a sense, for historians, this definition has encouraged the location of shame in pre-modern or primitive chronological contexts and perhaps indicates how far the informed use and application of this definition has so far remained the possession of anthropologists.

Generally speaking, in one of the early sessions on most university anthropology courses students will be confronted with the traditional view that in attributing blame or culpability to instil conformity, societies divide themselves into 'shame' cultures or 'guilt' cultures. Most analyses see the latter as a significantly more modern development built from the dissolution of the chronologically earlier shame cultures. These are characterised as overwhelmingly primitive since they generally express community norms and values rooted in established and traditional practices, carefully codified within the popular mind.

William Miller, for example identified the Icelandic society which produced the sagas as a shame society where honour was visibly lost by
those shamed, whilst onlookers were actively conscious that their
'gaze' played an essential part in this loss.[6] Such societies are also seen
to operate draconian sanctions upon their members. Here, perhaps,
is the crucial element in the function of these two definitions – that
modern society finds this marginalising treatment harsh and brutal.
This is where the historian's perspective takes up from where the
anthropologist might well leave off. Marginalisation and the use, and
often abuse, of shame are seen by some theorists like Norbert Elias as
not primarily important in representing the pain and anguish of the
individual, but instead as a wider method of discipline which allows
modern behaviour and restraint to develop.

Shame is a spectacularly powerful emotion as Arch's memories undiluted,
with the passage of time, testify. It is also an emotion to be taken
seriously and this dimension is noted as crucial to its definition and
importance. Miller argues that shame can be distinguished from humiliation since the latter is intent upon deflating pretension wherever it is
found – 'shame is the stuff of high-seriousness, while humiliation often
partakes of farce and fabliaux'.[7] Amongst psychologists it is accepted
beyond reasonable doubt that shame damages an individual's sense of
themselves. The sheer impact of shame upon their psychological makeup
and ego distorts their view of both the past and the future. Such individuals are sometimes said to have no sense of the present because they
are locked into a cycle of guilt, remembering the consequences of transgression or anxiously awaiting future social failures with foreboding. Such
individuals come to distrust their own judgement and discount the
sum of their experiences by which they evaluate the norms and the standards of the society in which they live. Thomas Scheff located shame
as a central part of the system of social relations suggesting:

> ...that the degree and type of deference and the attendant emo-
> tions of pride and shame make up a subtle and pervasive system
> of social sanctions. This system leads to experiencing social
> influence as compelling. Our thoughts and perceptions of social
> expectations only set the stage for social control. We experience
> the system as so compelling because of emotions – the pleasure
> of pride and fellow feeling on the one hand, and the punish-
> ment of embarrassment, shame or humiliation on the other.[8]

This collection of insights describes the leading characteristics which
distinguish shame cultures from their supposedly more modern and

more sophisticated counterpart – guilt cultures. The latter are generally considered more complex and supposedly modern, since they describe the individual (rather than the community) as the centre of the web of culpability, blame and atonement. 'Guilt' describes a collection of psychological tools possessed by the individual which persuades them to form their own personal deterrent, policing agent and judicial mechanism. This would also add credence to the work of some sociologists who emphasise that conformity involves individuals in an almost constant state of self-examination and evaluation against both norms and aspirations. This was characterised by Charles Cooley as the so-called 'looking glass self'.[9] Thus modern theorists suggest this produces a state of empowerment far divorced from the primitive and brutal communal sanctions of others. As S.P. Garvie suggests:

> The shamed self is thus either passive and helpless, or enraged. In contrast, guilt prompts the self to try to make amends for the wrong doing. Because guilt preserves some distance between the self and its wrongful act, it enables the self to become active and engaged in an effort to repair the damage the offence has caused. Shame supplies no such motive to repair.[10]

Alongside such speculations are those which see guilt societies as providing tools with which the individual can readily rebuild themselves after their encounter with their own culpability. These individuals are characterised as more flexible and civilised with a more impressive ability to recover from transgressive or embarrassing behaviour. As Thomas Scheff suggests:

> Guilt is about what one did, shame is about the self, what one is. Guilt also involves feeling that the ego is strong and intact: one is powerful enough to injure the other, and one is also powerful enough to make amends....Guilt is a highly individualist emotion, reaffirming the centrality of the isolated person; shame is a social emotion, reaffirming the emotional independency of persons.[11]

Shame – Origins and ancestors

In the West, aspects of shame are inherent in Judeo-Christian culture and perform explicit functions. Important aspects of Christian teaching involved the submission of the individual will and appetites to the needs of the wider Christian community. Certain aspects of Christian teaching also themselves prescribed behaviour and encouraged rituals of shame for those who transgressed these prescriptions. Early Christianity was arguably the classical shame culture with virtue residing in the community's women and problems around this negotiated by the community's men. Placing women in this position was arguably the essential quality inherent in the Pauline view of women. This view was also augmented by a distrust of sensuality and the flesh which emerged in the teachings of Saint Paul, but also latterly in the work of Saint Augustine who produced a developed and calculated conception of guilt. It has also been suggested that the idea of shame was preserved more obviously in Anglo-Saxon cultures, whereas Romance cultures were more inclined to develop the related emotions of embarrassment and humiliation. This characterised shame as already associated with social norms rather than conceptions of sin. This line of thinking also suggests that embarrassment replaces shame rather than guilt as the visible social emotion.[12]

Some historians have especially noticed that late medieval Christendom began to discipline its population with a renewed seriousness at the end of the fourteenth century. A crucial part of this discipline was the development of a central place for both sin and guilt in regulating the behaviour of the Christian community.[13] Importantly, this predated the Reformation and in England the development of the mature Puritan Protestantism described by Patrick Collinson as a driving force from the middle of the sixteenth century onwards.[14] Interestingly, others have described the Reformation as a revolt against the interminable psychological millstone of 'Original Sin' perhaps constituting liberation from primal guilt.[15]

Puritanism itself became closely identified with Biblical shaming practices in England whilst Scotland developed its own species of discipline centred on Calvinism and the power of the local Kirk. The eighteenth century saw the development of manners as a more refined and subtle method of controlling appetites and behaviour, although it would be wholly wrong to suggest that these replaced the need for more direct controls on errant individuals. Here we meet one of the clear historical paradoxes that cluster around the issue of shame. Does its existence demonstrate that it worked as a deterrent, or its use in action suggest its periodic failure? If obvious socially visible shame punishments were necessary to maintain order and decorum, then individuals did not have a sufficiently developed sense of shame which prevented them from transgressing. If it required cultures of manners to create embarrassment amongst more socially aware individuals, then we are at once required to qualify the distinction between primitive shame cultures and modern guilt ones. Shame punishments are frequently seen as the blunt instrument, yet equally it may be precisely this bluntness which suggests individuals punished by this regime had a comparatively developed sense of shame. Within more refined cultures of embarrassment the very fear of shame constituted a lasting psychological knowledge of it, even if it had never been actually experienced by the individual. Thus we might be forced to conclude that shame had a more real presence and effect on supposedly more modern cultures of manners and behaviour, than it may have done on supposedly more primitive shame cultures. As has been noted, the eighteenth century was characterised by a growth in politeness and manners, but there was also a complementary interest in the cult of emotions. This was driven by the culture and machinery of politeness in the form of instruction books and didactic literature of various genres. However, emotions were also increasingly foregrounded by enthusiastic and charismatic versions of Christianity which stressed the feeling and response to salvation – as Miller suggests 'emotions were in vogue among the high and the low'.[16]

The first half of the twentieth century saw the ideas of Sigmund Freud effectively remove human thoughts and actions away from the realm of public culpability and into the unconscious.[17] Other philosophers and commentators such as Nietzsche and Schopenhauer similarly eroded the power of blame, guilt and culpability; but also managed at the same time to associate these social feelings with nineteenth century Liberalism and those who had constructed it in the first third of the nineteenth century. From these early twentieth century attempts to discredit the absoluteness of some discourses about behaviour, we can also then construct a line of thinking which reaches to the post-modern ideas about morality.

The historiography of shame

Historical scholarship which has identified and analysed cultures of shame in a variety of contexts and locations, has served to compliment and build upon the work carried out by theorists, philosophers and anthropologists. Social historians, in particular, have addressed the concept of shame in a range of ways from the 'embarrassment' associated with the internal and external habits of the early modern body; the opprobrium associated with sexuality and sexual behaviour in the pre-modern period; and, more recently, the shame related to the aftermath of war, political atrocity and acts of social exclusion.[18] Although in some respects, shame cultures have been firmly placed on the social and cultural historical map, there remain some obvious gaps. In the genre of crime history, where we might expect to find a close and detailed analysis of shame due to its correlation with crime, deviance and the law, the subject has received relatively little attention. To date, there is no work which attempts to study the history of shame over a long chronology, nor has there been any attempt to paint a comprehensive picture of the reach and influence of shame within an extensive milieu. Thus, in the main, the historiography surrounding the relationship between shame and criminality has been limited in scope, in coverage and in detail.

Despite the relative inadequacy of research into shame by historians of crime, three fundamental areas of interest can be identified from the existing scholarship. These are victimology; community-based rituals and officially-sanctioned punishments. With respect to victimology, shame has been identified as a key factor in the under-reporting of certain types of offences throughout history. The deep sense of degradation and humiliation generated by offences such as domestic violence, rape or sexual assault in particular, has resulted in shame regularly acting as a catalyst for the so-called 'dark figure' of unreported criminal activity.[19] The understandable reticence of victims to recount the crimes committed against them has undoubtedly impacted upon the way in which these types of offences have been regarded, managed and 'policed' over time. This has largely transformed how the authorities have approached criminal encounters of a more personal and sensitive nature.[20] Certainly, it seems that the relationship between criminality and opprobrium has been recognised in relation to the victim's experience. Yet, historians who have studied these types of interpersonal violence have yet to fully explore the impact that shame had on the psyche of the victims involved, whether these emotions were experienced differently in distinct eras or contexts, and the extent to which assailants experienced any sense of shame on account of their actions.

The second key area of historical research which investigates the relationship between criminality and shame relates to the place of opprobrium within community-based punishment rituals, particularly during the early modern period. Although the scholarship on this subject extends across Europe and the United States of America,[21] in a British context at least, the research focus has been on episodes of 'rough music' (such as skimmington rides).[22] These were instances where individuals, who were perceived to have transgressed community norms, were forced to endure publicly prescribed ridicule of one form or another. This could involve anything from being ridden around the neighbourhood on a pole or a donkey, characters being burnt in effigy, or the production of elaborate street dramatisations of the misconduct which had taken place.[23] A variety of misdemeanours could result in the infliction of communally sanctioned shame punishments, but most commonly this occurred when accepted patriarchal values had been abused or inverted. An instance of cuckoldry for example, or the actions of a scolding wife, could often result in an individual being publicly shamed by their neighbours and peers.[24]

Historians have pointed out that community endorsed shaming punishments such as these were not random displays of mirth or indiscriminate attempts at plebeian aggression. Rather, shame, within this context had a clear intent and purpose. By shaming transgressors in the full glare of the public gaze, communities hoped to publicise scandal, to rectify bad behaviour and also to warn others of the likely consequences of similar indiscretions.[25] In sum, shame was used in early modern England as a tool to retain harmonious relations within communities where functional systems of justice were either incomplete or wholly absent.

Despite the range of interesting and valuable studies that have been carried out on community shaming rituals, the analysis of these episodes remains somewhat incomplete. For one thing, most of the scholarship concentrates on the English experience alone and even then, much of what is provided are largely narrative descriptions of localised examples. Little assessment has been made of either the effectiveness of this type of punishment, the impact it had on the participants involved, or the attitudes that the authorities had to this kind of practice. Moreover, much of the history of communal shame punishments is restricted to the early modern period, which might suggest to the reader that public humiliation ceases to exist after 1800. This volume will attempt to address this particular issue by looking at the way that shame functioned over a longer chronology, and how its nature and application changed over time.

The final area of crime history which investigates the link between shame and bad behaviour relates to officially sanctioned punishment regimes. This scholarship traces how shame was perceived to function within the sphere of judicial punishment over time. It has been traditional to show that the application of shame punishments entered a decline from the start of the eighteenth century onwards. This has been encouraged by the fact that the link between shame and punishment has led the historiography off in a somewhat different direction. The gradual arrival of incarceration as the mainstream punishment has also assisted in associating shame with the anachronistic, primitive and pre-modern. From other areas of analysis, this paradigm of change has also received considerable support. The central thesis of Foucault's *Discipline and Punish* required a translation from overt visible punishments to incarceration to be both rapid and universal. The episteme in which punishment was brutal, visible but supposedly 'honest' was replaced with regimes of incarceration, surveillance and control resulting in the individual's ultimate policing of the self.[26] Thus our histories of punishment, in moving on to studies of incarceration, left unresearched what evidence of shame in action remained.

Whilst it may no longer have been central to mainstream punishment, shame still existed in nineteenth century society and in places (such as dysfunctional marriage, the press and the workhouse) it was still considered an important (albeit sometimes unwitting) part of disciplinary cultures. Although shame was seen to have a part to play in a variety of corporal punishments, most academic attention has been given over to the ultimate sanction, that of capital punishment. In the initial phase, up to the end of the early modern period, historians have indicated that the punishment of the body (either prior to execution or post-mortem) was committed in order to shame the convict and indeed their family on account of the misdeeds committed.[27] The shaming of the individual had to be done in public not only to encourage the convict to atone for their crimes and to justify the merits of the judicial system to the wider populace, but also to deter the audience from felonious activity and bad behaviour. The pains inflicted on the body of the condemned, however, were more than 'a shameful side effect'. By witnessing the horrors of the scaffold and the shame imposed on the convicted individual, the audience were active participants in a dramatic ritual which played on their own fears and fascination relating to death and the afterlife.[28]

As Mitchell B. Merback describes, 'Popular fascination with the fate of criminals executed by the state has been a persistent feature in the history of capital punishment in the West.'[29] During the eighteenth century, however, the shame associated with executions gradually transferred from the body of the condemned, to operating within the mind of the gallows onlooker. Scholars, such as V.A.C. Gatrell, have described this transference as a 'battle' between 'propriety' and 'curiosity', which, over time, was eventually won by the former.[30] Executions were increasingly regarded as unseemly and inappropriate spectacles for the minds of a 'civilised' public. Gatrell recounts the actions of George Selwyn MP, who during the eighteenth century '...was said to have disguised himself in women's clothes at executions to avoid recognition, a conjunction of excitement, gender inversion, and shame'[31] which was symptomatic of burgeoning contemporary anxieties related to the 'shamefulness' of this type of morbid curiosity. The removal of these elements within punishment is generally seen as an important part of the process of modernisation. In this analysis, the use of shame as a component in punishments is seen as somehow primitive and barbaric as well as foregrounding this emotion as a part of this society's social relationships. As a result of this growing tide of sensitivity, convicts came to be increasingly regarded as political or psychological 'others', and their fate was eventually taken out of the public gaze and put behind the prison wall in 1868.[32]

Scholars have thus identified, that shame had a fairly nuanced part to play in the history of capital punishment. Shame, in this context, not only changed over time, but it was fluid rather than fixed, and was interchangeable between the individuals involved, as the case-study in Chapter 3 illustrates. The changing role and function of shame with regards to executions has also been analysed, as have the various factors which have impacted upon how capital punishment has come to be regarded in the modern era. This volume builds upon many of the theoretical perspectives that have been applied to the study of shame and capital punishment in the early modern period. It also uses these perspectives as a template with which to investigate wider cultures of shame and their history across Britain since 1600.

The importance of shame to the historian

Episodes where the 'social emotion' of shame is displayed intrigue the historian, providing an unrivalled window into the emotional and psychological lives of past individuals and societies. It is with this in mind that this book was written. Both authors, during the course of other research, independently uncovered 'cases' and examples that showed the negotiation of social relations through elements of shame. These covered areas as diverse as sexual impropriety, marital discord, atonement for crime, the use of shame punishment and challenges to respectable reputation. All of them involved the 'primary social emotion' of shame and were sufficiently rich in the potential for 'thick description' to provide inspiration for this project. The sources for these were material within the public domain and involved a particular emphasis upon records in which the individuals concerned were actively portrayed or spoke for themselves. These consisted of official records ranging from court reports of various kinds to state papers. However, our realisation that an important element of the argument concerns how printed media influenced shame and its portrayal, has meant we have also worked with newspapers, journals and pamphlet literature. The interplay between these sources has involved close reading of them and an assessment of behavioural choices and motives.

Shame, as we discovered, was fertile territory for sociologists, psychologists and anthropologists but currently not for historians.[33] This seemed a considerable omission since episodes where shame broke the surface in past communities ought to be telling us about the cohesion of community, the place and role of the community's power over the individual and particularly the changing importance of the self as an historical concept worthy of investigation. It ought also to be telling us about important issues relating to class formation and the orientation of individuals towards the phenomenon of time. These are both fundamentally important themes in eighteenth and nineteenth century cultural history. Much of the anthropological literature associated shame with the primitive and the rural, but it should also be noted that (as we have discovered) the nineteenth, or 'bourgeois century' contained its fair share of shame and anxiety for the respectable middle classes. The fear of a poverty stricken reversion to the class below, or indeed the relentless quest to reach comfort, status or prosperity (and the inherent pitfalls of doing so) are central themes of much Victorian fiction, thereby demonstrating shame's lingering potency as a pre-occupation.

Shame cultures, as social scientists have frequently told us, are associated with supposedly more primitive societies. This has generally provided the theoretical background to positivist explanations of such societies as 'backward' and 'undeveloped'. Whilst there is little room to investigate further here the ideological presumptions behind such categorisation, there is some consideration of this in the book's conclusion. The ability to look at the operation of 'shame' offers the chance to study past cultures in the processes of both construction and dissolution. This allows us to potentially understand how cultures, only a little removed from our own, established their priorities and their codes of behaviour. We can see societies in action disciplining and enforcing norms and standards, or indeed we can watch from afar individuals imposing these standards upon themselves or trying to negotiate new ones, and on occasion failing miserably.

Given these apparent opportunities, it remains further perplexing that the emotion of shame has not attracted the significant attention of socio-cultural history before this point in time, since the two major paradigms shaping the subject should, on the face of things, have much to gain from the study of the subject. If social history was governed by class, as sometimes its critics claimed, then the systematic study of shame should have been one of its central occupations. Similarly, the post-modern challenge to the paradigm of class-orientated social history ought also to have pre-occupied itself with exploring the narratives and discourses around shame since these involved the creation and use of highly codified language to describe social realities. This use of language would also have helped mould identities beyond the constraints of class-based analyses. Post-modernists should also have been wise to the importance of stories and narratives (and their sustained importance for societies and individuals) as central to the individual human experience of shame. Some sociological studies of conformity have noted how rejection and marginalisation is frequently characterised by the subjects pinning these on the narratives of their own lived experience. Scheff in his examination of Helen Lewis' psychological studies showed the memory of narratives (or stories) in which individuals who were shamed became pathological, to the point where their recollection of shame and its ignominy left them bereft of their decision making powers. Such individuals endlessly replayed such scenes and became obsessed with these incidents rendering them unable to interact with the present and thus 'subtly distracted'.[34]

Although much modernisation theory would tend to suggest shame cultures are a form of primitive behaviour left behind at a specific stage of social development, there are also arguments at work that see this process as crucial to the whole history of a society's capacity to modernise. Norbert Elias's famous conception of the 'Civilising Process' argued that marginalisation lay deep at the heart of social change. Far from inspiring static conformity, he preferred to see this as inspiring minute, yet profound, changes which advanced society at a slow if still inexorable pace. Marginalisation, embarrassment and shame at social 'faux pas' or misbehaviour may have produced intensely negative psychological effects for those that had these experiences, but for Elias these were an individual and collective learning curve that would produce a modern and emphatically better society. Shame taught individuals to conform to norms whether or not these were static or, as Elias argues, dynamic.[35] The result was an apparently civilised society which created interdependence and a noted reduction of violence within social relationships, alongside the marginalisation and regulation of errant behaviour patterns. These were either discarded or heavily adapted to allow for their existence within modern society in a safe and relatively benign form.

Norbert Elias's 'Civilising Process' has also encouraged historians to think of a clean break with the past. Elias had suggested that the middle ranks of society achieved dominance through their ability to control and manipulate social space and the interactions that occurred within it. It was through regimes of manners (or respectability) and through establishing harsh regulatory norms of behaviour that these ranks marginalised those below them in the social hierarchy. Thus Elias drew upon manuals and code books of behaviour which prescribed etiquette within domestic encounters everywhere from the dinner table to the bedroom. Many of these episodes where advice is given also contained a variety of harsh warnings about the consequences of poor or unseemly behaviour. Readers of this advice would be persuaded to feel shame and embarrassment since their demonstrably uncouth ways would attract the disapproving gaze of the refined and respectable. Because Elias saw this emphatically as an essential step on the way to modernity, it was also treated as an episode that had occurred firmly in the past.

In making us modern, Elias would have been anxious for us to leave the phenomenon of shame behind. If he was right, the very power of shame itself ought to have made our ancestors refine and reinvent themselves so that they might become relaxed participants in society, rather than marginalised by it. Similarly, the same process would also have seen our 'civilised selves' view shame punishments as an unpleasant and anachronistic reminder of past times and our less 'civilised' forebears. This would fit with the essence of the anthropological chronology which suggests a transfer from shame to guilt cultures in which the autonomous individual polices themselves for their transgressive behaviour, however slight. Yet some critics of Elias, taking a less optimistic view of modernity, have suggested that this autonomy ultimately alienates individuals from communal norms and desensitises them to shame. Such individuals, it is suggested, live with a loss of self-control that leads to species of disappointment. Other arguments suggest that the capacity for violence was merely replaced with consistently high levels of social anxiety. In contrasting a raucous thirteenth century dinner party with what might transpire in a Henry James novel, William Miller suggests that the choreographed behaviour required by the latter would produce intolerable levels of anxiety about shame filled lapses. In contrast, only a surprisingly small number of behaviours would cause problems in the medieval great hall.[36] This suggests that the equation between the inexorable growth of respectability and the decline of shame is problematic.

Although the ideas of Norbert Elias focus upon the historical consequences of events in the early modern period there are also arguments closer to the nineteenth century which the concept of shame revisits. Radical and labour historians of the 1970s worked constructively with the concept of 'social control'. This particular theory arose as a species of quasi-Marxist explanation for the failure of revolution amongst the mature industrial proletariat. It suggested that working-class revolutionary potential, in all its forms, was effectively trumped and 'bought off' by the apparently benign behaviour of employers and authority faced by the danger posed by the working masses.[37] Borrowing from ideas associated with Gramscian hegemony, the social control thesis explained the apparent social peace of nineteenth century Britain, whilst also highlighting the gradual gains which slowly enriched working-class social and cultural life throughout the period. Episodes of shame appearing throughout the nineteenth century may yet add further credence to models of social control or may alternatively add explanatory depth to the argument.

A still further and important reason for studying the history of shame is that the supposed ability of late nineteenth century society to supersede it and modernity's desire to erase it from public space emerge from this study as considerably less than successful. One element in our discussion is clearly the developing role and sophistication of various media in portraying shame that can twist and distort both fact and interpretation. This provides an important context for many, if not all the discussions and individual cases which are analysed. In this we rediscover that 'shame' had its uses to a society that should arguably have outgrown it. It tried to create and influence public opinion, but also on occasions became a trope central to entertainment and for constructing the uncivilised other. This particularly illuminates, and conceivably seems to be a precursor of, some elements of modern entertainment culture which have rediscovered both the innate power of shame and its efficient ability to convey other cultural messages.[38]

The ideas of the sociologist Erving Goffman are also crucial to an evaluation of shame's enduring importance beyond its supposed mutation into a modern guilt culture.[39] Goffman added new dimensions to the suggestion that shame was the social emotion through his substantial denial that individuals really possessed any sense of inner life. For Goffman, the modern autonomous self was an illusion since he argued that the self was more obviously socially constructed through various successful (and occasionally unsuccessful) public performances by the individual. The success or otherwise of such social performances rests upon the individual's ability to marshal resources to reflect and celebrate the attributes of the dominant culture in which they find themselves. Thus, according to Goffman, the preservation and enhancement of self-image is the central pre-occupation of social interactions. Goffman felt this could be observed through the close examination of specific situations where individuals might seek to increase their esteem and public image, which Goffman associated with the phenomenon of games. The opposite activity of protecting the public self was characterised as saving and preserving the self from the games and one-upmanship of others.[40]

Goffman's investigations involved the skilled use of narrative and regularly described episodes which he would unpack, to demonstrate their applicability to his theories conceptualised as 'Framing'. This ostensibly had the same purpose and function as both micro-history (for historians) and 'thick description' (for anthropologists). 'Framing' argued for a collection of the facts pertaining to individual instances and using the deep analysis of context to 'frame' what the observer might describe. It also elaborated the manner in which the participants would seek to order and classify events and in turn tailor their response to these. Thus, within this paradigm, Goffman might perhaps have considered social history to consist of cataloguing the individual's attempts to frame experience using the tools around them.[41] Within this, the relative power of the individual to shape events and make sense of them would be a further dimension which it should be history's purpose to record. This would unpack and describe codes and norms for us in some useful ways that would enable us to think more deeply about gender, class and wider identity as well as the operation of behavioural expectations and norms.

Given this conceptual framework, the ideas of Erving Goffman should be ideal for the social historian of emotions, but especially for those interested in emotions that involve the perception of the self and its interaction with the world of social encounters. In a sense, some of his methodology has been influential in devising the structure and intentions of this book, since we have sought to draw analysis from individual and specific incidents. Goffman's sense of performance and how this is fraught with dangers and opportunities for the individual also especially characterises the phenomenon of shame. This emotion would signal specific 'frames' where individuals have failed to negotiate their 'face' and 'self' before the expectations and norms of a given society. Their feelings and displays of shame, and the attempts of others to heap shame upon them, would emerge as the power struggles of individuals more readily than they would represent a conscious project as outlined by Elias. Goffman's focus upon situations should be especially useful to social historians who see them as demonstrating paradigms of behaviour either imposed, or in the process of dissolution. Moreover, the placement of such situations alongside each other, as in this book, also allows the prospect of comparison as well as the examination of different places (in all senses of that word) and dimensions of social life where shame might appear. A chronologically sensitive arrangement of such situations also fruitfully suggests both continuity and change over time.

However, criticisms of Goffman's approach suggest that his work consists of a collection of observations which, at times, does not appear to be anything like a systematic analysis of human interaction. However for the social historian this should not matter because a cohesive explanation is supplied by the context and the aforementioned comparative and chronological dimensions of viewing a collection of frames or situations. Many of the individuals and their actions described in this book show a failure of comprehension with significant consequences for their idea of themselves, or other's ideas of that social self. We might also note here that the wider 'framing' provided by newspapers and printed media, as suggested by Jurgen Habermas through his conception of the 'public sphere', constitute a much wider community for the portrayal of socially damaging and expressive incidents of misbehaviour.[42] In a way, the twin approaches of Goffman and Habermas placed faith in the ability of the social to both express norms and to mediate stress. But the social also empowered individuals to resist attacks upon themselves and preserve ideals of community acceptability.

The quest to become polite and peaceable may form a central part of the longue durée history of behaviour. However, we would certainly argue that the evidence offered here suggests that change was not homogenous, uniform nor complete. Other critiques have been prepared to see alternative sub-cultures challenge politeness or have seen the etiquette of politeness used to inflict physical or psychological cruelty. Others still have also seen how politeness has been harnessed and turned to use by women seeking to police and expose the cruelty of private violence.[43]

Our conclusions from our examination of the various definitions available, some general, some discipline-specific, should be placed alongside what we have so far gleaned from the historiography. These suggest that a substantially updated and more nuanced definition of shame is necessary for a full appreciation of its impact upon modern social and cultural history. The evidence of our examples suggests that shame is not, as previous definitions suggest, solely a monolithic and inflexible single culture that people live within or are constrained by. Our discovery of its survival into at least the late nineteenth century, beyond the reach of paternalist cultures, would argue that, especially in its latter history, it is a response reached for by both individuals and groups. This grasping of shame occurred when the individual sought to theorise, organise and articulate their response to their own behaviour. Yet it was also capable of being mobilised by groups against others as a method of articulating grievances and regaining some essence of control over situations which demanded this. Within this paradigm it is no longer helpful to view the chronological dichotomy between an old and primitive 'shame' and a separate distinctly modern conception of 'guilt' which has supposedly supplanted it by the end of the nineteenth century. Shame, as this book demonstrates, could borrow from old established ideas and idioms whilst still using the most modern forms of communication technology and social networks with astonishing effectiveness. We would further argue that any definition of shame must clearly appreciate the importance of dynamic interactions between people, institutions and ideas within its influence. Knowing as much as possible about context is thus crucial to examining shame and how it worked. Likewise we need to understand the importance of circumstances which triggered shame to operate for those involved. In this book, our construction of shame, illustrated through our examples, has sought to include, as far as possible, these many factors which influenced, and potentially dictated, the behaviour of our protagonists. These examples illuminate in detail the parameters of their behaviour possibilities and the potential choices open to them. Shame was not necessarily the only possible response and the choice to reach for this particular emotion requires much deeper analysis. This interestingly also takes us beyond the restricted, chronologically static and claustrophobic world suggested by existing definitions. Importantly, this allows us more readily to move beyond the dominance of the central actor in shame – as focussed upon in the OED definition. Beyond this we can see the actions and responses of those on the fringes of these shame episodes. They were, as onlookers, still fundamentally important participants in the actions of shame and shaming whilst contributing to its power and significance. Lastly, based on the evidence offered in this book, we would refute the crude hypothesis that shame is solely associated with pre-modern and primitive contexts. Nor do we accept that shame was effectively removed either by modernising cultures of politeness or Foucault's pessimism about pre-modern subjectivity. This book exposes a significant number of instances where the supposedly pre-modern emotion of shame exists and indeed flourishes in a thoroughly modern context. Indeed, one notable factor is precisely how modern media and modern popular culture seamlessly incorporated the power of shame and modes of shaming. Not simply did shame deal with the emotional and moral life of the individual like it always had, but at certain moments it was capable of being removed from this context to provide something as profoundly different as popular entertainment.

Thus our chronological understanding of shame becoming guilt is questioned by this book. The established definition of a guilt culture sees its focus upon the individual explicitly as what distinguishes this from a 'shame' culture.[44] This book however begins to write the later history of shame in which the individual plays a more important part, problematising the transfer to 'guilt' cultures. Shame lasted longer than previous historians have suggested and our evidence suggests it did not disappear quietly. Shame was not marginalised by modernising societies but incorporated within them and made malleable by them. As such they remained powerful responses and tools of negotiation; whether this occurred in community exchanges or in the mind of individuals involved, or even far removed from the central location of each episode. This book thus uncovers places where the older society clashes with the new, exposing moments where civilising projects come unstuck, question their own motives or are sometimes disappointed by their own ineffectiveness. Indeed most of the central debates about shame and shame punishments, during the period covered by the examples used in this book, represent a questioning of what behavioural standards are for, and what they were fundamentally seeking to achieve.

To many of the individuals and groups represented in this book, it was not always clear what the behavioural standards of their society would allow them to undertake or wish them to abstain from. We might conclude from this that anything from ignorance to arrogance were as predominant dispositions as courtesy and politeness. Or if we were more charitable, we might observe individuals adapting their behaviour in response to unusual or trying circumstances, for which conventional solutions or attitudes seemed ineffective. Witnessing (and reacting to) an infanticidal mother rising from the grave, or baulking at the behaviour of a drunken and bestial priest, or even heaping opprobrium upon the Victorian monarchy were all exceptional occasions. Nonetheless, they so often represented a common blend of old and new behaviours since measured and printed criticism still rubbed shoulders with carnivalesque depiction and variations on rough music. At the very least, a prevailing picture of populations becoming mannered and civilised, without themselves problematising and occasionally rebelling against this, needs to be qualified. We hope this book is a significant contribution to this analysis that will inspire other scholars to comb the backstreets of eighteenth and nineteenth century society and the forgotten corners of the archives, to give us a still richer picture of shame, guilt and embarrassment across time and cultures.

The structure of this book

After this initial chapter, there is an exploration of a number of individual cases in which the sexual behaviour of the individual in the early modern period was the subject of shame, inspired censure or was actively punished. The interaction of official discourses of shame alongside the collective action taken by communities is an especial feature of this chapter. The comparatively routine nature of such censure is striking, and gives us especial insights into the operation of communal sanctions providing cohesiveness to communities and the policing of them. Initially, the piece outlines the form, function and process of the so-called ritual of 'rough music' across European and North America before 1900. The chapter then moves on to an analysis of the types of misdemeanours which could be punished by community-based humiliation, emphasising in particular, the contemporary pre-occupation with patriarchal order and moral paradigms. The existing historiography of 'rough music', which has tended to focus on the English experience of these episodes is then explored, before the chapter turns to look at some specific forms of this kind of folk ritual. These have been largely neglected by historians to date because they predominate within parts of Britain often considered to be 'peripheral' and thus supposedly unworthy of more detailed scholarship.

The first type of punishment to be addressed is that of 'branking' which was used most extensively in Scotland. As the case-study of Jenny Forsyth shows, the 'branks' was an iron bridle used to restrict the tongue, and subsequently the behaviour, of a particularly loud, boisterous or unruly woman. Although not regularly considered to be a variant of the charivari-type ritual, it is clear from the evidence uncovered here, that 'branking' was regularly preceded by 'rough music' north of the border. This was in order to maximise the shame experienced by the offender and to amplify the lesson that her opprobrium offered to the local audience. 'Ceffyl Pren' or 'wooden horse' is the second form of communal shame-punishment to be examined in detail in this chapter. This Welsh sanction was a close relative of the more familiar 'skimmington ride' found throughout southern England in the early modern period. The case-study of Jane Davies used to illustrate the regularly brutal nature of this ritual, also testifies to the longevity of this practice, occurring towards the middle of the nineteenth century.

The analysis of these case-studies focusses on the involvement of church officials in shaming episodes and tries to identify why women, in particular, were so often the target for instances of 'rough music'. The adoption of a seemingly more serious approach to these punishments by the Scots and the Welsh is also scrutinised in order to determine why their practices stand in stark contrast to their English counterparts in the period before 1850. More generally in this chapter, comparisons are drawn between the Scottish, English and Welsh experiences of community-led shame and humiliation to provide a more nuanced, national picture of these ritualised events than has hitherto been drawn.

The third chapter discusses the strange and celebrated case of Margaret Dickson. Convicted of infanticide in eighteenth century Edinburgh, she was sentenced to be executed for her crime. Forced to endure a parade through the streets in which she was subjected to the insults, taunts, petty violence and opprobrium of a large crowd, Dickson suffered the dreaded fate of many before her. Yet astonishingly, Dickson survived the execution, to emerge from her coffin and surprise the carters taking her corpse for burial. This death-defying miracle turned Dickson from a pariah to a folk heroine and thereafter she was feted by the people of Edinburgh. The incident graphically suggests how shame could follow an established eighteenth century ritual in relation to crimes that were regarded as heinous and deserving of the ultimate penalty a community could exact. If shame can be chiefly characterised as the removal of status, then Dickson experienced the stark removal of her status as a Christian mother within the community. However Dickson's resurrection emphasises how communal feelings of shame were unreliable and were strongly conditional upon the two central ideas of atonement and providence. When such mechanisms were spectacularly overturned, the rhetorics of shame and punishment could be hastily rewritten by the popular mandate – Dickson was dramatically 'unshamed' and given a privileged status within the community.

Interestingly, Margaret Dickson's example gives us a unique and unparalleled method of witnessing an individual's own knowledge of their full atonement for the ultimate crime, and people's reactions to such atonement – a salvation generally denied to the executed! However Margaret Dickson's story was also rewritten by the authorities with specific ideological intent. Her escape and survival severely undermined conventional narratives of atonement and punishment, and the reaction of the populace itself added further concerns to this volatile mixture. Thus Margaret Dickson's story was rewritten on at least two subsequent occasions in order to 're-shame' her and to re-affirm the conventional narratives of atonement and repentance.

The next chapter investigates the history of punishment within the pillory. This was supposed to allow the community the chance to obtain a species of petty summary justice and to reconfirm the social and cultural order disturbed by the miscreant. This analysis, based upon the various uses of the pillory, allows us to look at the subsequent history of shame punishments up to the start of the nineteenth century. This emerges as a more varied and oblique history than previously supposed. Shame punishments were still considered powerful in some areas of the disciplinary system, yet the increasing failure of society and its members in producing a homogenous reaction to it came to place it as an object of intense debate. This chapter finishes with the appearance of Daniel Defoe and other ideologically motivated victims in the pillory as a vehicle for studying the efficacy and effectiveness of shame punishments and reasons for their decline.

The mid-point of this book comprises a chapter which leads on from the ambivalence of shame punishments to show how shame was discussed and debated amongst authorities which claimed patriarchal and intellectual stewardship over it. This shows legal theorists and prison reformers like Beccaria, Bentham and others throughout Europe and the United States investigating the long-term value of shame as a means of regulating society and morals. From this questioning, emerged a waning enthusiasm for the power and effectiveness of shame. Thereafter, the shame components of punishment, and official forms of it, became eclipsed by other agendas and imperatives. However, it would be wrong to oversimplify this change and the evidence offered here serves, in part, to problematise a model of teleological and universal change whether that offered by Foucauldians or more mainstream modernisers. This chapter also sets the scene for the following sections which suggest that the idea of shame left important legacies before its reshaping at the end of the nineteenth century. It retained significant power in specific circumstances where collective disapproval was deemed essential and it could still be surprisingly articulate and effective.

The next chapter is a demonstration of nineteenth century shame and covers the extraordinary case against William Hughes, the vicar of a small and apparently quiet parish in the Wexford of 1825. Hughes, however, was the centre of a controversy that saw him brought before the Archbishop's Consistory Court in Dublin. He was accused of drunkenness, indecent exposure, coarse behaviour, blasphemy and encouraging his dog to perform bestial acts before a disgusted audience. Hughes had upset the local landowner by opposing Catholic emancipation and had angered the local community through his harsh treatment of a Catholic priest. Hughes was acquitted but the evidence offered in the case raises many questions about the issue of shame. If he was in fact innocent, then the incident demonstrates how shame ridden accusations were skilfully constructed to attack unpopular authority figures. If Hughes was guilty, the accusations suggest how an individual could so dramatically misjudge his community, as well as his own standards of behaviour before his audience. Whether true or false, the accusations suggest that rural communities were prepared to use the law in quite sophisticated ways beyond merely arguing for customary rights. They were able to define and promote ideals of behaviour as well as to shame individuals and indict poor behaviour, without recourse to the unofficial sanctions traditionally associated with shame by existing historiography.

The subsequent chapter unpacks a story which illuminates the shame that could lurk within the dark corners of nineteenth century marriage. In 1870 John Le Roi was prosecuted on the island of Jersey for cruelty to his wife. He had been reported for confining his wife's head in an 'iron mask' and a 'cage'. When the case came to court, Le Roi admitted that the mask had been constructed to combat his wife's severe and long catalogued problems with alcohol. The whole venture had been designed to save both Le Roi and his wife from widespread shame in the wider community. Yet his actions were swiftly reported to the authorities and the shame of the court case exposed his failure as head of the household and questioned his status as a concerned husband. This episode demonstrates the enduring power of communal constructions of proper behaviour and the willingness of the community in practice to protect family and reputation. It also shows the conflict between such constructions and the laws proffering alternative legal solutions. Moreover, the story itself was written up in four conflicting ways in both local and national newspapers giving us an insight into how the issue of shame was tailored to specific audiences and actively consumed by these audiences.

The theme of creating and managing audiences for shame is continued in the next chapter on a somewhat grander scale. Centring upon the last third of the nineteenth century this particular chapter examines the construction of a thoroughly modern and urban culture of shame. Through sustained criticism of the Victorian monarchy, and in particular its sexual impropriety and neglect of duty, middle-class radicals gained assent for their own definition of morally upright behaviour. Criticising the monarchy's behaviour allowed middle-class cultures of propriety to gain confidence and set themselves in opposition to the behaviour of the ruling class. This section demonstrates the evolving modern functions of shame and similarly developing critiques of the idea of morally uplifting example associated with social status and respectability. It analyses motivations for cultures of abstinence and what these tell us about social change in the nineteenth century. The chapter also examines the use of media idioms (such as newspapers, publicly reported speeches and wide circulation pamphlets) within a wholly modern urban context. These constructed and operated modern mechanisms of shame – thus allowing individuals to be appalled by the moral behaviour of people they had never met.

The concluding chapter ends the book with an examination of how the late nineteenth century discussed wife-sale, rough music and the skimmington ride as historical curiosities. When Thomas Hardy introduced both these events into *The Mayor of Casterbridge*, he portrayed them as customs that were clearly dying out. Wife-sale in this instance also brought forth the further discussion of abstinence as a desired form of social behaviour. This chapter examines the late nineteenth century cultural attempts to close the door on what were considered to be plebeian practices that a civilised society had eradicated. It investigates the motives and conclusions of the late century folklorists who reported and made communal shame antiquarian in the skimmington ride and wholly manufactured it in relation to wife-sale. The latter in particular, was rewritten from its origins as plebeian divorce to become tainted with shame and impropriety. In particular, the opinions voiced at the 'death' of these customs, ultimately help us address the debate about whether the management, concealment and ideological use of shame was a part of the 'Civilising Process' still in action at the end of the nineteenth century.

Our book concludes by investigating the larger questions that the history of shame provokes for the wider and contemporary history of justice. Shame may appear cruel and barbaric, yet parts of it remain surprisingly popular in our justice system and some modern theorists who argue the function of justice is retribution and restoration are redefining what we think of this concept. Restorative justice and criminal/victim reconciliation strategies borrow heavily from traditional conceptions of shame and it clearly has a future within society and its mechanisms. Thus shame has an untold history, but also has a significantly larger reach into social and cultural history than historians, sociologists and anthropologists have hitherto realised. Appreciating and the understanding the extent of this and its possibilities is now an important task which the forthcoming chapters hope to achieve.

2
Private Passions and Public Penance: Popular Shaming Rituals in Pre-Modern Britain

Throughout history, humiliation has always functioned as the essence of punishment. In the 'official' legal sphere during the early modern period and beyond, shaming mechanisms were used in abundance to penalise offenders. In particular we should call to mind instances of the gallows march and dying speech, the branding of petty criminals, the use of the pillory, or the whipping of convicts at appointed stations through a given community.[1] All of these judicial-based punishments involved the spectacle of public shame in order to render the criminal penitent, to deter any like-minded contemporaries from criminal activity, and, of course, to reinforce the power of the judicial authorities of the day.

The notion that shame could be used as a tool to control personal conduct also pervaded the minds of the general populace since the earliest times and was put into practice through a variety of forms of what we could term 'street theatre'. These episodes, like their officially sanctioned counterparts, were similarly designed to humiliate the offender concerned, to dissuade others from behaving badly, and, depending on the offence committed, to either ostracise the perpetrator from the community, or to reintegrate them into the fold. However, given the apparent strength of judicial authority alluded to above, it seems strange that public punishment of this sort was ever deemed necessary. Why did societies feel the need to resort to public shaming for certain offences? Why was recourse to the law not sufficient in certain areas? Does the existence of communal shaming rituals testify to a popular belief that judicial retribution needed to be supplemented during the pre-modern period? How were these communal shaming episodes regarded by the authorities, and how did church and religious authority fit into the extra-judicial processes that took place? Were there specific guidelines for the distribution of communal punishment? How did these 'unofficial', community-based shaming practices compare with judicially informed versions? Did this punishment vary according to the crime, the criminal, or the individuals meting out the penalty? Were these shaming practices gendered in any way? Was location a factor; in other words, did different communities harbour different attitudes to this type of penance? Is there evidence that this kind of public shaming successfully curbed criminal behaviour? In order to answer these questions, as well as others, this chapter will look at examples of 'offences' or misdemeanours which could result in this type of 'unofficial' public shaming, and the forms that this community-led treatment took throughout Britain since the early modern period.

Evidence for the existence of community-led forms of public penance has been uncovered across Europe and North America from the early modern period to the mid-twentieth century.[2] These examples not only testify to the widespread nature of these practices, but also to the remarkable longevity of their existence. The significant impact of communal shaming is also evidenced by the various literary references which illustrate how humiliating, injurious and damaging public shaming episodes could be.[3] Commonly referred to, as 'charivari', this custom '…characteristically involved a noisy, mocking demonstration usually occasioned by some anomalous social situation or infraction of community norms.'[4] Despite the prevalence of these practices across time and between cultures, it is important to point out, that the experience of 'charivari' was not readily comparable or uniform. For instance, there are significant and evident distinctions between the types of ritual humiliation practiced in the United Kingdom, compared to that encountered elsewhere.

Natalie Zemon Davis's work on sixteenth century France, for instance, shows that episodes of 'charivari' took place on very specific occasions, most commonly in relation to proposed second marriages when there was a significant age disparity between the husband and his prospective partner. It was the youth of the community that took the lead in the shaming rituals that ensued, but in practice, the episodes do not seem to have been excessively rebellious or injurious, and there appears to have been a relatively jovial atmosphere to the proceedings.[5] Studies of folk rituals in the United States tend to demonstrate that 'charivari' were occasions for celebration, festivity and humour, rather than episodes of utter humiliation which had to be endured.[6] In Russia on the other hand, a different picture emerges, and it is one that is not unlike that of the United Kingdom in terms of the stigmatising and degrading treatment victims received, as well as the extensive nature of community involvement.

However, the main targets of charivari in Russia were thieves, rather than moral transgressors, and this is where the Russian and British experiences diverge.[7]

In Britain, historians have preferred the term 'rough music' rather than 'charivari' to describe the various forms of communal humiliation practiced there since the sixteenth century. Martin Ingram and Edward Thompson in particular, have written extensively on this subject and have contributed much to our understanding of these opprobrious episodes, although due to poor record survival, it is difficult to determine just how common these instances actually were in practice.[8]

Akin to 'charivari', instances of 'rough music' in the United Kingdom involved a brutal cacophony of sound, often accompanied by ritual or drama, which directed explicit mockery and humiliation to individuals who had transgressed particular community conventions. The types of 'rough music' in existence varied in form according to the specific circumstances of each individual case, but they were regularly '... a highly ritualised expression of hostility'[9] and could be both physically brutal and emotionally traumatic. As well as the din or 'rough music' itself orchestrated by members of the community meeting together to clash pots and pans in the proximity of the offender's residence to draw attention to the unfolding scene, the event might involve '...the riding of a victim (or proxy) upon a pole or donkey; masking and dancing; elaborate recitatives; rough mime or street drama upon a cart or platform; the parading and burning of effigies; or indeed, combinations of all of these activities.'[10]

Occasionally, the historiography of English 'rough music' provides examples of episodes where the ritual was activated against unpopular officials or related to industrial grievances. Usually, this type of incident was fairly isolated and restricted to the late nineteenth or twentieth centuries.[11] More commonly for the pre-modern period, however, 'rough music' occurred due to domestic complaints of one sort or another. These could include scolding, wife-beating, cuckoldry, and generally, offences against a patriarchal notion of marital roles. In addition, sexual impropriety such as sodomy or fornication was also targeted, and adultery, in particular, was one of the most frequent offences to be censured.[12]

The maintenance of patriarchal values was imperative in early modern society. As David Underdown explains: 'Patriarchal authority within the family was the cornerstone of Elizabethan and Jacobean political theory, the ultimate, "natural", justification for obedience to the state: to reject wither was to threaten the entire social and political order.'[13] Yet, from the mid-sixteenth century onwards, there was a growing pre-occupation with individuals whose behaviour represented a *threat* to the patriarchal system. In the main, this threat came from 'unruly', independent women, and was best evidenced by a significant increase in court business targeted against such women in England, from the 1560s period onwards.[14] Women who stepped outside the boundaries of 'normal', 'acceptable', 'feminine' behaviour, for instance by trying to rule their masters or husbands, had to be reproached and reminded of their place both within their own domestic arena and within wider society more generally.

The relationship between sexual impropriety and communal public shaming has an even longer history than the concerns with patriarchal authority just outlined. In Ancient Greece, for instance, public humiliation was regularly ordered against adulterous couples. Amongst other abuses, male adulterers could be subjected to genital depilation using hot ash, or made to suffer the pain and opprobrium of having a large vegetable (usually an overgrown radish) or a spiny fish inserted roughly into their anus, whilst the rest of the community looked on.[15] Their female counterparts, on the other hand, could be symbolically stripped naked in public, with their clothes literally torn from their bodies, and thereafter, they could be made to walk around the community so disposed.[16]

Disdain for extra-marital impropriety and sexual misadventure more generally, persisted into the pre-modern period. Shaming punishment functioned in the United Kingdom at this time as a means by which to publicise a scandal which had occurred and to maintain 'communal harmony' by reminding the populace of their moral duty.[17] Although in the main, sexual misdemeanours of this kind were usually not deemed 'criminal' and therefore they were not often brought before the judiciary, ecclesiastical discipline did its best to curb this kind of behaviour which it regarded as 'sinful', dangerous and a scourge on society due to the broken relationships and illegitimate pregnancies which were regularly left in its wake.[18] Initially, it did this within its own jurisdiction, but after the decline of the church courts from the late seventeenth century onwards, religious authority was best represented by the church's involvement in community affairs.[19] With that in mind, episodes of 'unofficial' communal humiliation were particularly good opportunities to demonstrate the resilient power of the church at a local level as we will see.

Aside from the observation that instances of communally organised public shaming occurred due to the commission of very specific transgressions, what else does the historiography of this popular custom tell us? In general terms, there are three further conclusions that can be made for what we currently know about the British context of this so-called 'obnoxious sport'.[20] The first of these is that although instances of 'rough music' were seemingly rebellious and raucous in form, these episodes were not necessarily casual and haphazard in terms of their preparation or execution. For instance, in order for 'rough music' to be effective, the proposed target had to be a recognised member of a community, and the directive to impose punishment had to be based on a deliberate decision by the majority of that community.[21] Random attacks on individuals which were not universally endorsed were seemingly proscribed, regardless of the strength of feeling or provocation to curb improper behaviour.

The second key point to make regarding the British version of 'charivari' is that class hierarchies do not appear to have restricted 'rough music' to plebeian culture in England during the pre-modern period. There are numerous instances of landowners and noblemen being either abused or directly involved, particularly during the early modern period.[22] In the main, however, the evidence largely reflects that this type of community-based degradation was committed between 'common folk'. As has been said above, the effectiveness of this shaming practice was dependent on widespread community agreement and involvement. If the custom had been solely instigated and enforced by community leaders or wealthy landowners and the like, it would not have been welcomed; the intended effect on the perpetrators and the communal audience would have been largely negated; and as a result, the ritual would simply not have survived over the centuries.

The third and final conclusion to be drawn from the existing historiography of 'rough music' is that the disgraced victims of this type of shaming ritual, at least in relation to pre-modern England, were more commonly male rather than female.[23] Moreover, when women were targeted in this kind of episode, they were regularly shamed in effigy, rather than in person.[24] The seemingly gendered nature of communal shaming punishments in England is fascinating, but along with so many aspects of this type of public penance, it has remained unchallenged, unexplained, and as yet, not fully understood for too long. Arguably, the work of historians on 'rough music' thus far, has tended to concentrate on the ritual elements involved in instances of communal opprobrium, rather than on the impact that these episodes had on the victims, or indeed the participants concerned. Little has been written about whether shame was an effective tool in the maintenance of community order and propriety, and no consideration has been given to authoritarian attitudes towards this type of 'unofficial' punishment. Moreover, much of the studies carried out on 'rough music' have focussed solely on the English experience of these customary practices, largely ignoring their equivalents in Scotland and Wales, and the potential for comparative analysis therein. For this reason, the case-studies provided in this chapter will focus on Scotland and Wales. English instances of 'rough music', which have already been extensively examined in the existing historiography, are used as a comparator. The chapter concentrates on two specific forms of unofficial communal humiliation. The first is the 'Branks' or 'Scold's Bridle' used most extensively in Scotland, and the second, is the skimmington ride, and in particular the Welsh version of this shaming punishment, known as 'Ceffyl Pren' or 'Wooden Horse'.

The Scots define the 'branks' as '...an instrument of public punishment [in the form of] an iron bridle and gag used to punish breaches of the peace or abusive language.'[25] In colloquial terms, to 'put the branks' on someone meant to restrain them, or to '...cut them down to size'.[26] In England, this implement was referred to as the 'Scold's Bridle' or 'the chastity belt for the tongue'.[27] Conventionally, this mechanism for humiliation has not been considered by historians to be a form of 'rough music'. This is because it was regarded as either an officially sanctioned form of punishment, usually meted out by the ecclesiastical authorities, or as a tool largely confined to the private context of the marital relationship beyond the public arena.[28] However, the community-endorsed, ritualised nature of this form of punishment in Scotland, which stands in contrast to the English experience of this punishment, might encourage us to think again about historical categorisations of the function, expression and implementation of 'rough music'.

The punishment of the branks was said to have military origins and its usage can be traced back to the late sixteenth century, when it was employed as a torture device to procure confessions from alleged Scottish witches.[29] From the 1600s onwards, however, the punishment was applied more generally, and rather than being confined to mouthy scolds (as was the case in England), it was used north of the border to curb *various* forms of specifically female waywardness; typically instances where traditional patriarchal roles or moral strictures had been abused in one way or another. In England, 'Scold's Bridles' were usually instigated by victimised husbands or authority figures operating in an official capacity, but in Scotland, the procedure was more public in nature and was often communally orchestrated, with the women of the neighbourhood regularly working in tandem with church officials to see that the punishment was properly meted out and ultimately effective.

All of the evidence uncovered for the use of the branks in Scotland testifies to it being a gendered punishment, exclusively reserved for

'The "Branks": These are examples of devices used for restraint and communal shame punishment in the early modern period. Similar examples survived into the 18th and 19th centuries.'

'deviant' women. After 1570 in fact, there are no surviving recorded instances of men receiving this type of humiliating punishment north of the border.[30] The nature and range of offences for which women could be 'branked' are evident from the following series of examples.[31] Marione Smyt and Margaret Huntare were made to wear the branks in Glasgow in 1574 after quarrelling with one another in a repeatedly vicious manner.[32] Similarly in late sixteenth century Glasgow, the 'evil-tongued' Janet Foreside was punished for her malicious slander upon Margaret Fleming and was ordered to be branked for as long as her victim Mrs Fleming chose.[33] In 1635, after reigning repeated blows on her husband with a hammer and a whip and 'because he now goes about in fear for his life,' Elspeth Hunter was ordered to be branked at the Canongate in Edinburgh.[34] Isobel Smart was similarly punished in Cupar (Fife) in 1699 for attacking her husband with a broken bottle 'with a passion akin to a savage beast'.[35] And in the borders town of Jedburgh, in 1706, Margaret Wallace was 'branked' for assaulting her father and a cattle dealer by '...throwing stones at them and whilst they were thus incapacitated, brutally hitting them on the arse with a red-hot poker.'[36]

The most detailed surviving examples of branking relate to women who had been either implicated or indeed caught in acts of sinful fornication in the eighteenth century. After having been communally punished, these women subsequently applied to the courts for a bill to secure their future well-being and protection. This was the case in the following example. In 1721, Jenny Forsyth was found in the hay loft of a Dumfriesshire barn with a man who wasn't her husband; Jenny being recently widowed at this time. Both of the individuals were naked when they were discovered, and their defence that they had undressed because they were too hot after working in the fields did not hold much weight, given that it was early January and snow covered the estate on which they were employed! Two additional factors counted against Jenny Forsyth in relation to the community's decision upon her fate. First of all, her indiscretion was initially witnessed by two young boys who, after apparently hiding in the barn for some time, ran off and reported the matter to their father. The evident corruption of innocent minds by (even accidental) public acts of indecency such as this was something the community was unlikely to tolerate. In addition, Jenny had been widowed for less than a fortnight when she was caught in her unfortunate situation. The local community may well have been less sympathetic to an individual whom they believed had not only shamed herself, her family and her neighbours by her actions, but had also arguably shamed the memory of her late husband who had only recently been buried, in the grounds of the estate near to where the 'incident' had occurred.[37]

Fornication and other forms of misbehaviour, when blatantly discovered, were rarely tolerated in Scotland during the pre-modern period, and certain areas of the country set up 'courts of immorality' to oversee the supervision and punishment of evident offenders.[38] To punish

Jenny for her indiscretion and for the shame she had brought upon her family and neighbours, the local church officials and community leaders ordered Jenny (but notably not her lover) to 'be branked'. As was typically the case with communal branking episodes, several women from the parish congregated outside Jenny Forsyth's residence. They raised a din by singing loudly and by crashing pots and pans together, so as to alert the rest of the population to the scene. The women then entered Jenny's house, dragged her outside by force, fitted the 'branks' on to her, and then paraded her about the populous parts of the community for a lengthy period. There seems to have been little regional variation in these practices north of the border. The humiliation lasted until the culprit swore to behave more appropriately in the eyes of God, and if this was not forthcoming, the whole debacle could be gone through again on successive days until acquiescence was achieved.[39] A repeat performance or a subsequent branking was rarely necessary however, as E.J. Guthrie describes '…the discipline never failed to effect a complete reformation.'[40] Indeed, to date, there have been no recidivist branking episodes uncovered in pre-modern Scotland. Most likely, the combination of communal and ecclesiastical humiliation served to utterly subjugate the 'patient' and render her penitent and compliant thereafter. From the evidence gathered here, it seems that the branks functioned effectively as a shaming tool for those Scottish women who were forced to endure it.

North of the border, the actual device used for the 'branking' of the victim was arguably more brutal than that used in England. It is unclear whether these devices were already at hand in different regions during the pre-modern period or whether they were dutifully constructed for each individual shaming episode. The 'branks' was a skeletal iron helmet which was secured in place at the back of the head by a padlock. There was an iron loop at the front for affixing a chain by which the offender could be led around. Affixed to the inner portion of the helmet was a piece of metal, which, when the instrument was properly fitted, pressed the tongue down, and effectively 'branked' or bridled it. The longer the length of the mouthpiece, the worse the punishment, as it would cause the offender to gag, especially if they struggled. Moreover, despite regional variations in the basic structure and ornamentation of the helmet, all of the Scottish 'branks' still in existence have elevated rasps or spurs attached to the mouthpiece that caused serious lacerations to the mouth when the offender was in motion, and of course, if not properly fitted, the mouthpiece could move about smashing teeth and pulverising gums with every pull of the chain-leash or every stumble.[41] Of course, all of this had to be endured in the public glare, and the psychological scars of this type of shame punishment must have persisted long after any physical scars had healed over.

Martin Ingram describes the branks as having '...a very brief history' in England and argues that it was rarely put into practice there during the early modern period.[42] The device does not seem to have been used in Wales or Ireland during that time, and its use had started to decline in England by the latter 1700s according to T.N. Brushfield.[43] The use of the branks in Scotland was also relatively rare, but it has to be borne in mind that patchy record survival, particularly in relation to burgh records, may well act to suppress the number of 'branking' instances that were recorded. For instance, in preparation for this work, the authors uncovered some 64 episodes of branking across Scotland during the pre-modern period (1600–1900), either from sentencing records or from victims' bills of complaint at the conclusion of their punishment.[44] Yet, John Harrison's detailed analysis of the well-preserved Stirling Burgh Records between 1600 to 1722 revealed more than 100 branking-related punishments directly sentenced in that area alone.[45] If record survival allows, a more detailed analysis of local sources may well reveal that the use of the branks was far more extensive than current thinking suggests.

Certainly, the use of the 'branks' in Scotland seems to have had a much greater longevity than was the case south of the border. From the early seventeenth century, English shaming rituals came to favour the cucking-stool or ducking-stool for scolding-based offences rather than the branks or 'Scold's Bridle'.[46] Yet this transformation does not appear to have occurred in Scotland. Numerous eighteenth century examples of branking exist north of the border, as does a case from as late as 1858 against a husband-beater from Paisley (near Glasgow) called Katherine Crawford.[47] The evidence suggests that the Scots retained the use of the 'branks' largely because the alternative, ducking, was fairly widely regarded as a largely ineffective shaming tool.

The ducking stool was a chair-based piece of apparatus to which an offender was secured and then dunked several times into a local river or cess-pool, whilst a crowd of onlookers jeered and mocked.[48] Martin Ingram has argued that ducking rituals could regularly backfire as the offender rebelled against their requisite punishment, giving private orations instead from the stool about the absurdity and iniquity of their circumstance.[49] In Scotland, it was observed that the branks '...was much to be preferred to the ducking stool, which not only endangered the health of the patient, but gave the tongue liberty between each dip.'[50] It seems unlikely, given the regular involvement of the Scottish church in these shaming episodes, that the authorities would permit anything other than total disgrace and effective humiliation at the communal shaming ceremonies they orchestrated. They were more likely to rely on 'branking' because it was a mechanism they had seen in action and one which they had confidence in, at least in regard to the punishment of unruly women.

'Branking' then was seen as a key mechanism for the shaming of women in pre-modern Scotland. Clearly, it was a humiliating and regularly brutal gendered punishment which was not solely restricted to scolding offences as in England, nor was it largely private in nature or only officially sanctioned as John Harrison has described.[51] The spectacle of 'branking' was often a community experience, regularly instigated by church officials and interestingly often played out by women against women. As Christina Larner has pointed out '...a patriarchal social structure divides women. Largely dependent for their livelihood on the goodwill of men, most women will not only conform, but will also attack women who by their nonconformity threaten the security of the conformist women.'[52] Perhaps the need to retain respectability and security goes some way to explain why Scottish women were often the key players in the ritualised use of the branks to shame their erstwhile, but now wayward, sisters.

The reason why branking was a gendered punishment specifically reserved for female 'offenders' is not entirely clear. It is likely that Scottish communities believed that shaming punishments, generally, were more effective on women due to the central part that respectability played in generating their right to status and esteem within a given locale. Certainly this notion is borne out if we compare how Scottish men were treated for committing similar misdemeanours to their female counterparts. On the whole, for 'offences' like fornication, minor assault and slander, men were ordered to be exposed on the 'govis' (pillory) or the ecclesiastical 'stool of repentance' for a period of time with a list of their offences pinned to their shirt.[53] Although, protracted and embarrassing to a certain extent, this type of punishment seems relatively timid when compared with the brutalising punishment of the branks, which (as we have seen) was often accompanied by a ritual enactment which culminated in the degradation of the female form.[54]

The need to make an example of sinful, indiscreet or unruly women within the community was also mirrored in the courtroom. Here the Scottish judiciary were keen to inflict exemplary punishments on women accused of more 'criminal' or 'unlawful' behaviour during the pre-modern period.[55] Scottish women, who behaved badly, had to be tamed. They could not be allowed to betray the notionally 'feminine' qualities of their sex, nor could they be permitted to offer encouragement to other like-minded viragoes. Rather, there was a perceived need, amongst the multiple layers of authority in Scottish society, to subject unruly women to the accepted values of patriarchy through shame and humiliation of one form or another. It was assumed that episodes of public opprobrium, such as a 'branking', would not only curb female wrong-doing *per se*, but would also serve to remind other women of their appropriate duties and obligations.

The other type of communal humiliation to be analysed in this chapter is the skimmington ride. This particular form of punishment is regarded by historians as the most typical example of 'rough music' or 'charivari' to have taken place in the United Kingdom during the pre-modern period;[56] although scholars have been quick to point out that it is extremely difficult to gauge just how frequent these episodes actually were over time.[57] Although shame was central to all the instances of skimmington rides, there were fairly significant regional variations in how this punishment was carried out.

Regardless of location, 'rough music' was the prelude to this particular variety of shaming event. As has already been described, individuals from the local community came together, usually outside the residence of the intended target, to make a lot of noise in order to attract the rest of the neighbouring population to the scene. In southern England, a skimmington ride would then involve the target being drawn from their house and then seated (usually backwards) on a donkey, in order to be led around the neighbourhood to the jeers and taunts of the community.[58] Sometimes the target would be punished in person; sometimes an effigy or substitute would be used instead, dressed up appropriately for the occasion.[59] The use of a donkey-ride as a shaming punishment can be traced back to at least the first century B.C., and it is clear that the classical examples presented by historians such as Violet Alford, do not differ that much in terms of form and function from their pre-modern counterparts.[60] Similarly, the notion of riding backwards as a form of shame punishment also has a long history, and a close association with attempts to permanently stigmatise the participants.[61] More often than not, the intention of English skimmington rides was not only to shame the individuals involved and to publicise the scandalous nature of their present situation, but it was also a blatant attempt to have the culprits removed or exorcised from the community on a permanent basis.[62]

In more northern parts of England and in Scotland, the version of the skimmington ride in operation was commonly called 'Riding the

'Hogarth's depiction of a skimmington ride taken from "Hudibras" (1725)'

Stang'. A 'stang' was a long, unshaven wooden pole, usually a tree trunk or a similar equivalent. The process leading up to this punishment was relatively similar to that of the skimmington described above, save for the actual ride itself. Instead of a donkey being used, the individual targeted had their hands tied behind their back, and they were then straddled over the 'stang' and their legs were tied together below the knees. The 'stang' was then lifted up and marched around the neighbourhood. At various stations during the riding, the pole was lifted high into the air and then swiftly lowered causing the victim to cry out in pain each time he or she was bounced off the 'stang'. As the tree trunk used was highly abrasive and often still had branches sticking out of it, the individual's thighs, legs and genital area were regularly 'fearfully torn and scratched', and by the end of the riding it has been recorded that some individuals were rendered unconscious due to the suffering they had endured.[63]

The Welsh version of the skimmington ride combines several aspects of *both* the northern and southern versions of this type of shaming punishment. Here the punishment was known as 'Ceffyl Pren' or 'wooden horse' and the men and women targeted for this opprobrium were carried round the community on a wooden apparatus of some kind (usually a ladder), often elaborately decorated to look like a horse. As with the northern and Scottish versions, 'Ceffyl Pren' could be injurious as well as humiliating, as we will see from the case-study below.[64] The emotional trauma, and physical suffering caused by undergoing this kind of treatment must have been considerable for the individuals involved and the stigma of enduring this kind of shame within the public glare must have often been overwhelming.

In more general terms, this kind of communal shaming punishment could be imposed for a variety of reasons, but as with 'branking' it was most commonly applied due to a perceived abuse of the moral or patriarchal order; usually adulterous behaviour.[65] The specific manner in which the skimmington ride was carried out, varied according to the offence that had been perpetrated, and it seems that the episode could escalate or indeed recede (in terms of the hurt inflicted and the humiliation received) entirely at the community's discretion.[66] Examples of this form of 'rough music' can be found as late as the first third of the twentieth century in England, although few examples can be traced for Scotland or Wales by that time, and in general, after the close of the nineteenth century, instances of its use become relatively rare and unusual.[67] Despite the relative lack of evidence for skimmington-type punishments in the north after 1850, and although it is difficult to judge how common these opprobrious episodes were in general, there is still little evidence to support Violet Alford's contention that throughout history, the practice was exceedingly rare in northern areas compared to southern ones.[68] A study of the Scottish records alone reveals numerous examples of 'riding the stang' across the country throughout the pre-modern period, and numerous other studies have pointed to a variety of northern English examples.[69]

There are some important and interesting parallels and comparisons to be drawn from the varieties of this type of communal shaming punishment in pre-modern Britain. There are three conclusions which are particularly worthy of comment. Firstly, the practice of this customary punishment in England and Wales during the early modern period differs from the Scottish experience as, in Scotland, just as with 'branking', episodes of 'riding the stang' were predominantly instigated by church officials.[70] This was rarely the case in the English or Welsh examples uncovered to date, and suggests that the dominance of the church was less pronounced in community affairs south of the Tweed, even by the seventeenth and eighteenth centuries.

Secondly, although in England men *and* women could receive this punishment – sometimes simultaneously if an adulterous couple were targeted – in Scotland and indeed in Wales, (again as with 'branking') women were more commonly the victims of this type of opprobrium. The English examples often replaced any potential female target with an effigy or a substitute male participant dressed in her likeness.[71] In English skimmington rides where women were targeted, the shame of the event, even if only by association, was deemed sufficient punishment. In Scotland and Wales, however, the humiliation ritual was seemingly regarded as incomplete or ineffective if the offender did not directly participate. Crucially, the gender of the offender could not be used in mitigation. Once again then, the evidence indicates a perceived need to overtly punish unruly women in some areas of pre-modern Britain which does not exist elsewhere. It is difficult to ascertain why this was the case, but it seems that offences against patriarchy or moral strictures, particularly those committed by women, were regarded with much more seriousness in the Celtic fringe than they were in more central regions. The reasons for this dichotomy are yet to be fully explored or understood, but they may relate to the more cohesive nature of social relations in the relatively communal-based and unindustrialised areas of Scotland and Wales in the period before 1850. Communities in these areas may well have felt the need to take authority into their own hands due to the inconsistent and incomplete reach of centralised justice. Women, in particular, who were regarded as the moral guardians for future generations, may have been seen as the appropriate target for much of this community-based regulation. The fact that so many of the Scottish and Welsh examples of 'rough music' relate to rural rather than urban areas in the pre-modern period, may well substantiate this hypothesis to a certain extent, although more analysis and investigation than there is room for here is necessary in order to come to firmer conclusions.[72]

This last point relates to the final comparative conclusion to be drawn from the experience of the victim in English skimmington rides (where typically the guilty party rode backwards on a donkey through a community to a raucous reception), actual physical abuse was largely avoided in favour of psychological intimidation or 'psychic terrorism'.[73] In Scotland and Wales, on the other hand, 'riding the stang' and 'Ceffyl Pren' could prove both shameful *and* injurious. On the whole, the English examples of this type of punishment appear more jovial and humorous in nature, whereas examples from the rest of the country exemplify abject hostility and anger.

For instance, on the 6th of April 1838, the *Carmarthen Journal* reported on an ongoing court case brought by one Jane Davies against Morgan

Thomas and others.[74] The defendants were charged with repeated acts of riot and assault against the said Miss Davies. More specifically, it was recounted that on the 20th of October 1837, Jane Davies had been returning from a Llandilo market where she was accosted by her assailants. She was tied to a 'Ceffyl Pren' (in this instance a wooden hurdle) and was carried around the village of Pontarllechau '...with a great procession and with guns firing before them.' She was then taken to a stream at Rhydsaint where she was grievously ducked several times. Davies went on to explain that she was then taken to two further neighbouring villages (Bailydyffryn and Felinissa) where she received similar treatment. In the last village she came to, she claimed she was thrown into a pool of dirty water at the side of the road, and she was then viciously punched, kicked and trampled on by her attackers in order to prolong the time she was held under water. Jane Davies believed her life was in danger during the assault; she was much bruised and bloodied after the attack; and further reported that she was unable to walk after her ordeal, and had to be sent home on horse-back. Two witnesses testified in support of Jane's version of events in court.

In their defence, Jane's persecutors tried to claim that the incident had been '...nothing but a piece of fun and frolic, very common in the neighbourhood' and was intended to make Jane '...a virtuous woman'. The defendants stated their belief that Jane ought to be punished for her indiscretion with an un-named married man from the locality. Moreover, the court was told that Jane Davies had received this kind of 'transaction' from the community before, but had not heeded its significance, and this might go some way to explain why this particular instance of 'Ceffyl Pren' was so prolonged and arguably brutal in its implementation.

The judge and jury, however, had little sympathy with the defendants' claims and returned a verdict of guilty on all charges. Morgan Thomas was sentenced to six months hard labour, in consequence of both the attack itself and because he had threatened to stab Jane Davies if she testified against him. Four of the remaining five defendants were sentenced to four months hard labour each, and the fifth, a young child called William Morris (who pleaded guilty), was sentenced to a fortnight's imprisonment in the common gaol.

This example shows that rather than merely having fun at someone else's expense, as was often the case in English skimmington rides, episodes of this type of 'rough music' from elsewhere in the United Kingdom point more towards communities taking justice into their own hands. It seems that in terms of the United Kingdom as a whole, the impact of more central systems of justice was patchy and incomplete in the period before 1850, and thus some neighbourhoods decided to retain for longer customary practices related to the regulation of bad behaviour. Despite nuances in practice, communal humiliation rituals were not simply regarded as random acts of boisterous behaviour.[75] Just as in the Jane Davies case, the participants believed they were legitimated in what they were doing. They were not only trying to help the specific offender better themselves through the process of humiliation, but they were also reminding their peers and neighbours that they could suffer the same fate if they did not conform to community codes of appropriate behaviour.

Clearly, the Celtic versions of this particular form of 'rough music' could be brutal, and in this respect both 'riding the stang' and 'Ceffyl Pren' compare well to the Scottish instances of 'branking' already outlined. There are two main contrasts between these types of shaming rituals, in a specifically Scottish context. The first is that men were also made to ride the 'stang' on occasion, whereas branking was solely reserved for women.[76] In addition, individuals could be made to 'ride the stang' on multiple occasions in Scotland if the community saw fit, whereas branking was seemingly effective enough to only require a single, one-off application.[77]

Another obvious difference between humiliation rituals across the United Kingdom is that although the range of offences for which individuals could attain communal shame in Scotland and Wales was similar to that of England, neither the Welsh nor the Scots appear to have adopted the full repertoire of forms of 'rough music' evident in England. No instances of effigies being used or burned and no miming, dancing or acting have as yet been uncovered.[78] As we have seen, the Welsh and the Scots seemingly preferred to remove the more theatrical or dramatic elements from episodes of 'rough music' and to substitute them for physical abuse and psychological terror.

The second key difference to point out is that again, unlike the English examples we have, the Scottish and Welsh instances of 'rough music' were not entirely customary in function or fully divorced from state-sanctioned authority. Several of the recorded shaming episodes were carried out as a prelude to a court case, as if it was imperative that the community had their say on a given matter, before the issue was dealt with in the formalised legal sphere. In addition, Scottish church officials in particular, had an intriguing part to play in the regulation of bad behaviour. Ministers were commonly involved in the initial investigations of wrong-doing. They then led and orchestrated the 'rough music' in their parishes, and, as if to see the case through to its formal conclusion, they regularly testified for the prosecution in court proceedings. This interplay of multiple jurisdictions particularly evident in early modern Scotland is fascinating, as is the almost symbiotic relationship between customary practice, the church and the law, with church ministers acting as a conduit between the parties involved. Scottish churchmen evidently worked hard throughout the pre-modern period to retain their authority within and across Scottish society.[79]

The involvement of the church in Scottish 'rough music' probably explains why (unlike in England) there were comparatively few claims in Scotland for defamation or assault made on the back of the surviving examples of community shaming rituals.[80] This suggests that there may have been an acceptance of these traditional mechanisms for 'control' amongst the Scottish populace. However, it is clear that this was not always the case, and as time went on, it seems that these customary practices were increasingly frowned upon and curbed by the law. For instance, a petition to the Regality Court of Huntly (Aberdeenshire) in 1734 by several women asks *permission* to have a tolerated or legalised 'riding of the stang' for a local wife-beater.[81] In the petition, the women say that they want to avoid being punished for their actions, but that the man deserves this treatment. The court refused their petition, but undeterred, the women made the culprit 'ride the stang' but after ensuing litigation, they incurred a twenty pound fine.[82]

John Harrison's analysis of this petition is to count it as evidence of folk-based punishments being suppressed in pre-modern Scotland by the law.[83] Yet we have already established above, that examples of 'branking' and indeed 'riding the stang' continued to exist north of the Tweed long after 1750. Throughout the pre-modern period and in relation to more 'minor' offences or indiscretions, it was still the accepted duty and role of the church, coupled with community support to deal with individuals who behaved badly. Nevertheless, it is clear from the Huntly-based petition and indeed from the growing number of complaints and court cases in England and Wales (of which the Jane Davies case-study above is a good example), that tensions did develop between communities and the legal establishment. Certainly it seems that shaming punishments are arguably another example of the slow encroachment upon customary rights which occurred over the course of the pre-modern period. Nonetheless, the pace of this encroachment should neither be overstated nor its triumph assumed to be inevitable amongst contemporaries. Crucially then, we need to know more about the relationship between the community, church and state and why the reaction of these to bad behaviour, which at one time was fragmented but complementary, was transformed to be the sole preserve of a single sovereign authority represented by the secular state. Over time 'rough music' was declared as 'rough justice' and outlawed to the relief of many unruly Welsh and Scottish women in particular, but we need to know more about when this transition took place and what the precise reasons were for these changes.

Public shaming episodes have been in existence for thousands of years and yet the theory, form and function of these instances had changed very little over time. Shame was regarded as an essential part of punishment in the pre-modern era, both in relation to officially sanctioned penalties, and in the wider communal arena of 'popular' justice. Within the latter sphere, communities regarded public shaming as a useful tool to curb minor indiscretions, particularly those which challenged the accepted patriarchal order or moral code. Through humiliation rituals of one form or another, offenders would be reformed, potential criminals would be deterred, and the neighbourhood would be reminded of their duty to behave properly. Within this context, and as the above examples have shown, shame was not merely a one-dimensional tool used to influence the actions and behaviour of individuals as traditional definitions suggest. The audience for shaming rituals were also an essential element of the process, and their participation in such action to supplement the justice of courts indicated a craving to see justice in action. When organised by a community, shaming rituals facilitated the articulation of grievances and enabled groups to regain or claim control over situations which demanded forms of 'public' intervention or expression. In these episodes, shame should not be considered as an inflexible entity, but rather as a dynamic interaction which held enduring significance for all of those involved.

The examples and case-studies presented in this chapter clearly demonstrate just how humiliating and tortuous forms of communal punishment could be. The employment of 'rough music' as a precursor to a prescribed shaming ritual was fairly universal, although there were marked regional variations in how the episodes played out. The English versions of unofficial community shame-based punishments, such as the ducking-stool or skimmington ride, have been extensively written about elsewhere, and on the whole, appear to have been rather mocking and jovial in tone and practice. By way of contrast, the Scottish and Welsh versions, which have been largely neglected by historians up to this point, were seemingly implemented as 'real' punishments and were more of a calculated blend of prolonged shame and physical harm. Certainly, although there was an obvious ritualistic side to Celtic episodes of 'branking', 'riding the stang' or 'Ceffyl Pren', they appear to have been regarded with far more seriousness by the participants concerned, when compared to their English equivalents. The frequency and effectiveness of these types of episodes is very difficult to gauge, and more detailed work on local source material is necessary before any more definitive conclusions are made. It can be suggested, nonetheless, that in Scotland and Wales at least, the ferocity of the punishments meted out, as well as the inevitable and lasting stigma involved, probably resulted in repeat performances being unwarranted and unnecessary.

Two further significant points of interest are illuminated by the preceding analysis. The first is that unruly women who participated in sexual transgressions or boisterous behaviour were particular targets for communal shaming punishments in Scotland and Wales during the pre-modern period. Such women had to be made examples of, as it was believed that through their 'deviant' actions they had not only shamed themselves, their families and their local neighbourhood, but they had also shamed their gender too and had betrayed the notional qualities of their 'fairer' sex. All of these factors, coupled with the fierce nature of the pre-modern shaming episodes in the Celtic fringe, served to enhance the perception that these disruptive women would make 'good candidates' for specific types of opprobrious punishment. From the community's point of view, the subjugation of these women would bring peace to the neighbourhood and would result in a restoration of the established order. Moreover, it was believed that the women themselves would ultimately benefit from the perceived remedial qualities of public shaming; through the reformation of their character, through private penitence and public absolution, and then through their subsequent reintegration into community life.

Another interesting factor identified above is that, particularly in the Scottish context, communal shaming punishments could function and work alongside other more 'formal' or 'official' practices such as church appearances and legal indictments. Rather than operating as a separate, autonomous entity, the community played its part within a complex web of societal layers concerned with the regulation of the bad behaviour, with the authority of the church dominating the various proceedings. Episodes of communal shaming are one instance during the pre-modern period where the Scottish church could retain its influence and demonstrate its power at a local level, despite the fact that more centrally, the strength of its authority had been undermined and diminished.

Despite abundant evidence which testifies to the longevity of public shaming, there are nonetheless, various indications which point to the growing encroachment of the state upon popular practices of this sort. Over time, instances of communal public shaming came to be increasingly regarded as inappropriate and were thought to be uncivilised and overly riotous, rather than reconciliatory and reformative.[84] This wider transformation in attitude towards the use of shame as a crude tool for subjugation and improvement marks something of a social and cultural shift. However this change was complex and can by no means be equated with either civilisation or modernisation. Important aspects of that change and their history will now be investigated and explored in the subsequent chapters of this volume.

3

The Shame and Fame of 'Half-Hangit Maggie': Attitudes to the Child Murderer in Early Modern Scotland

In a variation upon the previous chapter, where the shaming rituals described were community-based, this chapter relates to the more state-sanctioned forms of opprobrium that operated in relation to formally recognised crimes. More specifically, this chapter is centred around an intriguing and famous infanticide case from early eighteenth century Scotland, involving a woman called Margaret (or as she was better known Maggie) Dickson. This particular example and the reactions to it, can tell us much about how crimes committed by women (such as infanticide) were regarded not only by the general public, but also by the legal and moral authorities of the day. In the Scottish context at least, there appears to have been a clear distinction (or ideological clash) between the opinions of these two social interest groups with regard to the 'degree' of shame and humiliation that should and could be afforded a female felon. Consequently, given the concerns of our particular study in this volume, the seemingly conflicting experience of shame and repentance north of the Tweed is important to our investigation. Moreover this example suggests to us how shame could live beyond the strict confines of a regulated and understood primitive culture and how it was, even in the eighteenth century, a response capable of being fashioned and reshaped to suit the different purposes of protagonist, authority and onlooker.

In order to demonstrate the disparity of opinion regarding the pertinence of shame punishments, we need to look past the formal records of criminal behaviour (such as depositions and indictments) and look towards the more popular forms of literature that were readily produced and widely available during the early modern period. Certainly, the implementation of shaming rituals associated with the penal regime in eighteenth century Scotland seems from the outside at least, to have been rigorous, necessary and accepted by all. However, by delving deeper into cases such as that of Maggie Dickson, we can learn that for some criminals, the humiliation associated with their offences (whether self-imposed or sanctioned) only went so far. Moreover we can discover that the belief in shame as a just and appropriate element of the judicial process was not as widely diffused throughout society as the authorities hoped and believed. When 'rebellious' instances which overturned the established moral order became visible, as they did in the case of Maggie Dickson, the authorities felt the need to react, to re-impose their authority, and ultimately, to re-shame the individual concerned as we will see.

Many historians have already identified the close relationship that exists between the concept of shame and the crime of infanticide. Indeed, it is generally accepted that the notion of opprobrium lies at the very heart of new-born child murder.[1] For instance, infanticide is usually committed in the first place to avoid the humiliation of an illegitimate pregnancy.[2] Proven sexual relations outside marriage could impose permanent dishonour upon a woman and her kin, especially in the context of a staunchly Presbyterian country such as Scotland where women were charged to make appearances before the church court (known as the Kirk Session) as punishment for their participation in acts of so-called 'scandalous carriage'.[3]

In addition, if an act of infanticide was discovered and an indictment brought, the charge was considered one of the most dishonourable offences on the statute book as predominantly the crime was committed by women, who were not supposed to participate in interpersonal violence. Moreover, because infanticide was perpetrated by a mother against her own child the crime suggested something dark, sinister, anti-maternal and unforgivable. The killing of a new-born child by its mother openly contradicted normally understood and expected maternal instinct and was regarded as a wholly unnatural transgression. Infanticide was clearly seen as a crime against womanhood, and more importantly a crime against the perceptions of how women, and mothers in particular, were expected to behave. Women who contravened this norm and killed their newborns had turned their backs on civil society, humanity and their gender. During the first half of the eighteenth century in particular, these women were commonly given the appellation 'monster' or 'demon' in court indictments as a reflection of the abhorrence provoked by their crimes.[4] Clearly, and in order to protect notions of gendered normality, infanticide could not be tolerated in a more 'enlightened' society. Consequently, infanticidal mothers came to be shamed both on account of their actions, and on account of their sex.

We must remember too, moreover, that the opprobrium associated with the committal of infanticide was not merely personal and private to the specific individual involved. Rather, infanticide was very much a communal offence in the early modern period. At nearly every juncture in the judicial process, members of the local community (particularly church elders, magistrates, midwives and other 'authority' figures) were called upon to expose the behaviour, character and particular actions of the women accused of killing their new-born infants.[5] Here we can see that shame regularly also functions outside of the individual psyche, and that the context in which it occurs is crucial to its efficiency, longevity and success.

In Scotland, criminal investigations of child murder were commonly presided over by Kirk Session ministers if the body of a new-born infant was found in their parish, or if one of their parishioners was suspected of carrying illegitimate offspring. Within the staunchly Calvinist context that was prevalent north of the Tweed in the early modern period, arguably, having the chief church elder at the forefront of this kind of investigation must have encouraged a higher degree of communal involvement in this type of episode than was the case elsewhere.[6] Through private interrogations, the minister prevailed upon his parishioners to reveal all they knew about the woman accused and/or the circumstances of the case whether it be good or bad, or whether it be based on fact or merely on local gossip and rumour.[7] The intensified community interest in this type of offence, north of the border, meant that the women who perpetrated new-born child murder in the Scottish milieu were seemingly less likely to be ignored and their crimes less likely to remain undiscovered. Not only did this scrupulous environment potentially increase the indictment rate for this kind of crime in Scotland compared with elsewhere, but it also ensured that those Scottish women who were accused of infanticide and new-born child murder would find it especially difficult to escape the opprobrium associated with that type of offence.[8] The life and crimes of infanticidal women became public knowledge very quickly and the shame associated with this crime in particular, appears to have resounded far and wide for the majority of the women so accused.

For Scottish women in particular, the weight of shame associated with this type of crime seems to have been intensified by the way in which the offence was dealt with by the judiciary. Unlike most other crimes for which women were indicted north of the border during the early modern period, convicted infanticidal mothers were more likely to receive 'exemplary' forms of punishment compounded with 'shame'. These could include hanging followed by the spectacle of public ana-tomisation, rather than the hidden and less obviously public sentences of banishment or transportation.[9] Such forms of post-mortem punish-ment were usually reserved for the most violent of male felons (such as murderers or robbers)[10] and their application to female infanticide con-victs, indicates just how unfavourably this crime was regarded by the Scottish legal authorities of the early modern period.

On their way to the gallows and even after meeting their fate, the shame usually levelled at infanticidal women was quite deafening and unremitting. In Scotland, during the eighteenth century, popular broad-side literature about infanticidal mothers significantly outnumbered publications produced about other forms of criminal activity (regard-less of gender) by three to one.[11] Child murder was something of a pre-occupation with the moral and legal authorities in Scotland. Often dripping with religious rhetoric, as we will see, this broadside material repeatedly convinced the populace that infanticide was a dreadful sin and a heinous crime. Thus it argued the degrading and shameful punish-ments meted out to the women who committed this crime were entirely appropriate and just. For the women accused of new-born child murder in Scotland and indeed elsewhere in the early modern period, shame was simply inescapable.

It was within this context of humiliation and opprobrium that Maggie Dickson was brought to the public's attention, when she was tried for parricide and the murder of her own child at the High Court of Justiciary in Edinburgh, during the summer of 1724.[12] The court heard that the body of a new-born male child was discovered, washed up on the banks of the River Tweed near Kelso (in the Scottish borders) on the 19th of December 1723. There were no obvious marks of vio-lence upon the child, but in any case (and as was standard procedure in such instances) the community authorities ordered a search of the vicinity to be conducted in an attempt to find a female who bore the symptoms of a so-called 'green woman'; in other words, a woman who had lately given birth to a child.[13] After carrying out several physical examinations upon suspected individuals, the authorities came across a woman called Margaret (or Maggie) Dickson who had 'ripe' milk in her breasts alongside other post-partum symptoms. After further investiga-tion, Maggie confessed that she was the mother of the child found dead. It is unclear, from the indictment evidence at least, who the father of Maggie's child was, although it is intimated in the associated publications and pamphlet literature produced at the time, that the child was the result of a 'shameful' extra-marital affair.[14]

As part of her confession, before the Justices of the Peace for Roxburgh, Maggie Dickson claimed that the child had been still-born, and that she had kept the corpse in her bed for well over a week before disposing of it in the nearby river.[15] The retention of the child's remains may indicate, or at the very least suggest, that Maggie was suffering from some form of mental malaise which had set in either during, or immediately after, the birth of her child.[16] However, such a supposition was of little interest to the court authorities of early modern Scotland. Maggie had admitted that she had concealed her pregnancy and had not called for help or assistance in the birth. With this admission the court was able to sustain that her actions conformed to the infanticide statute of 1690 with regard to concealment. This was despite the fact that as a married woman, several elements of the act and its assumptions were judicially irrelevant and inapplicable to the specific circumstances of her case.[17]

As the trial proceeded, witness testimony was heard from four individuals called by the prosecution: a surgeon, a midwife and two women who resided in the local community where the crime had been committed. Interestingly, the testimony of these witnesses did little to embellish the facts associated with the case, and instead their evidence merely served to substantiate the information offered by Maggie in her own confession. The only exception to this was the testimony of one Margaret Lenman, who reported that when Margaret Dickson was initially arrested on suspicion of new-born child murder, she steadfastly refused to confess to the crimes charged against her. According to Lenman, Maggie only changed her mind about her judicial position, when she was brought before the local minister, Mr Ramsay, and it was he who 'persuaded' or 'shamed' her to enter a confession before the Justices of the Peace for Roxburgh.[18] The evidence of Margaret Lenman serves to reiterate just how crucial the role of the church and the wider community were in 'managing' instances of infanticide or new-born child murder in early modern Scotland.

In any event, the jury returned their verdict against Maggie Dickson on the 3rd of August 1724, finding her guilty by a unanimous verdict upon the details of her own judicial confession.[19] The jury also found the defence that the pannel (or accused) had actively revealed her condition during her pregnancy to be not proven. The judge in the case described Maggie's offence as a '...horrid and barbarous occult crime' committed by '...an unnatural woman', before going on to sentence her to death by hanging upon a gibbet.[20]

In many respects, the case brought against Maggie Dickson in 1724 was fairly typical of Scottish infanticide indictments from the early modern period. Maggie, along with most women accused of infanticide north of the Tweed, appeared penitent before the court. Yet she defended her actions by arguing that her infant had been still-born and, due to the post-partum panic that ensued, she had disposed of the dead body in a hurried and haphazard manner.[21] In terms of motive too, Maggie was not unlike the vast majority of her criminal counterparts when she declared that she had (largely) concealed her pregnancy in order to avoid the opprobrium associated with bearing an 'unlawful' child.[22] As has already been indicated, the determination on the part of these women to avoid the shame associated with illegitimacy must have been all the more pressing in the context of a country where inappropriate behaviour of a sexual nature was rarely tolerated or accepted. Finally, and as was common in the Scottish Judiciary Court in the first half of the eighteenth century, the court's treatment of women like Maggie Dickson appears to have been somewhat calculated and instrumental. Despite the regularly flimsy nature of the evidence presented in indictments for new-born child murder, there was seemingly little room for leniency amongst the Scottish legal authorities of the day. Their reactions were often predictable when faced with women who were accused of stepping outside the accepted boundaries of what was considered 'normal' gendered or maternal behaviour. The conviction rate for infanticide indictments in Scotland at the time when Maggie Dickson's case was brought to trial was considerable, and it was exceedingly rare for non-capital sentences to emerge from these judgements.[23]

Up to this point in the story at least, Maggie Dickson's case is only unusual in two respects. Firstly, it was relatively rare in the early modern period for a married woman to be indicted for new-born child murder.[24] It was far more common for married women to dispose of their infants through 'exposure', where they would simply leave the child in a crib on the steps of a church or a similar perceived place of care.[25] Alternatively, it was easier for married women to commit child murder through more deliberate neglect, as an infant death could be more readily explained by a married woman as a natural occurrence, as married women would have less of an obvious motive for infanticide compared to an unmarried mother.[26] Most married mothers, who had indulged in illicit extra-marital affairs during the early modern period, may well have been able to hide their pregnancies within the confines of their marriage. However, as Maggie Dickson's husband was an itinerant labourer at this time, we can surmise that it may have been difficult for her to pass off her child as a product of their marriage. The absence of married women indicted or prosecuted for new-born child murder appears to be a common feature of this type of crime in western cultures during the early modern era. Accordingly then, the Maggie Dickson episode provides us with a fairly unique example of the desperate circumstances often associated with pregnancy and childbirth during this period.

The second element which makes Maggie Dickson's case unusual, at least, in a specifically Scottish context, is that her actions do not appear to have been violent at any point. Yet, as has been written elsewhere, the overwhelming majority of Scottish women who were indicted for infanticide had perpetrated the offence in an overtly aggressive and blood-thirsty manner. In at least 63 per cent of the indictments for infanticide brought to trial against lowland Scottish women between 1750 and 1815, blood had been shed in the committal of the crime; 48 per cent of these infants had been killed after being attacked with a sharp instrument and 51 per cent had been battered to death.[27] The levels of excessive violence that appear to have been perpetrated by Scottish women stand in stark contrast with the methodologies associated with this crime elsewhere. Rather than adopting more overt forms of violence, asphyxia was the principal means of infanticide in Europe during the pre-modern period.[28] As Laura Gowing has observed, generally, infanticide was '...understood to be a crime not of violent activity but of passivity or neglect.'[29] It is very difficult to explain why Scottish women were seemingly so much more violent in the perpetration of this kind of murderous activity than their counterparts elsewhere during the pre-modern period. Shame must have been a significant factor, although economic issues, revenge, jealousy, feelings of abandonment and loneliness as well as manifestations of mental incapacity might have had a part to play too.[30]

Despite the prevailing pattern of violence amongst Scottish infanticidal women, there is no evidence to suggest that Maggie Dickson was overtly cruel towards her new-born child.[31] This, along with her marital status, makes Maggie's case fairly unique in terms of the Scottish context of this crime, and both of these anomalies together, make her conviction rather remarkable. In the fierce judicial context in operation north of the Tweed, the Scottish authorities were principally preoccupied with prosecuting violent, unmarried mothers accused of killing their new-born infants, yet Maggie Dickson did not belong to either of these categories.

The prosecution brought against Maggie Dickson appears to have been even more problematic than was usually the case in infanticide trials in pre-modern Scotland for a variety of reasons and, as a result, a great deal of legal wrangling is evident in relation to this case. For instance, aside from the standard defence of still-birth already alluded to, Maggie Dickson's legal team offered several other arguments on her behalf in an attempt to negate the relevance of the 1690 statute and to have the indictment dismissed. Firstly, the defence claimed that Maggie had been 'coerced' or 'forced' into making her original (extra-judicial) confession, and only did so because she was confused and frightened at the time. The defence also criticised the search for suspects that had been carried out by the local authorities which, it was argued, had not been conducted thoroughly enough, but had simply come to an abrupt end when it was discovered that Maggie Dickson exhibited the symptoms of a 'green woman'. It was argued that had the search been carried out in a more professional, meticulous manner, several other suspects may have arguably come to light. Moreover, the court heard, if a proper interrogation of the defendant had been carried out at the time, it would have revealed that Maggie had the symptoms of a 'green woman' because she was still suckling her youngest child, and not because she had recently given birth.[32]

Probably the most 'persuasive' of the defences offered by Maggie Dickson's legal team was that of her marital status. The defence lawyers reminded the court of the typical interpretation of the 1690 statute: 'The said act of Parliament, has always been understood and interpreted by your Lordships, to extend only to single, not to married women; and that justly, because married women having husbands (who by law are obliged to father their offspring) can be under no temptation to murder their children.'[33] Accordingly, the defence argued that as a married woman, not only would Maggie Dickson have no motive to murder her 'legitimate' child, but she would also have little opportunity to conceal her pregnancy from her husband.

Aside from the relatively robust defences offered, it would appear that the incriminating evidence offered against Maggie Dickson was rather slim and circumstantial. For instance, there was no evidence that the child found dead had actually been murdered; similarly there was no direct physical evidence produced to connect Maggie to the said child or indeed to its demise. Perhaps more importantly (at least from a statutory perspective), the defence team claimed that they could prove that Maggie had revealed her condition to others during her pregnancy and thus had the tacit acceptance of her neighbours. In addition, the language used by the prosecution witnesses in this case suggests a rather tentative approach to the delivery of testimony which is indicative of a rather sympathetic attitude towards Maggie's plight on the part of the local community. This kind of attitude is fairly unique in the Scottish context of new-born child murder. The benign and conciliatory descriptions offered to refute the indictment reveal a different, more compassionate attitude towards infanticide not usually encountered in the courtroom. This is especially obvious when set against the fierce, intimidating and condemnatory hyperbole used by the prosecuting lawyers and authorities in this case which seemed intent on activating shame as a tool against Maggie Dickson. A good example of this contrast in language is exhibited around descriptions of how the infant's body had allegedly been disposed of. The Advocate Depute declared that the pannel (accused) '...wickedly and malevolently threw the body of the deceased into the River Tweed.'[34] In contrast, witnesses like Ann Pringle, Margaret Lenman and Janet Scot described how the pannel 'put' or 'laid' the body of the child in the Tweed.[35] Although apparently a subtle difference in semantics, the perfunctory and more sympathetic testimony given by prosecution witnesses at Maggie Dickson's trial is certainly unusual and adds to the precariousness of the evidence against her.

Perhaps because of the flimsy nature of the evidence, the relatively robust defences offered and the apparent sympathy for the accused, Maggie Dickson's legal team seemed to have felt confident that the verdict would be in her favour. So much so, in fact, that despite applying for 'Letters of Exculpation' to call three defence witnesses to the trial to testify to Maggie having revealed her pregnancy, none of these three individuals were called into the courtroom during the trial.[36] The defence clearly believed that there was insufficient evidence to warrant a conviction against Maggie Dickson, and thus they assumed that evidence in exculpation was neither warranted nor necessary. Clearly, this was a fatal error of judgement.

As suggested above, Maggie Dickson's case occurred at a time when the Scottish judicial authorities were preoccupied with convicting and executing women suspected of killing their new-born infants. In the first half of the eighteenth century in particular, the courts (both religious and secular) were particularly keen to expose and shame infanticidal women as dangerous traitors to their sex who ought to be eradicated from society. Consequently, the lack of incriminating evidence against Maggie Dickson was outweighed, not only by contemporary establishment attitudes towards the crime she was accused of, but also by other factors related to her own specific circumstances. For example, although the extra-marital affair which resulted in Maggie's pregnancy was not referred to directly in court, it was certainly alluded to on occasion.[37] In any case and, as has already been indicated, Maggie's personal circumstances were well documented at the time through contemporary publications and pamphlet literature.[38] It seems likely that the 'public' nature of Maggie's 'private' life may have condemned her. She was conceivably damned for breaking the boundaries of acceptable behaviour, not once but twice; firstly by indulging in an immoral and illicit relationship out of wedlock which had resulted in an 'unlawful' pregnancy, and then by being accused of infanticide, which at that particular moment in time was the key concern of the Scottish legal system. In other words she appeared as an individual which the authorities had a clear and vested interest in both shaming and punishing.

Another, arguably more subtle, explanation for the determination of the Scottish authorities to convict Maggie Dickson on the back of limited and insubstantial evidence comes in the indictment papers sent to the High Court of Justiciary by the Justices of the Peace for Roxburgh.[39] In this documentation, the Justices repeatedly refer to Maggie as a 'stranger' to the local community, and it appears, that she was targeted as a suspect, initially at least, because she was an itinerant alien. Seemingly the local authorities were more hostile to Maggie Dickson and her circumstances and therefore more determined to bring about her conviction, because she was regarded as an outsider. It is certainly possible that the pressures on women with illegitimate or unlawful children were greater in areas where they were regarded as interlopers. The shame levelled at these women may have been more intense because the 'host' community wanted to be rid of them for moral or more likely, for economic reasons. The fact that Maggie had committed her crime in an unfamiliar locality worked alongside her other personal circumstances to negate the strength of the defence case, and expose her to the rigour of the Scottish legal authorities.

The determination of the authorities to convict and punish infanticidal women (which seems to have been all the more prevalent in the case of Maggie Dickson) resulted in the confessions of some women convicted of new-born child murder becoming matters of shame, notoriety and obvious didactic purpose. Many confessions appeared as pamphlets prior to their execution and were readily distributed to the populace. Not only was this done in order to invite individuals to attend the hanging, but the confessional material was also circulated to encourage the public at large to participate in the shaming rituals so closely involved with the spectacle of execution.[40]

The authorities used every device available to them to maximise the message that an execution could deliver to the public at large.

Public punishment of this nature was acknowledged to be '...pure theatre'.[41] In the absence of a police force, according to the historian R. McGowen, the spectacle of execution was regarded as the most economic and effective way of instructing the population to respect the law.[42] In Scotland, as well as England, executions were always held on a market day to ensure a significant number of people saw them[43] (as many as 30,000 people turned out to witness executions in Glasgow in the pre-modern period)[44] and various forms of pamphleted information 'advertising' the spectacle were regularly distributed to target audiences further afield.[45] Furthermore, the impact of a public execution was made doubly severe due its largely localised nature, as many members of the crowd of spectators would actually know the condemned individual about to be 'launched into eternity' to meet their fate.[46]

In Ancien Régime France, according to J.R. Ruff, there were five ways of carrying out a sentence of execution, namely drawing and quartering, burning at the stake, breaking on the wheel, hanging and decapitation.[47] In Scotland, the favoured practice was hanging by the neck on a gibbet. After having all their goods and gear forfeit to the Crown, a convicted individual would be imprisoned and fed on bread and water up until the day they were to be hung. For women this period of imprisonment lasted 39 days on average, for men 37.5 days. The experience of the actual process of execution in Scotland and England appears to have been remarkably similar. The day of execution, what Foucault would describe as a 'social ritual'[48], began with the condemned individual being taken from prison in a horse-drawn cart along with a chaplain to be shamefully paraded through the streets and amongst the crowd until the place of execution was reached.[49] Having arrived at the gallows, the condemned individual would stand up in the cart, and was asked to deliver what was commonly known as a 'dying speech'.[50] The accused would usually give a list of past indiscretions in order to '...remind spectators that the death they were about to witness should constitute an awful warning.'[51] It was not enough that the criminal should die accepting his or her fate penitently and passively, the condemned had to publicly acknowledge that the justice they were about to receive (along with their present opprobrium) was both a correct and necessary purgative shaming ritual. These speeches were regularly given on the gallows in Scotland during the eighteenth century and were advantageous to both the state and the church[52]: 'They legitimised not only the punishment being suffered by the individual felon, but also the whole structure of secular and religious authority.'[53]

Despite occasional departures from normal practices from time to time, the executioner's task in the case of a simple hanging was relatively straightforward. The scaffold consisted of three posts, ten and 12 feet high, held apart by three connecting cross-beams at the top.[54] Whilst standing on the cart, in the presence of the chaplain, the criminal's feet were bound and a mask (usually a night-cap) was placed over the face. The hangman attached one end of a rope around the prisoner's neck and the other end to the gibbet. A handkerchief was dropped as a signal for the executioner to whip the horses causing the cart to dart forward from under the prisoner's feet. Death was humiliating, seemingly slow and resulted from asphyxiation.[55] For this reason, according to J.A. Sharpe, 'It was apparently customary to curtail the death-throes of the condemned by pulling on their legs.'[56] This was how executions were carried out in Scotland until the late 1780s when a new 'mechanical' system was introduced.[57] In the earlier period, however, and in the absence of more humane, modern technology, it is clear that shame had a key part to play at every stage of the execution process.

The confessional element of capital punishment was the key tool used to ensure that the populace took away the 'appropriate' message from the spectacle they were about to witness. In addition, and as indicated above, these criminal biographies also served to publicly humiliate the convict, and render them penitent, powerless and obviously exposed before their peers. One of these broadside confessions was circulated prior to Maggie Dickson's execution.

Maggie Dickson's gallows speech was a fairly substantive publication and not untypical of this kind of pamphlet literature, as it provides a detailed account of Maggie's past indiscretions and chronicles how she eventually came to commit the crime for which she was to be executed.[58] The documentation goes to great lengths to emphasise that initially at least, Maggie had been brought up by her parents to respect the Protestant religion and to hold its teachings and principles in high regard. As the speech recounts: 'My parents...discharged a faithful duty, educating me not only in reading the Holy Scriptures, but also in making me to understand the duties therein contained, and the Sins therein forbidden; as also the rewards promised in case of obedience, and punishments therein threatened in case of disobedience.'[59] The confession claims that Maggie remained dutiful and reverent in her younger years, until she left home at the age of 19 to be married to a man disliked by both of her parents. From that time onwards it seems that Maggie '...decayed every day in her [sic] spiritual life, left off to seek the Lord, forgot him, slighted and rejected the offers of Grace and

Mercy, and sought satisfaction in the creatures more than in God the creator.'[60] Clearly, the pamphlet is intimating that by ignoring her parents' advice and marrying a man they disapproved of, Maggie had entered a new, darker phase in her life history.

The description offered of Maggie Dickson's marriage in the gallows speech is far from idyllic, as various references are made to chronic poverty, alcohol abuse and various cruelties committed against Maggie by her spouse. These issues and circumstances culminated in an initial separation between the marital partners and then a desertion, as Maggie left for Newcastle (where some of her relatives resided) with two young children in tow. On route, however, she slept with a young man after becoming inebriated in his company, and this shameful misadventure, resulted in her being with child for the third time. The gallows speech expresses Maggie's remorse and shame for her ill-judged behaviour saying: 'The next day I wept very sore, and was cast down in a great measure, and ever afterwards I walked with a bowed down back, for fighting against God, taking part with the Devil even to the ruin of my soul and the dishonour of God; I became [sic] a discredit unto religion, and now by the destruction of my body, a discredit to the place I was brought up in.'[61]

The confession then continues with a detailed description of the specific circumstances relating to Maggie's conviction, and how she concealed her pregnancy and the birth of her 'unlawful' child from her friends, family and fellow lodgers. She confesses that what she had done was '...a most heinous Sin, being against the light of my own conscience, for which God may justly condemn me among many others.' She continues declaring: '...I own the justness of the sentence, as also I desire to bless God that hath brought my Sin to light, for if I had gone on as I was, where would I have landed, or if I had been freed at this time, I might have gone from one Evil to worse [sic], until I had arrived at the utmost height of wickedness, and indeed I have come a great length already.'[62]

The speech then comes to a dramatic conclusion with Maggie asking for forgiveness for what she has done and then she finally declares '...it is my earnest desire, that all into whose hands this may come, may take example by me, particularly young persons, that they may not go astray as I have done...Farewell vain and sinful world, and welcome Jesus and eternal life through him, unto whose hands I commend my spirit.'[63]

The extent to which Maggie Dickson actually penned or even dictated her own gallows speech can certainly be debated.[64] However, the identification or validation of authorship is surely less significant, when compared with the three-fold message that this type of literature was meant to convey – namely that the sentence meted out against Maggie was justified; that she had been rendered duly penitent and remorseful for her crimes and misdemeanours, and that the shame she had been subjected to in making this public confession ought to serve as a warning to deter other potentially like-minded women.

Given the rather unexceptional nature of the circumstances surrounding the crimes allegedly committed by Maggie Dickson, and the rather unconvincing nature of the evidence against her (as indicated above), it seems rather remarkable that a fairly lengthy pamphlet publication has been entirely dedicated to her case. Perhaps the fact that Maggie was married may go some way to explain the heightened levels of attention and publicity that she received. Indeed her committal for new-born child murder within the confines or sanctity of marriage enabled the authorities to use Maggie Dickson's case as a vehicle by which to emphasise and publicise the resilience of the Scottish judicial system. It is possible that the humiliation and opprobrium launched in Maggie's direction was greater as a result of this, compared to say an unmarried mother who had terminated the life of an illegitimate offspring. Was the fact that she was deemed to be an outcast or 'stranger' to the community where she committed the crime an important factor? It is difficult to discern evidence for these assertions and questions with any certainty, but in any event, by circulating this type of broadside material, which was almost saturated with Calvinist rhetoric, the scene was psychologically set for Maggie Dickson's execution. The publication unequivocally sent a clear message to the general public of the justice of the fate about to befall her, and the perpetual humiliation and shame associated with her crimes.

However, matters didn't exactly work out as the authorities intended. After Maggie Dickson had been hung, she was cut down and placed in a coffin which was to be transported to Inveresk, near Musselburgh for interment. During this process, a scuffle broke out between Maggie's friends and some apprentice surgeons who wanted her cadaver to dissect. Using a hammer, the medical students broke down one side of the coffin, but being prevented from removing the body inside, they ran off. On the road to Inveresk, the men entrusted with transporting Maggie's body, stopped off for refreshments about two miles into their journey, and whilst they were supping their beer, they started to hear noises from within the coffin. When the coffin lid was removed, Maggie Dickson sat up in a rather befuddled state complaining of a dry mouth and a sore neck! At the time, the authorities believed that when the medical students damaged her coffin, Maggie was given some air, and this, accompanied with the jolting of the funeral cart, revived her and rejuvenated her vital signs. Maggie was thereafter examined by a doctor and a phlebotomist who let her blood, and she went on to make a full recovery from her ordeal.[65]

Although execution survivals were not unheard of during the early modern period,[66] Maggie Dickson's case is certainly unusual in this respect. What is even more remarkable, however, is the amount of evidence we have concerning the *reaction* to her survival. Numerous press reports and publications remain which recount how the Scottish populace were utterly fascinated by Maggie's story; how they came to visit her after the event; how she made money out of what had happened to her and indeed, how in effect, she became an early modern celebrity, on the back of surviving an execution for new-born child murder.[67] As one report noted in 1724 'She is at present in her Brother's House at Musselburgh, in perfect health and judgement, and had been visited by almost every body here, high and low. She has had a great deal of money given her by those who have seen her, and several others have sent her money from this place.'[68] Another account notes that upon Maggie visiting a local church after her 'reanimation' she was '...almost overwhelmed by a vast crowd of people, who could not satisfy themselves with gazing upon one thus, as it were, alive from the dead. She was finally obliged to take refuge in a house, and escape by the backdoor.'[69] Clearly, Maggie Dickson's ordeal had given her cult-heroine status among the people of central Scotland during the early eighteenth century. Through her providential survival and resulting celebrity status her shame was converted to fame.[70]

Aside from the more generalised and formal narrative accounts of Maggie Dickson's life history, what is even more interesting still is the growing popular voice that could be heard after Maggie's botched execution. This sympathised not only with her plight specifically, but more importantly perhaps, with the plight of infanticidal mothers in general. Poems, letters and commentaries were circulated by all manner of people in the wake of Maggie's hanging which described infanticidal mothers as 'unfortunates', as 'victims', and as women who merited pity rather than persecution.[71] In relation to Maggie's case more specifically for instance, one commentary states: 'The observation to be made on this uncommon affair amounts to no more than a lesson of caution to juries to be careful how they convict the culprit on circumstantial evidence: for the evidence against this woman was at best but circumstantial; and her steady denial of her guilt after her wonderful escape from the grave, is a strong presumptive argument that she was not guilty.'[72] This was arguably citing Maggie's providential survival as a reason to shame an overzealous jury. One intriguing possibility is that Maggie's survival may have triggered, in some, feelings of shame about how ruthlessly contemporary Scottish society treated infanticidal mothers.

The surge in sympathy from the more populist voice is interesting when considered against evidence which suggests that infanticidal women in Scotland were more violent than their counterparts elsewhere. Moreover it provides us with a stark contrast to the hyperbole and rhetoric emanating from the legal and moral authorities of the day north of the border, who as we have seen, labelled such women as 'monsters of inhumanity'. Indeed, the Scottish authorities were very unhappy and perturbed by the widespread reaction to Maggie Dickson's trial, and they felt the need to quash the emerging sympathetic noises being voiced, in order to reinforce the power and prerogative of the judicial and moral system.

Engaging in a form of ideological warfare with the general populace, the Scottish authorities employed a range of tactics in an attempt to quell the burgeoning tide of sympathy not only for Maggie Dickson herself, but also for the plight of infanticidal women more widely. They 'encouraged' some of the outspoken or sympathetic voices to recant their opinions in print, and a few individuals observed this request, most notably those who were church ministers.[73] Next, the authorities carried out a detailed investigation of what had happened with regard to the execution itself, and they published their findings in the process papers for the High Court of Justiciary. Eventually they issued a directive that should a similar problem occur again, then the hangman responsible would be executed in the place of the convict who had escaped the ultimate punishment! A bill was also filed by the King's advocate against the sheriff responsible for overseeing capital punishment procedures in Edinburgh, charging him with omitting to fulfil the law and abandoning the duties of his office.[74]

Finally, and in a blatant attempt to reignite the shame process in the direction of Maggie Dickson and women like her, the authorities published two further 'confessions' on Maggie's behalf, both of which were unusually written in a more obviously 'populist' style, in the form of poetic stanzas. In a traditional oral culture, the use of memorable rhyming poetic stanzas was intended to ensure a wider and deeper absorption of the moral message of Maggie's narrative. The first of these publications, entitled *A Warning to the Wicked, or, Margaret Dickson's Welcome to the Gibbet* was produced shortly after Maggie's botched execution in 1724,

'Half-Hangit Maggie', a popular eighteenth century woodcut depicting Maggie Dickson's 'miraculous' recovery from execution.

and although it does contain a wealth of religious anecdotes and pious sentiment, it is far coarser in language and style than the earlier gallows speech.[75] For instance, when outlining Maggie's offences, the pamphlet declares:

> Her Heart grew fear'd, loath'd every Thing was good,
> And she indulg'd the De'il of Flesh and Blood.
> The Flame of Lust no Opposition meets,
> Commits Adultery, and the Crime repeats,
> Then Satan drives the Nail into the Head,
> Pushes her on to slay her new born Seed;
> Lying and Drinking did the Work begin,
> 'Till she's a Master-piece, and consummate in Sin.

The principles of penitence and repentance, which usually lie at the heart of this type of publication are wholly absent from this particular broadside. Instead, this document is a blatant attempt on the part of the Scottish establishment to besmirch Maggie Dickson's character once more. By doing this, the authorities hoped to re-establish an 'appropriate' antagonistic attitude towards infanticidal women amongst the public, and to vindicate the tough stance taken by the Scottish courts towards the women accused of this offence. Indeed, whilst the poem recognises that Maggie was spared from the 'ultimate' punishment, it goes on to predict that 'justice' will inevitably come to bear and that the eternal suffering to be endured, will act as an appropriate substitute for the failed execution. As the pamphlet describes:

> Tho' she survived the executing Cord,
> She can't survive the Justice of our Lord,
> The Terrors of the Gibbet soon abate,
> Her seeming sanctity and holy Hate.
> The more she Mercies get, she sins the more,
> Is ten Times greater Devil than before…
> The Miscreant kills the Fruit of her own Womb,
> To make Damnation her eternal Doom.

The notion that Maggie Dickson remained unrepentant and remorseless after her reanimation and survival, was not simply confined to this particular pamphlet, but rather it appears in various accounts of her remarkable case and at various junctures.[76] It is likely, the Scottish authorities acted to 'encourage' publishers to sully Maggie's character and to humiliate her all over again, just as they had previously 'encouraged' local correspondents to retract their sympathetic letters and poems in the wake of her bungled execution.

The second confession published by the authorities in the aftermath of Maggie Dickson's 'resurrection' was entitled *Margaret Dickson's Penetential Confession*.[77] It was far removed from the style employed in *A Warning to the Wicked*, and even more penitent and pious in tone than any of the previous publications produced in relation to her case. Yet, once again, the document insinuates that Maggie remained impenitent and sinful after her 'salvation'. For instance, her miraculous escape from the gallows is described as follows:

> But God, whose Mercy does so far extend,
> That from one Pole to th'other it doth not end,
> Did me preserve, as an Example high
> Of divine Omnipotence, which humane Sight can't spy.
> So I'm absolved from Men's servile Laws,
> Who dive into th' Effects, but not the Cause,
> A Life of Sanctity I purpos'd hence to lead,

But nat'ral Corruptions did almighty Grace exceed.
Had it but pleas'd my Great, Almighty Maker,
To take my Soul when finish'd was the Creature,
Into his High, Celestial Courts above,
Then I'd been blest with his Almighty Love;
At his Tribunal then could I appear
With joyful face, nor shed a sinful Tear:
My Life, I hope, shou'd ended been in Glory,
And not relaps'd to a more fatal Story,
But all of new my Crimes I do repeat,
Nor thinks upon the Terrors of my Fate.

This document was produced more than four years after Maggie Dickson was first sentenced to death by the Scottish courts, and arguably reflects that the ideological battle of wills between the authorities and the general populace simmered under the surface of Scottish society for some time. Arguably it also represents a reactionary attempt to shame the populous for their culpability in accepting and embracing the story of Maggie's survival and further prosperity at the hands of providence. Providence appeared to exonerate Maggie and her survival awkwardly appeared to be a retraction of her original confession! In the end, commentators report that Maggie lived for a further 30 years after her supposed execution date; she remarried her former husband and lived to a good age, with numerous children and grand-children about her.[78] The effectiveness of the attempts to re-shame Maggie Dickson can then certainly be debated given her apparently peaceful longevity and subsequently cosy family idyll. However the fact that the authorities felt the need to go to fairly extreme lengths to re-establish 'control' of her story in 1724 and beyond, tells us much about the nature of early modern Scottish society and the function of shame within it.

Opprobrium and shame lie at the very heart of the crime of infanticide. Child murder was usually committed in the first instance, in an attempt to avoid the shame of an illegitimate or 'unlawful' pregnancy. If discovered, the perpetrator was typically humiliated and vilified publicly, due to their betrayal of 'normal' maternal and gendered practices. During the early modern period and in the first half of the eighteenth century in particular, the Scottish establishment were preoccupied with the control of female criminality and the eradication of infanticidal mothers more specifically. Women indicted for child murder were shamed more aggressively than other offenders, and if convicted, they faced the types of augmented punishment normally reserved for the most callous or vicious of male felons. Moreover, the shaming process escalated for infanticidal women post-conviction to deafening levels, where the public at large got to hear of their aberrant lives, their deviant characters and their wicked behaviour. In the Scottish context, the shame process was delivered by a bilateral strategy between the Church and the State. For that reason, to outward appearances at least, the applied and skilled use of opprobrium seemed a pertinent, necessary and effective mechanism used to control the Scottish populace.

The remarkable case of Margaret Dickson (who came to be affectionately known as 'Half-Hangit Maggie') serves to raise various important issues about the process of shame and attitudes towards criminal women in early modern Scotland. Certainly this case-study of shame highlights the need for us to rethink attitudes to infanticidal women and indeed criminal women more generally. As the reaction to Maggie Dickson's case shows, the judicial condemnation of female offenders and the exposition of their shame was not the only opinion to be voiced on these matters. Popular concerns can also be heard, and it is only by listening more closely and engaging in this kind of case-study-based micro-history, that we can build up a truer picture of how criminal women and their crimes were regarded. Moreover shame was an essential vehicle for conveying these feelings and the reception of this emotion was crucial to the success of Scotland's moral order and this appeared coherent and credible to both the high and low of Scottish society.

Yet the case also shows that the shame process was scarcely an infallible one; the general populace did not always assimilate the message meant to come from the humiliation of offenders as broadly or as readily as the authorities often intended. Shame, it seems, had its limitations; and the populace at large may have been perturbed, at least on occasion, with how offenders were treated and regarded. In consequence of this, as we have seen, the legal and moral powers of the day could sometimes resort to rather desperate measures in order to appear resilient and to maintain the impression (to outward observers at least), that shame was a useful and acceptable tool by which to control standards of behaviour. In this way, we can see again that shame should not be regarded as a static, simplistic, one-dimensional entity. The fact that it always functioned within a complex context of social interactions meant that as a process it was flexible and could be modified depending on a particular set of circumstances, even if these were sometimes unusual or unexpected. After all, up to the point of Maggie's execution the ritual of shame followed a standard and traditional state and communally sanctioned pattern. It was only after its embarrassing failure that the dialogues and narratives of shame began to fragment in unexpected ways. As we have seen shame may have induced the wave of sympathy evident in the pamphlet literature for mothers guilty of infanticide, or the unusually harsh treatment of a married woman. Similarly those who were well disposed to Maggie and created her celebrity after her execution may have privately felt shame for their actions, or those of compatriots, in abusing one who God had providentially spared. Even the reactions of the authorities, those who most wished to control and limit dialogues and definitions of shame, were not immune to this fragmentation. Their recapitulation of Maggie's confession in many different guises eventually offered diverse flavours of her shame and repentance which themselves may have targeted different audiences out of necessity. Although the case of Maggie Dickson is unusual in terms of her own personal experience, the episode is significant nonetheless as it illuminates the vastly differing influence that shame could have upon a whole range of people, institutions and ideas.

4

'To Make Men of their Honesty Afraid': Shaming the Ideological Dissident 1650–1834

In pre-modern society, shame punishments were central to the operation of the law in England and many parts of Europe, and these seemingly reached their heyday in the seventeenth and early eighteenth centuries. They constituted an important and visible method of demonstrating the culpability and contrition of malefactors to the community at large. For a society without developed theories of criminology or penology they were, arguably, surprisingly effective. As we heard in the chapter before last, the fear of shame punishment constituted a significant deterrent to immoral and poor behaviour amongst the populace at large. As we are also aware, this was effective in strangely unforeseen ways which could alert society to its potential unpredictability. Although shame could strictly govern behaviour it paradoxically could also persuade individuals to commit still greater crimes, demonstrated by the numerous women who committed infanticide to escape prolonged and painful public censure for the visibility of their sin. In this, the fear of shame was balanced against the ignominy of the crime; ironically indicating its sustained effectiveness within the psyche of certain vulnerable groups. Like many areas of crime and legal studies, this also has a 'dark figure' in which those silently deterred from both immoral or subsequent criminal behaviour are hidden from view and the historical record.

Whilst we have already been made aware of the comparative success of shame punishments, this chapter attempts to look at the extent to which the intrinsic power of shame-based penalties was limited. These limitations were especially exposed when authority confronted crimes, and indeed criminals, that were ideologically motivated, and thus had significant tools of resistance to draw upon in their refutation of shame punishments and their power. We can particularly see this distinction in the difference between those whose infractions against authority involved conscious thought and dissension rather than simpler offences against the established moral order.

The scope of shame punishments constitutes a considerable range of both physical and psychological interventions upon the integrity of the individual. These range from types of mutilation and burning, to forms of public penance and display. This chapter focusses particularly upon the punishment of the pillory, since this was used quite widely in England until it began to fall out of favour towards the end of the eighteenth century. It was eventually formally removed in 1834,[1] by which time it had fallen almost completely into disuse. Whilst the pillory was ubiquitous as a punishment, it was also malleable and allowed a number of important messages to be exchanged between authority, miscreant and onlookers. It is particularly worth remembering that this last role was fundamentally crucial in conveying the sentiments of the society that punished the criminal. Because this was quasi-official, open ended and unstructured, the behaviour of the crowd was unpredictable. It reassured and justified authority when it demonstrated hatred and opprobrium for the individual in the pillory. Indeed, it constituted an agent of legitimised justice in a manner that Church and King Mobs also fulfilled, when the government sought to target dissenters and other marginal groups.[2]

Looking at how this and other shame punishments functioned is an important element in discussing cultures of shame. This is because they tell us much about how societies before the nineteenth century formally constructed episodes in which shame played a leading part, in contrast to more obviously unofficial customary justice. Indeed, we might go as far as to say that these shame punishments were the only place in which shame was formally and officially constructed after the erosion of ecclesiastical control over morality and behaviour. To get further into the psychological assumptions of those who participated in the application of shame punishment, it is worth recapping some of the assumptions that seem to have underpinned its use. Some of these issues were discussed in the chapter before last but they are worth restating before we consider them in more detail. We obviously have to consider the pillory as a very public display of both culpability and penance. Individuals were sentenced to appear secured within a wooden structure for anything ranging from a single hour to a whole day. This sentence could be repeated over a number of days and it seems intrinsic to the punishment that this display of the individual should occur at separate locations, often related to the nature of the offence. This last proviso will surely make us conclude that the visibility of punishment was an important aspect of its power, an issue emphasised by the fact that the wearing of hats was forbidden enabling the recognition of the individual. Clearly a greater level of exposure to the community was equated with the increased gravity of the sentence. This public exposure enabled the community to exact its own unofficial punishment upon the criminal whilst the individual who was confined came, literally, face to face with the community's opinion of them and their crime. The time spent in the pillory could be arduous to say the least, and there is ample evidence that it was greatly feared by contemporaries. Treatment could be harsh and brutal whilst long confinement could produce considerable suffering to the individual sometimes deprived of food and drink as well as the opportunity to discharge bodily functions.

So what were the assumptions made by the authorities in seeking to apply the pillory as a shame punishment? One of the central assumptions has to have been the idea that the community was a powerful and coherent whole. Within this there is a clear suggestion that being part of this community, and subscribing to its ideas and morality, was by definition, conferring benefits upon the individual. Membership of the community gave individuals access to all sorts of physical, economic and psychological support, which they arguably refuted and denied at their own peril. Displaying the criminal in a manner that would allow the crowds to seek retribution emphasised the miscreant's sheer isolation from this sense of community, however briefly this stylised form of contrition lasted. This also emphasised that the individual displayed in this way would feel and engage with this intense sense of loss, and that this would constitute a significant element of the punishment.[3] It was almost as though the criminal were a part of the community, then temporarily ostracised from it, but at no time was he or she allowed to become an independent autonomous individual. This particular aspect was arguably further enhanced by the frequency with which the sentence insisted that such individuals were to wear a sign, or carry a placard, proclaiming their offence to the multitude.[4]

If shame punishments such as the pillory were to have anything more than a momentary effect upon the criminal, then some assumptions about the criminals themselves had also to be made. The decision to make individuals feel shame for the crime they had committed could only function properly if the criminal had grasped their culpability. It was emphasised to them that they had stepped away from community norms and that passively facing the anger of the community was very clearly a method of forcibly demonstrating contrition. This also assumes that in some senses the will and ego of the criminal was fragile and had either been broken before the sentence, or would certainly be broken by the application of the punishment. Revisiting some of the theoretical writing in the area of shame, which we discussed in the first chapter, tends to suggest that the early modern individual was considered to have no ego or independent will. Shame punishments demonstrated that they had lapsed from community, but could be restored to it with remarkable swiftness, even if they were to endure and carry with them physical or psychological scars. There is also clearly an assumption about the homogeneity of values which gave punishments their strength and legitimacy in seeking to penalise those who had deviated from them. This might explain why some shame-based punishments, and the pillory in particular, were intended to punish challenges to the moral order.

The administration of shame punishment with communal involvement also made a number of judgements about the behaviour of onlookers at the physical location of the punishment. In seeking to expose the

HUDIBRAS

and Ralpho in the Stocks

"BOLD COUPLED IN ENCHANTED TETHER
BY PUNISHED LEG BOUND TOGETHER"

Engraved by J. Romney from the Original by W.ᵐ Hogarth.

'Hogarth's depiction of the stocks taken from "Hudibras" (1725)'

criminal to the reaction of the crowd, forms of authority clearly assumed that onlookers subscribed to the dominant values of that authority. It further assumed that any action taken by such onlookers would invariably promote and sustain such values. Thus the performativity of penance reaffirmed the values of the society that enabled and implemented the punishment, whilst taking part in this process was a further act of subscribing to those values.[5] It seems generally to have been the case, that the pillory was used to punish criminals who had damaged aspects of society where the maintenance of order and reputation were crucial to its ability to function. These were often challenges to the safety and stability of the community itself, and punishment through the application of shame functioned here as a species of restorative justice. Challenges to the authority and reputation of the community's infrastructure and machinery were those most likely to be punished through the sentence of the pillory.

Forgery was regularly punished with the shame sanction of the pillory. This is largely because the integrity of documents and official papers was absolutely necessary for the conduct of society and day-to-day business, and sometimes this caught out some highly placed individuals. Henry Byrde, registrar to the High Commission in Ireland, was sentenced in 1585 to 'stand on the pillory and suffer a year's imprisonment for forging certain warrants in the Lord Deputy's name.'[6] In the early 1630s, Henry Jones was found guilty of forging a passport in which he claimed he was one Robert Shelton. The document also allowed him to travel to parts of Western Somerset 'commending him to the charitable consideration of perusers of the document'. Jones was to be '... sett upon the pillory one hower in Uxbridge upon a markett day with a paper upon his head shewinge his offence.'[7] Some of these issues of confidence and credibility also concerned the integrity of the armed forces, and conceivably the defence of the realm and community. In 1696, Richard Burke went to the pillory for one hour for forging a receipt in the Hand of the Earl of Ranelagh, the Paymaster-General of His Majesty's Forces, whilst in 1702, Charles Power received the same sentence for forging a ticket of leave 'such as lieutenants in His Majesty's ships of war are used to make out and give to mariners.'[8] Coining was another offence which also required authority to act in concert with the populace and a steady stream of these offences were punished in the pillory until the middle of the eighteenth century. In 1696, Henry Mitcham was convicted of 'procuring clipped and counterfeit money of criminals at low rates, and putting it off for good', and was made to stand in the pillory on three separate occasions.[9]

Punishing the various dimensions of fraud was once again about maintaining confidence and the credibility of authority. Sometimes this sought to uncover and shame those who had defrauded the wider commonwealth. Thomas Swaddon of Calne in Wiltshire was convicted of providing a certificate that exempted several in his local community from paying the hearth tax. For this crime, he stood in the pillory three times.[10] Individuals could also find themselves punished for alarming the local community. For instance, Matthias Browne had to serve a pillory sentence for 'spreading a false rumour of taking of the city of Limerick, which was not taken, when he made that report.'[11]

Deception, and what we would today term 'confidence trickery', was another area of misdemeanour punished through the use of the pillory. Thomas Amis defrauded William Head in 1685 'out of a beaver hat worth fifty shillings' claiming it was for a non-existent member of the gentry. Amis was sentenced to pay a three shilling fine and 'to stand on the pillory for an hour of some day between 10 and 12 a.m. near Shoreditch Church, with a paper on his hat, inscribed with these words, to wit, "For cheatinge severall persons of their goods."'[12] A further species of deception which challenged authority was the counterfeiting of goods, the quality of which were otherwise guaranteed by an Act of Parliament and the assay system. In 1667 David Venables, a London silversmith, was found guilty of 'making and selling several little bottles, small cups, snuff boxes, tumblers, and other small things of impure and base silver, not up to the standard, for which offence he was ordered to stand in the pillory and fined £500.'[13]

There were also strong arguments for the use of shame punishments such as the pillory to aid and abet the legal process itself and to protect its reputation and integrity. The pillory was sometimes used to punish those who refused to take oaths. In 1684 15 individuals from the parish of Stepney refused to take the oath required of them by the Justices of the Peace who had been enquiring into dissenter activity within the parish. In the end, a variety of sentences were passed which resulted in two of these individuals serving sentences in the pillory. This particular offence resembles a kind of contempt of court – again a challenge to the ability of authority to enforce its system of values and will upon the populace.[14] A still more serious offence than this contempt of court was the attempt to sabotage and undermine due legal process through the offence of perjury. This was considered an especially serious matter and Elizabethan statutes prescribed the pillory and altogether more stringent corporal punishments, although sometimes in practice this was a punishment attendant upon failing to pay a fine.[15] In 1615 for example, Edward Etheridge was prosecuted 'for perjury upon a trial before the Justice of Common Pleas at Westminster.' His sentence was to be 'respited to prison for six months without bail, to pay to the lord the King and the injured party £20 or else to stand in the pillory, and to find sureties for good behaviour in the place where he formerly dwelt and in the Strand.'[16] Also in 1615 in Middlesex Matthew Hitchcock, a common informer, was indicted for giving false information against three men and his sentence was 'to be set upon a horse with his face to its tail, and to ride thus to the pillory, and there to stand for two hours in the open market with a paper over his head inscribed "for unjust compounding upon severall informacons without licence."'[17] Perjury remained a significant offence punished by the pillory, and was one of the few still attracting this punishment into the early years of the nineteenth century.[18]

Seditious words also attracted shame punishments, even if these were sometimes spoken in anger or haste and certainly, the reaction of the authorities to this, was generally coloured by the immediate political situation. In 1685 Deborah Hawkins:

> designing and maliciously intending to procure and rouse ill feeling against the said Lord the King &c. audaciously and seditiously uttered, in the course of conversation with Mary Bennett spinster of and concerning the death of the late King Charles the Second, these wicked and seditious words, to wit, "Before the King (to wit, King James II.) shall be crowned, this head of mine shall goe off, and before that day comes there will be a greate deal of bloodshed," and also spoke in presence and divers of the said now King's lieges and subjects these words in contempt of the said king, to wit, "Hee is noe King but an Elective King, and if there were warrs as I believe there will be, I will put on breeches myself to fight for the Duke of Monmouth."[19]

Hawkins received a sentence that 'she should be put on the pillory for an hour near the Turnstile in Holborn, having on her head a paper setting forth her offence.'[20] Others were obviously made bolder by drink and sometimes they were also turned in to the authorities by their fellow drinkers. In 1715 William Wide for instance, spoke the seditious words 'God damn King George, he has no Right to the Crown' after staggering drunk into a Billingsgate alehouse. The sensitivity to this behaviour may also have been linked to contemporary concerns about Jacobite sympathies amongst the populace at large. The unusual nature of this oath was corroborated by others who stated that 'they had known, and convers'd with him a great while', and never heard him 'say any Thing against the Government; but that he often drank King George's Health, particularly on the Day he landed.'[21] Similarly, Peter Matson in 1725 cursed a number of soldiers in a Petticoat Lane Alehouse and proceeded to drink the health of the Pretender, whereupon he was apprehended by the watch which had been swiftly sent for. Both Wide and Matson were sentenced to the pillory for their unfortunate outspokenness whilst under the influence of drink.[22]

Blasphemy was also an offence that attracted shame punishments throughout Europe from the medieval period onwards.[23] This was largely because blasphemy was the crime which was the ultimate challenge to authority. Moreover, it was linked to pertinent issues of providence and the fate of those in the community who witnessed or came to know of this blasphemy.[24] Communities and states who did not punish blasphemers, regularly believed themselves to be in peril, and behaviour intended to appease conceptions of providence centred around this offence. European punishment regimes used against blasphemers blended shame and ridicule bringing to bear the laughter and action of the community upon the convicted individual.[25] In Dutch and German evidence, blasphemers were punished by public exhibition of them in penitential (sometimes women's) clothing, or a clumsy barrel-like contraption.[26] To the south, Catholic Spain shamed its blasphemers by muzzling their faces and making them ride backwards upon a donkey.[27] Further north, Sweden punished blasphemers by compelling them to run the gauntlet of the community in a local street, whilst those present were enabled to lay blows upon the miscreant with wooden branches.[28] Calvinist countries, in particular, increasingly vested this sort of power in the Consistory Court which would use everything from neck irons, mock crucifixion, kissing the earth, mutilation and the pillory to curb blasphemy and reassure the community.[29] In both France and England, shame was associated with the practice of having a single copy of seditious and blasphemous works burned by the common hangman.[30]

The pillory and other shame punishments were able to function adequately against this range of petty offences and offenders. As we have noticed, most of these miscreants were those who challenged the reputation and integrity of systems of authority. As such, the community at large had a significant interest in observing and regulating the punishment of these individuals. Their actions, either through deception, fraud or breach of the assay system challenged the social life and economy of society at large. Even the blasphemers, who were punished, were those whose behaviour had been impulsive in reviling the powers of the almighty or who had sought to acquire his attributes or powers for themselves. These people, who were endangered, stressed or under the influence of insanity or drink, were some distance away from the late medieval heretic whose dissidence was calculated and serious. Interestingly, the ceremony of abjuration contained an overarching shame element which signified that the resistance of the heretic had been broken before the individual appeared contrite in public.[31]

Punishing this considerable range of individuals in the full view of society, for their challenge to authority in all its forms, was a cost effective method of dispensing restorative justice. Certainly we can come across evidence that the pillory, and the fear of its application, was effective as both a punishment and a deterrent. A convicted gentleman in 1683, a Mr Manfield, pleaded the King's mercy in an attempt to avoid 'that ignominious punishment of the pillory' whilst another individual noted that a woman's threat to 'have my ears in the pillory' had resulted in significant loss of trade for him in his local community.[32] Another man in 1696 expressed considerable contrition for his crime and wanted a judicial pardon in order to enter military service in the King's name. Interestingly, his request for a pardon suggested that his sentence to stand twice in the pillory 'will render him incapable of what he designs.'[33]

Yet even within this group of individuals punished for these crimes there remained those who were recalcitrant and did not accept the culture of shame which went with their punishment. In 1667, an unnamed forger did not take his pillory punishment lightly and simply refused to be penitent:

> The fellow was very stubborn at first, and did not stand quietly till the mayor directed handcuffs to be put upon him, which could not be done till four or five seamen went up and forced him to it. He is a very bold audacious rogue, and did not value the disgrace, but took a pride in saying that he had made many tickets, and was only sorry that he was apprehended for such a small sum, and many other stories in pride of his roguish actions.[34]

However, what really started to unravel the power of the pillory as a cohesive community punishment strategy, were those who were, what we might call, dedicated dissidents. These were individuals who had, in various ways, ideological arguments against the political, social or religious authorities of their era. These people had significant advantages as distinct from the others who simply offended against species of order. Those who had internalised and made their opposition coherent to themselves had obviously rather more in the way of psychological defences against the onslaught of the community. Certainly, we can encounter individuals unmoved by the shame they were confronted with, and still less displayed the supposedly more modern emotion of guilt. Individuals even used the site of punishment to demonstrate elements of underground subcultures that revelled in their dissidence.[35]

In 1698 one Captain Rigby, a naval officer, was convicted of blasphemy and sodomy and sentenced to pay a £1,000 fine, to stand in the pillory on three occasions and, to find sureties for his subsequent behaviour.[36] Evidently, the pillory sentence did not work as the authorities had assumed, and Rigby hijacked it to forward his own agenda. Their indignation is clearly evident in noting his behaviour and the failure of the punishment:

> Capt. Rigby stood to-day upon the pillory, not with his head in it, dressed like a beau; so attended with constables and beadles that nobody could throw anything at him. This was in the Pall Mall, by the tavern, where he endeavoured to play his pranks. We shall see whether he will escape so well tomorrow, when he shows himself at Charing Cross, and the next day at Temple Bar.[37]

It is intriguing to speculate upon what happened on the next and subsequent appearances in the pillory, since when Rigby came to petition the King for mercy in July 1700, he was able to claim that he had undergone the pillory 'almost to the danger of his life'.[38] If true, we may have to consider the distinct possibility that Rigby was excessively 'paid back' by the authorities who, stung by his show of bravado, arranged for his especially rough treatment after the Pall Mall pillory appearance.[39] If, however, Rigby was being economical with the truth about what had transpired, he was hoping the authorities had forgotten the reality of events. If so, it is a potentially interesting reminder of how transitory the experience might have been, at least for those witnessing or condemning individuals to the punishment. Harsh treatment at the hands of the pillory crowd also spawned its own public order concerns. Famously, Titus Oates, the miscreant who invented the Popish Plot of autumn 1678, was treated so harshly he had been left for dead. Whilst the authorities might have predicted some reaction, there was a surprising failure to acknowledge this from the King. James II empowered the Earl of Sunderland to enquire of the Sheriffs of London about the resulting disorder expressing he was 'much surprised

at it and does expect that greater care should be taken to prevent anything of that kind to-morrow and at all other times.'[40]

Matters were complicated still further when shame punishments
were used against fanatical and committed dissidents. Lodowick Muggleton and John Reeve for instance, had excited consternation in London
through their practice of entering taverns and other public places to curse
individuals who did not subscribe to their conviction that they were the
last two saintly witnesses upon earth. Muggleton's opinions were considered blasphemous yet, motivated by religious conviction, he stubbornly
refused to defend them at his own trial despite entering a plea of inno-
cence.[41] Muggleton continued in his obstinacy despite an appearance in
the pillory and his ideas continued to circulate.

One of the most famous seventeenth century individuals to receive
shame punishment and mutilation was James Naylor.[42] In the course
of proclaiming his Quaker faith, Naylor and his errant behaviour were
a constant problem for the authorities which oversaw the issue of law
and order during the Commonwealth. This was important since the
ecclesiastical courts which had functioned under William Laud had
been dismantled. Indeed one aspect that had fuelled opposition to the
Crown both before and during the Civil War had been the entire issue
of religious authority and where it lay. The removal of this authority
left something of a vacuum which Parliament and Oliver Cromwell as
Lord Protector made several different attempts to solve.[43] Nonetheless,
this was emphatically a problem that the Commonwealth had also created
for itself. The coming of religious tolerance under the Commonwealth
had unleashed religious sectaries whose doctrines challenged the very
fabric of authority within society. Naylor's Quakerism was confront-
ational and a profound challenge to the religious authority of the day.
Whilst previously persecuted sects were allowed to worship unmolested,
Naylor's Quakers disrupted the church services of their opponents and
staged inflammatory and blasphemous public displays of their own faith.
His interpretation of the 'inner light' gave Naylor sanction for all his
actions and contemptuous flouting of authority. In imitation of Christ,
he gathered 12 disciples around him and entered Bristol on a donkey and
was apprehended for blasphemous words and behaviour.[44] Yet the Naylor
case was the source of considerable problems for those seeking to maintain and enhance public order. Parliament undertook a vote on his fate,
narrowly sparing him the death penalty. Instead his sentence was com-
muted to whipping, appearance in the pillory, branding, boring through
the tongue (a regularly employed punishment for blasphemy throughout
Europe) and life imprisonment with hard labour.[45] Certainly it becomes
difficult to consider that Naylor was either shamed or deterred by his

punishment and the limitations of shame punishment against the highly motivated miscreant become apparent. Certainly, Quakers who viewed all religious authority other than their own as anti-Christ were more than prepared to meet martyrdom.[46]

But for our purposes, the whole debate around the Naylor case shows something else important at work. The whole issue provoked a distinct crisis of authority – the very authority which had sustained and promoted the coherence and effectiveness of shame punishments. No longer was it homogenous, since this had been compromised by the coming of toleration. Henceforth it became difficult to believe that authority had any right to enforce conformity, especially in respect of those who had fought in the parliamentary army against species of tyranny, just as Naylor himself had done. Certainly, we can get a clear sense of this when we look closely at the subsequent debates in 1656 surrounding the issue of how Parliament should deal with the Quaker menace, and this illustrates the problems of dealing with the ideologically committed. Members like Sir William Strickland noted that:

> They are a growing evil, and the greatest that ever was. Their way is a plausible way; all levellers against magistracy and propriety [property.] They say the Scriptures are but ink and paper. They are guided by a higher light. They deny all ordinances, as marriage, &c.[47]

But some noticed just how difficult it had now become to take action against those who held opinions or beliefs. A Mr Robinson noted astutely:

> I am against referring it to a Committee to bring in a law against them, under the name of Quakers. Some may be called Quakers that are not so. It is an offence, indeed, to keep on their hats before the magistrate; for, lay aside magistracy, and expect confusion. I would have the petition considered by the same Committee, and see how far the offences extend to the disturbance of the peace.[48]

Most damning of all was the opinion of Colonel Sydenham, who noted how the power and legitimacy of orthodox opinion was capable of misuse and corruption:

> I cannot but wonder to see the strange temper of the House in this business; how zealous they were for that high sentence

against Naylor, though there was no law at all for it, and never
quiet till it was done. I doubt you have opened a gap to prostitute both life, member, and liberty, to the arbitrary power of
men, who by a vote may do what they will.[49]

What this series of exchanges suggests to us, is that using coercion
that was likely to involve shame punishments to discipline conviction
and opinion was questioned as early as the middle of the seventeenth
century. Once it had been admitted that there was some capacity for
ideological dissention that could neither be tamed nor eradicated, the
power of shame and the urge for rehabilitation into conformity was
starting to be problematised. Social and political organisation was no
longer an unquestioned orthodoxy, nor could it be legitimately self-
perpetuating. Instead the room for doubt, trail blazed by religious and
political dissenters, had made the construction and operation of society
a potentially discursive subject.

What really began to erode the coherence of shame punishments
like the pillory was the availability and access to print culture. More
specifically, the coming of print culture that discussed and addressed
issues that centred around punishment and its legitimacy, made the
whole process of using shame punishment gradually become considerably less than consensual. We have heard from many historians about
the didactic power of last words of advice and dying speeches from
those about to be executed, but it is worth investigating some of the
literary responses which the pillory, specifically generated. Some of these
are capable of showing us how the traditional terrors that the pillory
offered could be reconsidered in the hands of the skilled, the articulate
and the prepared. What many of these 'dialogues' with the pillory and
nature of shame punishment itself have in common, is a determination
to undermine the one dimensional presentation of culpability, which
the presumed communality of shame punishments had previously represented. No longer was the miscreant unequivocally and acceptably
the sole recipient of the community's psychological and physical disdain. Instead this whole issue had become discursive since the written
statements of those who found themselves in the pillory asked the
crowd to reconsider the justice of the 'criminal's situation'. Some went
further to indict elements of authority which they considered far more
worthy of punishment than they were themselves. Occasionally, this
was demonstrated by crowds at the sites of shame punishment. In
1680 for instance, Benjamin Harris was tried for printing and publishing *An Appeal from the Country to the City* and sentenced to a spell in

the pillory, yet the crowd supported the supposed miscreant since 'no one dared cast any thing at him and one that only spoke against him was in some danger.'[50]

The most widely celebrated example of this occurred in the first years of the seventeenth century with the experience of Daniel Defoe. Defoe, outraged at the threat to undermine the religious toleration offered to dissenters under William III, replied through a satirical, caustic and hyperbolic pamphlet entitled *The Shortest Way With The Dissenters*.[51] This outrageously argued for their summary execution as a method of removing the problem for the authorities. Defoe clearly had high Tory attitudes and concrete enemies in view, and they in turn were unstinting in their pursuit of him. Defoe's authorship was discovered and he was arrested in London, charged with seditious libel and thrown into Newgate Prison. J.R. Moore argued that Defoe's sentence – to stand in the pillory for the length of three whole days at three separate locations – was astonishingly severe and was a consequence of his published belligerence towards his enemies.[52] But Defoe also appealed still further afield to a wider public (a public that might well have been expected to gather at the pillory and its environs) with his arguments about the justness and efficacy of religious toleration. However, Defoe's real contribution to making his culpability discursive, and revoking the supposed shame he was intended to feel in the pillory, was his creation of a literary work which openly addressed the machinery of his punishment whilst deflecting its power. Defoe's *Hymn to the Pillory*, dated the same day as his first appearance in the pillory, was printed and circulated around the site of his punishment. It was a tour de force of accusation and blame which was intended to deflect the gaze away from Defoe to those who had contrived and conspired to put him in the pillory.

The poem's first stanza unequivocally attempted to undermine the symbolic power of the pillory as an engine of punishment by dissecting its effect upon men whilst emphatically putting it firmly in its place:

> HAIL hieroglyphic state machine,
> Contrived to punish fancy in:
> Men that are men in thee can feel no pain,
> And all thy insignificants disdain.
> Contempt, that false new word for shame,
> Is, without crime, an empty name,
> A shadow to amuse mankind,

Daniel Defoe in the pillory at the Temple Bar, from 'The National and Domestic History of England' by William Hickman Smith Aubrey (1858–1916) published London, c.1890 (litho) by English School, (19th century) Private Collection/Ken Welsh/The Bridgeman Art Library Nationality/copyright status: English/out of copyright

> But never frights the wise or well-fixed mind:
> Virtue despises human scorn,
> And scandals innocence adorn.[53]

From here, with a species of pathetic fallacy, Defoe noted how the pillory's use was neither discerning nor discriminating, and that history itself had a habit of rehabilitating those it had ridiculed alongside those seemingly deserving of contempt and ire:

> Tell us, great engine, how to understand
> Or reconcile the justice of the land;
> How Bastwick, Prynne, Hunt, Hollingsby, and Pye,
> Men of unspotted honesty,
> Men that had learning, wit, and sense,
> And more than most men have had since,
> Could equal title to thee claim
> With Oates and Fuller, men of later fame:
> Even the learned Selden saw
> A prospect of thee through the law.[54]

Judges, churchmen and city stock jobbers were all indicted in the poem for their culpability in deluding the populace through hypocrisy, corruption and destructive behaviour. In doing this, Defoe recognised the power of shame within his punishment and sought to transfer this back to where he tried to convince the community at large it actually belonged:

> Shame, like the exhalations of the sun,
> Falls back where first the motion was begun;
> And they who for no crime shall on thy brows appear,
> Bear less reproach than they who placed them there.[55]

In one section of the poem, Defoe focussed upon how shame punishments could inspire the apparent destruction of individual personality and conscience. It was a censorship of thought and deed that a supposedly tolerant society should no longer bear:

> What are thy terrors, that for fear of thee
> Mankind should dare to sink their honesty?
> He's bold to impudence that dare turn knave,
> The scandal of thy company to save:

He that will crimes he never knew confess,
Does more than if he knew those crimes transgress;
And he that fears thee more than to be base,
May want a heart, but does not want a face....
...To make men of their honesty afraid,
That for the time to come they may
More willingly their friends betray;
Tell them the men that placed him here
Are friends unto the times;
But at a loss to find his guilt,
They can't commit his crimes.[56]

The punishment of the pillory was only reluctantly being used for disciplining the ideological offender by the end of the eighteenth century.[57] Yet this, paradoxically, did not stop radicals voicing a wistful regret and wishing it could be used against the corrupt society that had engendered it. The author of the 1820 poem *Ode to the Pillory (Ode the Second)* implored the pillory:

Oh! Clasp 'em tight; and, perjuries to check,
Break every parasitic scoundrel's neck,
And grind their tongues to powder, if you please!
'Twill be of lasting service to mankind,
To rid the world of such a scurvy groupe;
A mean, unprincipled, subservient troop,
To every object but their interest blind!
Mankind would deck thee with the mural crown,
For purging thus the sewers of the town.[58]

Interestingly, this particular poem appears to have surfaced in the wake of the Queen Caroline affair of 1820 in which radicals supported Queen Caroline of Brunswick against her husband George IV's attempts to discredit her behaviour and sue for divorce. This incident has also been cited as an influence upon the creation of later middle-class domestic ideals. The Queen Caroline Affair was an occasion where the issues surrounding shame and its performativity had been transferred into the wider public sphere to indict supposed moral exemplars.[59] Here, shame was invested with a popular sanction, since the systems of authority which had overseen the administration of shame punishments were themselves made to confront and feel shame.[60]

Certainly, it would be impossible to argue that there was a linear or progressive abandonment of the pillory in punishing ideological offenders. Some 60 years after Daniel Defoe appeared in the pillory, the infidel Peter Annet found himself confined to the pillory for publishing blasphemous libels contained in *The Free Inquirer*. Annet appeared at Charing Cross and again at the Royal Exchange with a paper on his head proclaiming him to be a blasphemer. Yet in many histories and in the views of contemporaries the mention of Annet's case usually involves citing his advanced age (68) as clear indication that the punishment was barbaric and anachronistic even by this date.[61] However, as we have seen, we can say with greater certainty that the shame punishment of the pillory was certainly of limited use against the determined (sometimes fanatical) ideological opponent who could use the punishment to embrace martyrdom, or enter into dialogue with their fate and its machinery. Historians have suggested how the growing distaste for disorder and violence had undermined the pillory's place in the punishment regime of eighteenth century England. We should add to this that the shame element, so potent before the eighteenth century, became eclipsed.[62] The system of punishment, of which the pillory was a part, ultimately failed to address the determined or ideological dissident unafraid or capable of manipulating their fate.

It is perhaps salutatory to think of the late eighteenth century ideological opponents of political and religious authority and how their punishment through shame proved spectacularly inadequate. When Thomas Paine published his eventual runaway best seller and radical primer *The Rights of Man*, the verdict of the court in the author's absence was that a copy was to be burned by the common hangman. In amongst the repression of this work which involved seizure, confiscation and imprisonment, a single London Corresponding Society activist John Frost was sentenced in 1792 to the pillory.[63] As we know, such sentences scarcely brought widespread ridicule and popular opprobrium upon Paine and his ideas, except from those who were in any case hostile to them. Indeed the reaction of the authorities readily fuelled the consumption of Paine and his oeuvre. *The Rights of Man* sold exponentially, so that upper estimates suggest it sold 250,000 copies with ideas clearly reaching far beyond this. Daniel Isaac Eaton was treated with compassion and kindness on his appearance in the pillory in 1812 for publishing the *Age of Reason*.[64] Paine and his works were not shamed or driven out of public life but eventually became the cornerstone of early nineteenth century radicalism. Interestingly, what was central to them was indignation against the pretensions of authority and its regularly overblown claims for legitimacy and how these could be dismantled through the careful application of thought and argument. The relationship between these sentiments and what Shoemaker sees as a waning of interest in mass and mob forms of behaviour can only be speculated upon. They also represent a dimension of reputation being more in the control of individuals and being discussed through the printed word, again an important development noted by Shoemaker.[65]

In the 1820s and 1830s, radicals and atheists who flourished in the years leading up to the pillory's final demise in 1834 give further demonstration of this failure. When Richard Carlile, his wife, his sister and their numerous compatriots were serially prosecuted for blasphemy, their quasi-seditious words challenged the religious and political authority of the state every bit as much as Defoe, Naylor, or Muggleton had done. Whilst the Carliles, James Watson, Susannah Wright and others could not be prevented from having their say in court, their eventual punishment was something of a different story. All defendants in these blasphemy cases found themselves confined to prison safely away from view.[66] No longer was the defendant able to try the sympathy of a crowd gathered from a homogenous community. Instead, the Carliles and their friends had to run the gamut of sophisticated censorship of the printed word in order to address a diffuse and discursive reading public.

Whilst the pillory had evolved as a punishment against assaults upon authority, the absolute nature of the authority concerned began to be diluted from the seventeenth century onwards. This power appeared especially ambivalent, precisely where it was called upon to police and punish those whose opinions deviated from established orthodoxy. Within this it became all too clear that the application of communal sanctions and the ostracisation of individuals from society had a diminishing effect upon both the perpetrators and the audiences for what were now ambiguous and as time moved on, infrequent shaming punishments of the pillory. It is here that we realise that the example of the pillory shows us the early-modern conception of communal shaming as a form of all embracing and monolithic culture was dissolving. In this respect this chapter illuminates the cracks that were starting to appear in official attitudes to shame as a component of punishment. Nonetheless we can also see elements of the new forms it would potentially take and the new emphases at work within it. Diminishing the success of the pillory demonstrated the importance of dynamic interactions between individuals, institutions and ideas that were to be fundamental to shame's later history as outlined within this book.

As we shall see in the next chapter, the discredit of shame punishments was contemporary with wider debates about the whole purpose of shame within punishment. However the outcome of these debates were not the relentless and simple modernisation that previous commentators have claimed.

5
Conservatives, Humanitarians and Reformers Debate Shame

By the end of the eighteenth century, as we have discovered in the last chapter, the centrality of shame within punishment, both officially sanctioned and popularly prescribed, was falling into disuse. It was arguably no longer important to society's policing of its population nor central to its moral geography. The mid-point of this book is an appropriate place for us to consider how the idea of shame was perceived by those who theorised about issues associated with control, policing and punishment. As we should be aware, the whole issue of punishment came under the spotlight from the early eighteenth century onwards stimulated by individuals who approached the problem from considerably different perspectives. Whilst writers upon punishment had obvious social agendas in mind, we should also remember that many critiques that inspired such investigation had their roots in the enlightenment discovery and promotion of the individual as the building block of society. This was, after all, the age of the Scottish Enlightenment, the French philosophes and Locke's intensive investigation of mankind's cognition of the world.

Much of this investigation explicitly explored the composition and workings of the human mind and this was also bound to produce a wider and deeper consideration of the self and the impact of society upon this. From this questioning emerged a waning enthusiasm for the power and effectiveness of shame. However, as we shall discover, this approach and these dialogues about the issue of shame were not entirely one-sided, nor were they obviously polarised between entrenched positions. Conservative organisations (such as the Society for the Suppression of Vice) argued that shame was an intrinsic part of social cohesion necessary for an organically harmonious society.[1] Others offered versions of what we might call a modernisation approach whereby the feelings and widespread social use of shame should be transcended as a society matures and becomes civilised. Yet what is perhaps still more surprising is the discovery that the idea of a simple modernisation and rationalisation of punishment alongside the coming of supposedly humane approaches to the philosophy of penality is overdrawn and simplistic. Although change was fundamental to both theoretical and imagined regimes of punishment in the second half of the eighteenth century, as Foucault and others have argued, we should be wary of seeing this as an obvious part of the transition away from a supposed shame culture. What emerges from a study of the leading theoreticians in the area is how much notions of shame and its power were instead recast into other forms – forms which were arguably not as objective and modern, as writers like Foucault would have us believe.

Attempting to trace the debate about shame into all corners of eighteenth and early nineteenth century society and culture would represent a truly enormous task. Instead, the historian can only hope to identify the main currents and investigate the central characters and theoreticians whose thought and writings are known to have been widely published or especially influential. Thus these works and their definition of shame, represent a point at which social critics put their own perspective on these subjects into words. In doing so they gave voice to both philosophical and practical arguments that showcased the viability, desirability or otherwise of shame within punishment.

In many respects, some crucial issues relating to shame punishments and their function emerged in Montesquieu's wide ranging *The Spirit of Laws*. In his consideration of ancient societies, Montesquieu saw the regulation of public morals as a clear species of censorship and noted that severe punishments were associated with despotism, whereas republics were associated with a culture of honour and virtue.[2] These so-called 'moderate' governments, so Montesquieu argued, were entitled to use shame and the 'fear of blame' as a wholly legitimate method of governance. Shame appeared within this scheme as a natural and organic phenomenon which had a legitimate, if unwelcome place where it was defined as the antithesis of civil virtue. Those who were not shamed by punishment were in a society which did not support and value virtuous behaviour over its opposite.

> Mankind must not be governed with too much severity; we ought to make a prudent use of the means which nature has given us to conduct them. If we inquire into the cause of all human corruptions, we shall find that they proceed from the impunity of criminals, and not from the moderation of punishments. Let us follow

nature, who has given shame to man for his scourge; and let the heaviest part of the punishment be the infamy attending it. But if there be some countries where shame is not a consequence of punishment, this must be owing to tyranny, which has inflicted the same penalties on villains and honest men.[3]

Montesquieu also saw that religion played a central part in the maintenance of good order and in gaining assent to govern through the collective approval of moral schemes of behaviour and virtue.

In order to raise an attachment to religion it is necessary that it should inculcate pure morals. Men who are knaves by retail are extremely honest in the gross; they love morality. And were I not treating of so grave a subject I should say that this appears remarkably evident in our theatres: we are sure of pleasing the people by sentiments avowed by morality; we are sure of shocking them by those it disapproves.[4]

The debate about shame also appeared in material more obviously concerned with the theory and practice of justice and the treatment of society's criminals and criminality. Cesare Beccaria's work has been regularly cited as a fundamentally important influence upon the foundation and development of modern criminological thinking and methodology. Beccaria's opinions about the nature of law, justice and punishment were most readily distilled into his celebrated *An Essay on Crimes and Punishments* which went through several editions after it was first published in 1765, finding its way into many European languages and into English in 1767. Beccaria at no point mentions the issue of shame explicitly, but central to his ideas about the nature and practice of punishment, was an assault upon the philosophy that allowed and promoted shame punishments. His critique of existing modes and philosophies of punishment was a systematic attack upon the whole phenomenon of arbitrariness in their practice and administration.

Beccaria argued that, hitherto, laws had not been rationally constructed and were more readily the product of passion rather than individuals considering the utilitarian ideal of 'the greatest happiness of the greatest number'.[5] He also suggested that the motives for rational punishment did not naturally exist amongst the populace at large, noting that the 'passions of the individual' were generally opposed to the notion of the 'general good'.[6] The quest for rationality was clearly given further credence through Beccaria's insistence that the codification of laws was utterly essential to avoid uncertainty and arbitrariness. Indeed he went so far as to suggest that precise mathematical calculations could in reality be applied to a scale of punishments.[7] Crimes should be punished according to their direct and measurable impact upon society, not some spurious judgement about the dignity of the person so offended. According to this, so Beccaria argued in true enlightenment style, it became an absurdity that blasphemy was regarded more seriously than the assassination of a reigning monarch.[8] This was part of a wider assault upon the whole concept of 'Leze Majesty' which insisted that hierarchies were the governing legal principle, rather than the rationality and coherence of the law. As he argued 'on this occasion, as on a thousand others, men have been sacrificed, victims to a word.'[9] This was ostensibly an attack upon punishment as a demonstration of retribution and as a visible example of the display of power. Moreover Beccaria was adamant that the application of punishment as a species of torment (which by implication included shame) was absolutely anathema to his proposed system.

> From the foregoing considerations it is evident, that the intent of punishments, is not to torment a sensible being, to undo a crime already committed. Is it possible that torments, and useless cruelty, the instrument of furious fanaticism, or of impotency of tyrants can be authorized by a political body.[10]

Torture could not be rationally defended because it effectively punished the weak and its proposed ability to purge sin was nothing other than a barbaric anachronism. Torture was fundamentally irrational because it ultimately punished the innocent who were subjected to punishment for a crime they did not commit.

Implicit in this text was also a request that all punishment should be proportionate to the crimes committed. It also argued that the codification and regularisation of the nature of punishment would also allow individuals to minutely calculate the 'inconveniences attending every crime.'[11] This was also a cue for Beccaria to discuss the nature of the individual, which he saw as partly created through the concept of honour. Whilst at first sight this would seem to equate with a society that would set high value upon the concept of shame, Beccaria pushes the idea in a different direction when he uses it to describe the creation of the autonomous individual arguing

> ...the esteem of men becomes not only useful, but necessary, to everyone, to prevent his sinking below the common level.

> The ambitious man grasps at it, as being necessary to his
> designs; the vain man sues for it, as testimony of his merit; the
> honest man demands it, as his due; and most men consider it
> as necessary to their existence.[12]

Throughout his essay, Beccaria was anxious to stipulate that the exercise of the law was not to be the demonstration of power, but functioned most effectively when there were obvious limits to its reach and rationale. Thus he argued that all acts of punishment engaged in by authority should, in strict definition of the term, be absolutely necessary. Importantly, he qualified this, by suggesting that anything beyond this stipulation was clearly tyrannical. Similarly his definition of justice indicated that he considered it to be 'that bond, which is necessary to keep the interest of individuals united; without which, men would return to their original state of barbarity.'[13] Alongside this, the positive virtues of esteem, pride and merit were those deemed essential to the rise and prosperity of an enabling society.[14] These virtues, bonds and merits were all damaged by the phenomenon of shame within punishment.

Beccaria also appeared as a champion of the power of print culture and its didactic capacity. This would further enhance his conceptions of honour, publicise a codified general law subscribed to by all, and promote a detailed understanding of the nature of punishment alongside the crime it was inscribed for.[15] This was further emphasised through the suggestion that it should be abundantly clear to all when they were either breaking the law or were conforming to it. This was a further attack upon the perceived arbitrary nature of the laws of Beccaria's own time. A corollary of this came in the assertion that punishment could never be just, if the laws had not done their utmost to prevent the crime that they sought to punish.[16]

This imperative for the communication of the law and its consequences also appeared to motivate his interest in the rapidity of punishment to reinforce the sense of penitence within the individual, but also to strongly associate the crime with its punishment. Similarly he was anxious to ensure that the punishment should have the greatest effect upon others with the least possible pain for the miscreant themselves.[17] Although within this essay Beccaria never mentions the issue of shame itself, much of what he has to say about both punishment and systems of justice clearly indicate an antipathy to the systems which sustained shame within punishments. He foresaw a system in which crimes were punished solely within their own terms and only for the benefit of society. This rejected the notion of the affront to power or dignity that was central to the philosophy and culture of traditional shame punishments. He wanted systems of punishment to be constant, intelligible and predictable. When punishment occurred, only out of necessity, it was to be the obvious last resort and was to produce the maximum possible effect upon the onlookers and minimum effect upon the individual. This, it should be noted discounted the importance of shame and its deterrent value within punishment. However it did highlight the importance and role of onlookers which may curiously have unwittingly allowed a role for shame within Beccaria's system.

However examining the utility of punishment as the primary consideration stood in opposition to the material reality of shame as a social phenomenon and shame punishments more widely. Firstly, Beccaria considered that trusting punishments to the passions of individuals was a fundamental mistake for an enlightened system of laws to be bound by. Similarly, the considered application of shame through punishment manifestly failed Beccaria's search for a strongly codified and regulated response to crime. Its use was irrational and could never undertake a satisfactory measure of the psychological pain inflicted upon the miscreant. Such punishments were even unpredictable in terms of their physical effects upon criminals. Indeed a cornerstone of the pillory's power lay in the fact that the reaction of the populace was unpredictable, and thus the feelings of the individual so punished were obviously impossible to determine. Shame within punishment countered his desire to see an implicit link between the scale and nature of punishment. Similarly this would have offended Beccaria's search for certainty and rationality within punishment, as well as compromising his arguments to preserve and promote mutually respected 'honour' within society. For Beccaria's rational enabling society, the opportunity to be psychologically dragged backwards through the mire of shame and opprobrium was significantly damaging.

Beccaria even seems to have his own conceptual replacement for the phenomenon of 'shame' with what the *Essay on Crimes and Punishments* described as the concept of 'infamy'. Importantly, Beccaria noted that this should ideally rely for its power upon the law, although he recognised that this was not always possible. Infamy was 'a mark of the public disapprobation, which deprives the object of all consideration in the hands of his fellow citizens, of the confidence of his country, and of the fraternity which exists between members of the same society.'[18] This concept of infamy was to be identified through a common standard of morality and not the arbitrary decisions of those who oversaw or regulated its application. The punishment associated with infamy was also to be associated with an individual's commission of a specific crime, so that summary collective punishment was to be avoided since 'the infamy of many resolves itself into the infamy of none.'[19]

Although Beccaria himself did not mention shame, the commentary upon his *Essay on Crimes and Punishments* by Voltaire (which is usually bound with it) in its first pages noted the corrosive power of shame. Voltaire chose to cite the example of a young woman within his own neighbourhood who had left a child born out of wedlock exposed to the elements, as she herself returned home to, in Voltaire's words, 'atone for her shame'. She was arrested, condemned and executed. Whilst acknowledging her crimes, Voltaire asks the reader if the retribution visited upon the mother was in anyway just, since she abandoned the child, rather than played a direct part in its murder. Moreover, Voltaire also notes that the role of shame in this episode prompted the young woman to admit and acknowledge her weakness, a fault for which she was subjected to the most draconian of punishments. This punished an individual who ultimately intended no malice and 'she hath already been severely punished by the pangs of her own heart.'[20] This seemed to suggest that shaming in this instance promoted neither remorse nor served the needs of the wider community with any degree of satisfaction.

Perhaps particularly indicative of the 'pure' enlightenment approach to punishment, is the work of the American writer Benjamin Rush which was elaborated in its most distilled form in his paper *An Enquiry into the Effects of Public Punishments upon Criminals and upon Society,* which was read in Philadelphia in March 1787. Rush took a close look at the public nature of punishment and brought to bear most of the consequences of enlightenment thought upon it. Within this work there is a quest for reformation, but especially an attempt to investigate the impact of shame and public punishment upon the psyche of the individual and whether this was beneficial for society. Rush began with the assertion that '...all public punishments tend to make bad men worse' and gave a detailed list of reasons why the reformation of the miscreant could not be achieved through using public corporal punishments. Firstly he asserted that public punishment associated the criminal with species of infamy destroying 'the sense of shame, which is one of the strongest outposts of virtue.'[21] He also believed that its generally short duration, compared to incarceration at least, did not produce any lasting and distinctive change of mind. Public punishment, so Rush believed was also capable of stimulating feelings of revenge within the criminal:

> A man who has lost his character at a whipping post, has nothing valuable left to lose in society. Pain has begotten insensibility to the whip; and shame to infamy.[22]

In constructing his own psychological picture of the criminal, Benjamin Rush's argument suggested that those punished, developed 'fortitude, insensibility or distress.' 'Fortitude' could numb the prisoner against the fierce, but temporary, assault upon their person and self. 'Insensibility' was dangerous since its promotion of bravado and cheerfulness as a reaction to severe punishment was further capable of eroding its meaning and effectiveness. On occasions, as Rush noted, it was even capable of stimulating retaliation against an audience of onlookers.[23]

What we have here is Rush portraying existing forms of punishment in a pejorative manner as a playground of emotions scarcely within the purview and control of the authorities who were duty bound to oversee its practice. Distress was, in Rush's eyes an even more compelling enemy of effective punishment regimes. This was liable to produce in the observer feelings of sympathy and compassion and a 'disposition to relieve it'. Rush believed that sympathy had an important part to play in the normal operation of emotional daily life, so important that he felt it irretrievably diluted, weakened and distorted when exposed to the spectacle of public punishment. He was concerned that:

> Misery of every kind will then be contemplated without emotion or sympathy...when the sentinel of our moral faculty is removed there will be nothing to guard the mind from the inroads of every positive vice.[24]

Thus shaming public punishments were liable to incite a serious want of respect for the law. Punishment, not closely linked to the crime in proximity or proportion, and devoid of explanation, appeared to the casual observer to be 'mere arbitrary cruelty.'[25] On the subject of the casual observer, Rush was also concerned about the impact of public punishments in their capacity to acquaint people with criminality of which they would otherwise be in ignorance. In suggesting the dangers associated with the example this might set the ignorant, Rush pointed out evidence that viewing such punishment had created a propensity to commit crime where it might not otherwise exist.[26] Rush was even baffled that public shame punishments had lasted so long and could see neither logic nor rationality in their persistence.

> It is therefore to the combined operation of indolence, prejudice, ignorance and the defect of culture of the human heart, alone, that we are to ascribe the continuance of public punishments, after such long and multiplied experience of their inefficacy to reform bad men, or to prevent the commission of crimes.[27]

Whilst Benjamin Rush, like other commentators, pondered the external factors that influenced the nature of punishment and its effects, he was distinct in providing psychological explanations about how punishment and shame impacted upon the human psyche. He noted how the human mind exaggerated all things that were distant from it in space and time, as well as its ability to magnify and give 'extreme qualities' of importance to the uncertain and the unknown. He also expressed awareness of the fact that the contemplation of evil retribution, if considered long enough, eventually ceased to have impact upon the miscreant individual. Most tellingly, he noted how the connection with community and kindred was essential for the psychological well-being of individuals – an important factor noted in the previous chapter around how the pillory and its related shame punishments were deemed to function.[28] Although Rush considered these as arguments about the failure of public shaming punishments, he marshalled them to support his proposal for a more gloomy and terror ridden concept of incarceration – one which would create for itself a place of fear in the mind of the local populace and its children, a so-called 'house of repentance'.[29]

In his focussed arguments against the prevailing customs around public punishments involving shame, Rush noted how members of the populace were exhibiting their own objections to these. Citing individuals moving away from execution sites alongside the well-documented loathing of the executioner, he exhibited a collision of sentiment and rationality in his critique of this:

> These things are the latent struggles of reason, or rather the secret voice of God himself, speaking in the human heart, against the folly and cruelty of public punishments.[30]

Rush arguably summed up the classic enlightenment position arraigned against the persistence of apparently irrational and anachronistic shame punishments which were unregulated, unrestrained and brought the forces of order into disrepute:

> I cannot help entertaining a hope, that the time is not very distant, when the gallows, the pillory, the stocks, the whipping post, and the wheel barrow (the usual engines of public punishments) will be connected with the history of the rack and the stake, as marks of the barbarity of ages and countries, and as melancholy proofs of the feeble operation of reason and religion upon the human mind.[31]

Debates over the nature and purpose of punishment were also present in Scottish writing in the early modern period, although much of that which relates to the Enlightenment era grew from the work of the late seventeenth century judge and politician Sir George Mackenzie of Rosehaugh (1636–1691). In his seminal publication, *The Laws and Customs of Scotland in Matters Criminal* published in 1678, Mackenzie states that:

> Punishments are inflicted, not only to satisfy, either the publick Revenge of the Law, or the privat Revenge of the Party, but rather to deterr others for the future; and yet they are rather inflicted upon either of these Designs, than to punish the Offender, and make him insensible, for what is done can no more be helped.[32]

Here, Mackenzie suggests that the chief impetus of punishment should be reparation and prevention, rather than the reformation of the criminal himself, and as such, he propounds Beccaria's view that punishment is a display of power which functions purely as a spectacle for those who witness it. Within this context, shame cannot function and has no role to play in the penal process.

Less than a century later, however, theories about punishment in Scotland had shifted, rather dramatically, as evidenced by the writings of the Enlightenment commentator Baron David Hume (1757–1838). For Hume, shame or as he prefers – 'ignominy' – had an important part to play in punishment regimes both public and private in nature. Moreover, it is also clear from Hume's writings that by the eighteenth century period, the reform of the criminal had become one of the key considerations of the Scottish judicial establishment, alongside deterrence and recompense.

In his two volume work *Commentaries on the Laws of Scotland Respecting Crimes*, Hume builds on the work of Mackenzie to produce a more theoretical and detailed account of the nature and process of the criminal law in Scotland. Hume's aim in this work was to introduce readers to the distinctive merits of Scots Law. Indeed, Hume argues early on in his work that the system of punishment in Scotland, in particular, was more 'eminent' than that of England.[33] South of the border, penal policy was pre-determined, as the judiciary followed the statutory provision to the absolute letter of the law. In Scotland, although the law was rigorous and authoritative, sentencing practice was more discretionary in nature. The judge determined each case according to its particular circumstances. This more flexible and accommodating Scottish system was '...sufficient to maintain a great degree of good order and peace, than exists in any other land so far advanced as this in the arts and refinement of life, and consequently so much exposed to the vices which attend them.'[34] In England, the law had to be tempered after the fact through a system of appeals and pardons, but there was no need for a similarly remissive policy in Scotland.

Although more discretionary, when compared to its English equivalent in terms of sentence delivery, Scottish penal policy arguably, in other respects, contained more precision. One of the most common complaints amongst eighteenth and nineteenth century legal theorists was that the time lag between sentencing and actual punishment was too protracted and unpredictable. Yet, in the Scottish context, definitive guidelines existed to determine when punishment should be administered. For instance in capital cases, regulations (such as that of 11th of Geo. I) insisted on execution sentences being carried out within 30 days south of the Forth estuary and within 40 days north of that dividing line.[35] As well as a specific day of execution being named as part of the judge's condemnatory declaration, the court had to ensure that the prisoner had been given adequate time to see to his or her 'spiritual concerns' to avoid a situation where '...death would so ill serve any of the purposes for which the spectacle of punishment is appointed by the law.'[36] Convicts had to be penitent and accepting of their fate, not angry and belligerent. There had to be an obvious blend between humanity and justice, and executions in particular had to be devoid of cruelty, unjustness or indecency.[37] Even with regard to more minor offences, a delay between sentencing and punishments was '...found to be troublesome, and a discouragement to the trial of petty offenders.'[38] If justice was to be effective, it had to be swift. Thus, even for these minor crimes, 3. Geo. II, c. 32 allowed between eight and 12 days of a gap between sentencing and '...any punishment short of death or demembration' which the Scots happily enforced.[39]

Scottish penal policy in the eighteenth century, at least according to Hume's description, appears comparatively elegant, refined and wholly appropriate to an enlightened society. It had managed to strike a balance between discretion and humanity on the one hand, and precision and stringency on the other. To many of the theorists who debated the short-comings of the legal systems in other European countries in the eighteenth and early nineteenth centuries, the Scottish example presented itself as an efficient, effective and highly desirable system.

As with many of his contemporaries, Hume does not discuss the concept of shame within punishment directly or specifically, but instead, like Beccaria, he concentrates on the notion of 'infamy' or 'ignominy'. Hume explains that after execution and transportation or banishment, the remaining punishments available to the Scottish judiciary '...consist chiefly in the ignominy, or the open exposure of the culprit to contempt and derision, and to the public knowledge as a base and an infamous person.'[40] In this description, Hume suggests that in order for humiliation to function within punishment, it had to operate on two levels. Firstly, and as Montesquieu noted, shame had to be internal and personal to the criminal as an individual based on their natural instincts. Secondly, and in addition to this, shame had to be externally visible and involve reproach by the audience who were watching. Clearly, this binary form of psychological discomfort was considered to be the essential element of effective shame punishments, but Hume is quick to point out that '...some degree of bodily distress' was also commonly suffered alongside the infamy itself.[41] Unlike other aspects of the Scottish penal system already discussed, the application of this particular type of 'distress' seems to have been somewhat arbitrary and immeasurable north of the Tweed. The 'unpredictability' of individual suffering within shame-based punishments and indeed penal strategies more widely, gave rise to widespread criticism from later legal theorists such as Jeremy Bentham and William Smith as we shall see.

Unlike his native predecessor Sir George Mackenzie, Baron David Hume *was* exercised by the purpose of punishment in relation to the individual felon. He argued that in order to achieve the successful 'reformation of the offender', it was necessary to apply *both* bodily distress *and* personal shame simultaneously.[42] Only under these particular circumstances, would sentencing policy be appropriate and effective for all those concerned. Within this model, opprobrium was clearly an essential element. As Hume describes '...such a stigma seems to be a suitable pain, where such malversations occur on the part of persons in situations of public trust.'[43] For Hume, 'public trust' extended to all elements of Scottish society: public as well as private.

Although Hume did express what he believed should be the necessary outcome of bad behaviour, he did not appear to be wholly convinced about the general effectiveness of this sort of punishment regime in relation to certain types of crime. He says 'It is open...to difference of opinion, whether infamy ensues on the undergoing of punishment, though in itself ignominious, such as whipping or the pillory, if it happen that this has been inflicted for an offence not of an infamous nature.'[44] For Hume, ignominy as a punishment was ineffective if the offence for which it was implemented was generally 'supported' by the populace at large, for example smuggling or rioting to raise wages, etc. As he explains:

> The crime is the act of the pannel [accused criminal], and the stain of infamy must attach to him, if such is the natural character of his crime; but the sentence is the act of the Court, and degrading pains may sometimes be applied unsuitably, owing to the rashness or ignorance of an inferior Judge. It is a different question, whether a man's credibility can be considered as entire, who has once undergone, even though improperly, such a public and disgraceful correction.[45]

By this argument, the opprobrious elements of punishment could only function effectively if the sentence itself was supported by all of those involved: offender, audience and authority. The exclusion of any part of this triumvirate would undermine the efficacy of the whole process. Although he offers no obvious solution to this problem, Hume's concerns regarding the appropriateness and effectiveness of shame-based punishments clearly echo some of the criticisms of other pre-modern legal theorists such as Benjamin Rush who we have already encountered above, and Jeremy Bentham whose work was contemporaneous with that of Hume. Yet shame, characterised once again as 'infamy' or 'ignominy' still had a role within Hume's conception of law and punishment although he clearly argued that this was to be discretionary and calculated.

Jeremy Bentham's influence around the philosophy of utilitarianism is especially pertinent for this volume since one of the subject areas in which he methodically sought to apply his philosophy, was in the area of governance and punishment, where the pain and pleasure principle was at its most apparent. This was elaborated within Bentham's influential tract *The Rationale of Punishment* which provides one exemplar of the case offered against shame punishments. Like Beccaria and others, this was not a single-minded assault upon the barbarity or lack of rationality shame punishments embodied. Instead it was a bi-product of the desire to make punishment fulfil other functions. In defining punishment, Bentham lists its supposed aims as 'reformation', 'disablement', 'determent', 'self-defence', 'self-preservation', 'safe custody' and 'restraint'.[46] Within this, he was clear that punishment could be categorised as either corporal or as a species of forfeiture, thus ruling out any explicit dimension of shame punishment for its own sake.[47] Further propositions argued that the chief end of punishment was the prevention of crime and that, as a result of this, it was ostensibly an act of safety not of 'wrath'.[48]

These suggestions were the cornerstones of Bentham's clear contribution to discussions about the nature of punishment which straddled the end of the eighteenth century and the start of the nineteenth. The major proposition, which was intended to turn penology in a specific direction, was the strong assertion that all considerations of punishment should turn around their obvious utility. Some of this clearly echoed Beccaria and it is obvious from the number of references to the latter's text that Bentham operated, to some extent, in the shadow of his work.[49] Perhaps the apex of this argument was the suggestion that punishment was unproductive, of minimal value for society and that it could certainly be done in a more cost effective manner.[50]

Not surprisingly Bentham was also anxious to implement a regime in which punishment was closely and scrupulously regulated. In this respect, the Scots practice of discretionary sentencing discussed above would have been frowned upon by Bentham and his followers, as it encouraged inconsistent and irregular practice. Rather, Bentham argued that punishment had to be exact and predictable – 'that is, it should present to the mind not only a part, but the whole of the sufferings it includes.'[51] Punishment, within a utilitarian model, was to conform to a tightly focussed collection of rules and regulations. All of these were intended to make the operation and function of punishment clear and coherent to all who played a part in its various processes. Punishment, so Bentham argued, must outweigh any profit potentially gained from the offence and thus it clearly should be dreaded more than any profit from the offence committed. Similarly, the scale of punishment should directly reflect the magnitude of the offence and the punishment itself, should be no greater than was necessary to sustain conformity. Bentham was also certain that it was especially desirable for the punishment to be implemented as closely in time to the offence as was reasonably possible. This was to ensure an identification of punishment with crime that seems to have been an enduring obsession amongst the reformers, despite the effective exemplar that the Scots had already provided. There was also an imperative for the suffering within punishment to be measured and for it to be capable of being measured. Mindful of society's role in the administration of punishment, and for its wider acceptability, Bentham stressed that any form of punishment must not be unpopular amongst the populace.[52]

All of this ran counter to the previously understood philosophy of shame punishments, such as it existed at all. It was the polar opposite of the open ended and boundary free nature of shame as a central part of punishment. Neither the magnitude, nor the effect of shame could be quantified or predicted in the manner Bentham deemed essential. This issue became manifest in his denunciation of the unregulated and disordered nature of punishment through the pillory. In particular, it is interesting to note that Bentham failed to understand that any aspect of the pillory's use as punishment, and the outcomes from it, could be devoid of intention on the part of the authority which implemented it.

> The pillory is a plank fixed horizontally upon a pivot, on which it turns, and in which plank there are openings, into which the head and hands of the individual are put, that he may be exposed to the multitude. I say to the gaze of the multitude – such is the intention of the law; but it not unfrequently happens, that persons so exposed are exposed to the outrages of the populace, to which they are thus delivered up without defence, and then the punishment changes its nature; – its severity depends upon the caprice of a crowd of butchers. The victim – for such *he* then becomes – covered with filth, his countenance bruised and bloody, his teeth broken, his eyes puffed up and closed, no longer can be recognised. The police, at least in England, used to see this disorder, nor seek to restrain it, and perhaps would have been unable to restrain it. A simple iron trellis, in the form of a cage, placed around the pillory, would however, suffice for stopping at least all those missiles which might inflict dangerous blows upon the body.[53]

As we can see from this description, the conventional operation of the pillory spectacularly infringed everything that Bentham believed punishment should entail. It was unpredictable, was beyond the control of measurement, was inordinately cruel, could render the victim unrecognisable and was significantly detached from the nature of the crime committed. Most disastrous of all, from Bentham's viewpoint, was the quite obviously corrosive effect upon many elements of authority. Its unpredictability cultivated contempt for authority which could regularly manifest itself in the differential treatment of prisoners consigned to the pillory. This broke Bentham's proviso that punishment should never be unpopular. It also appeared to be an especially risky form of punishment since it displayed, all too graphically, the limits of state power in controlling the populace, thereby further inviting the ridicule and contempt of authority.

Bentham was also concerned that other shame punishments conflicted with his notions of social utility and that they fundamentally stood in the way of a modernising society. In his discussion of the use of branding as a shame punishment, Bentham noted that this took punishment from a single isolated event, with calculated shock value, into a lifelong stigmatising punishment. This latter state of affairs, seen as permanently marking out individuals as exiles from society, was something which would remove any benefit their putative subsequent work or labour might have for that society. As Bentham suggested, society needed to take these issues into consideration, since stigma damaged both wealth creation and the wider well-being of society:

> ...this mark is an attestation that the individual has been guilty of some act to which contempt is attached, and the effect of contempt is to diminish goodwill, the principle that produces all the free and gratuitous services that men render to one another; but in our present state of continual dependence upon each other, that which diminishes the goodwill of others towards us, includes within itself an indefinite multitude of privations.[54]

Bentham's own assertion that punishment was to be regulated, and uniquely focussed upon benefiting society, criticised the singular and set-piece nature of punishments such as whipping, since they precluded adequate time for reflection on the part of the miscreant. Bentham was adamant that this would provide the impetus for reformation and catalogued the process through which the offender would pass, if adequately deprived of outside influences.[55] Nonetheless, even Bentham, in places, could be ambivalent about the proposed role of shame in his system of incarceration. On the one hand, he was clear about the supposed benefits of shame generated by lengthy periods of solitary confinement; something he considered was undone by allowing the miscreant to associate with other prisoners.[56] He also commented upon the medieval shame punishment of heretics as a process, which despite a need for regulation and reform was nonetheless 'good in itself'.[57] However, Bentham also noted that the emotion of shame was potentially counterproductive and arguably served to hinder his scheme of criminal reformation. Shame, as Bentham styled it, was a phenomenon which constrained and prevented offenders from displaying the required levels of contrition in front of fellow prisoners.

> From pride, each man will endeavour to make his own sense of his own sufferings appear to others as slight as possible: he will undervalue the afflicting circumstances of his situation: he will magnify any little comforts which may attend it, and, as the common phrase is, will put as good a face on the matter as he can.[58]

Similarly, although Bentham was vehemently opposed to the infliction of physical stigma amongst those sent back into society, he saw this issue rather differently when it was applied to those confined for longer terms within his structure of incarceration – '...let a stigma be inflicted; and let that stigma be perpetual.'[59] Shame also existed within his system as a consequence of guilt from undertaking questionable or immoral actions. In avoiding, or seeking out, close compatriots after this, individuals inevitably felt themselves confronted by 'the sting of shame'.[60] Once again, with an eye to the utility of forms of punishment, Bentham believed making individuals live through a state of infamy would invariably create alienation, rather than the state of reformation which he sought.[61]

However, in the later stages of Bentham's treatise, there are also clues about what was happening to the issue of shame in the context of the law. The third chapter of Book Three of the *Rationale of Punishment* contains a lengthy discussion about the issue of libel and its function within society and systems of law. This convoluted section outlined the nature of libel laws, but gave an instinctive clue about how the sophisticated state should have a credible and lucid method of dealing with situations where the issue of reputation was involved. This was qualitatively different to administrations using the power of libel to place people in the pillory. Bentham cited the case of Shebbeare, Williams and Beckford, in which the crowd's support for those in the pillory accused of libel, did not result in a satisfactory outcome. 'Shame, did not then, I think' follow the finger of the law.'[62]

Last of all, we should bear in mind Bentham's continued ambivalence concerning the role of infamy and that of shame within an enlightened and modernising society. In the discussion of his Panopticon scheme in the text of the *Rationale of Punishment*, it is possible to see distinct elements associated with shame surviving in this new, supposedly revolutionary and modern form of punishment. The Panopticon, so Bentham strongly argued, fulfilled its clear purpose and function best when it was placed prominently in a residential neighbourhood. This was intended to fulfil an exemplary function within the 'metropolis' at a place:

> where the greatest number of persons are collected together, especially of those who require to be reminded, by penal exhibitions, of the consequences of crime. The appearance of the building, the singularity of its shape, the walls and ditches, by which it is surrounded, the guards stationed at its gates, would all excite ideas of restraint and punishment, whilst the facility which would be given to admission, would scarcely fail to attract a multitude of visitors – and what would they see? – a set of persons deprived of Liberty which they have misused; compelled to engage in labour, which was formerly their aversion, and restrained from riot and intemperance, in which they formally delighted; the whole of them clothed in a particular dress, indicating the infamy of their crimes. What scene could be more instructive to the great proportion of the spectators?[63]

It is also possible to see elements of the debate surrounding approaches to punishment appearing in a number of lesser works which discuss the nature of crime and the reform of penal policy. In 1818, T.F. Buxton's brief treatise on the best method of treating prisoners focussed upon how important schemes aimed at their reformation would be to society in the long run. He noted that 'punishments are inflicted that crime may be prevented, and crime is prevented by the reformation of the criminal.'[64] He also echoed the Benthamite predilection for solitary incarceration suggesting that 'seclusion will humble the most haughty, and reform the most abandoned.'[65] Interestingly, in his criticism of the existing system and its failure to provide for the reformation of the miscreant, Buxton focussed upon the pejorative and damaging role shame played when prisoners were exposed to its effects.

> The prisoner, after his commitment is made out, is handcuffed to a file of perhaps a dozen wretched persons in a similar situation and marched through the streets, sometimes a considerable distance, followed by a crowd of impudent and insulting boys; exposed to the gaze and to the stare of every passenger.[66]

In 1823, William Roscoe borrowed several ideas from earlier writers and effectively elaborated upon some of them to portray the outmoded nature of shame in punishment. Roscoe himself noted that there remained far too many individuals who were advocates of unadulterated physical punishment. He also displayed a marked preference for the custodial and penitential approach. In advocating this, he believed that shame punishments, such as the pillory, were particularly ineffective since they tended to return the miscreant too quickly to society. In this, the criminal was permitted 'to renew his depredations or starve', so that to Roscoe an effective penal regime was one that concentrated upon isolating the offender from their community.[67] We also get the impression that Roscoe considered the longevity of penitential punishment to be more obviously advantageous. However, the reasons for this opinion relate to his opposition to shame punishment. As we noted, he considered this to be all too brief and the shame element an inadequate challenge to the determined miscreant. This he sought to replace with an extended contemplation of culpability so intense and individualised; it resembled the modern theoretical construct of guilt:

> the pangs and sufferings of an evil conscience, opened to the scene of its own enormities, abominations, and crimes – the overwhelming sense of self-reproach, contrition, and shame – the daily and nightly tears that must be shed before these stains can be washed out; and the dreadful apprehension that reformation has arrived too late, and that the sinner may be cut off before he has had an opportunity of expiating his offences by a better course of life, are, perhaps, the most acute sufferings incident to our nature.[68]

In the late eighteenth century, the growing tide of criticism against the piecemeal contemporary punishment regime grew ever more vocal and articulate. In the context of constructing critiques of punishment, and of advocating incarceration as an alternative, a number of commentators also obliquely discussed the role and issue of shame in punishment. These views cover a considerable cross section of opinion and scarcely support the idea of a consensual and unified push for forms of modernisation.

William Smith's *Mild Punishment* commences with a fairly standard humanitarian critique of the 'bloody code' era of punishment, noting that such draconian measures were indicative of a society which exhibited a 'ferocity of manners'.[69] He also adopted, and articulated, some of the standard arguments against this punishment regime; notably that it rendered punishment unpredictable and uncertain and that this chance element actively encouraged careers centred around criminality. Smith argued that this removal of 'certainty' severely undermined the supposed consolation offered by religion, which otherwise offered a contract leading from atonement to forgiveness and salvation. The arbitrary nature of punishment, which arguably short-circuited the hope for forgiveness, resulted in a 'scoffing' attitude towards the hope of salvation. Smith also wanted to introduce and sustain the, by now, familiar assertion that punishment should be as far as possible analogous to the crime committed – an idea we encountered earlier in the writings of Bentham and others. Yet there was a clear and obvious twist to Smith's line of thinking that is somewhat unexpected. He was at one with the modernisers in his pejorative views about the death penalty, but this drove him to take a radically different view about the role and function of public atonement and shame punishments. In suggesting that the use of capital punishment was arbitrary within the existing system, Smith argued it had lost its potency and meaning. For Smith, death no longer functioned at all as a 'deterrent against iniquity'.[70]

Instead, Smith suggested that corporal punishments for small offences (with a distinct and obvious shame element) 'would make a greater impression than capital punishment.'[71] Somewhat at odds with many of his contemporaries Smith appeared convinced that the solution to the eighteenth century's enduring issues with the application of capital punishment was a greater resort to public shame punishments. He argued that this tough approach to small offences would 'prevent greater enormities'.[72] Smith further suggested that all corporal punishment should be exposed to the public gaze so '...that the unthinking multitude may be taught to distinguish the degrees of crimes by distinctions of punishment' and noted that 'The sight of criminals being punished produces a repeat feeling of dread amongst the populace if it happens over and over again to the same individual.'[73]

Whereas others had linked punishment and public dread together as iniquities of the same failing system, William Smith had as seen them as fundamentally different approaches to solving the issue of crime and punishment. In reality, this envisaged a considerably enhanced role for shame within the punishment system. The declining credibility of capital sentences went hand-in-hand with their declining effectiveness. The arbitrary nature of their application and the uncertainty that surrounded this removed the emotional effects of execution from the public mind, a fact exacerbated by its infrequent and irregular use. For Smith, the restoration of punishment's regularity would restore its psychological power and hold over the minds of the populace. This would constantly present individuals punished, and arguably those who witnessed this punishment, with the spectacle of their own wretchedness as the observer 'judges by his own sensibility of what passes in another's mind.'[74] Although Smith does not mention the concept of shame within this context, it appears later in his work in a somewhat telling phrase. He notes that women enter prostitution after being exposed to public shame which he characterises as 'that guard which nature has planted round virtue.'[75]

A peculiar variation upon this theme is exemplified in George Onesiphorus Paul's address to the Gloucester magistrates in 1789. Whilst Paul argued in familiar fashion that the public shame component of punishments was clearly 'repugnant to reformation', he nonetheless believed that it had a useful purpose.[76] Paul was certain that exemplary punishments exposed their victims to forms of public degradation, but was prepared to argue that these should be reserved for individuals that could be 'selected from amongst the desperately depraved'. This particular assertion sits oddly with the rest of this text which seems an unapologetic examination of the consequences of instances of prison mismanagement and neglect, wherever Paul could find them. Moreover, it is singularly unclear what Paul intended through this statement. Whether the exemplary punishment of the depraved would have a didactic effect upon the onlookers is unclear. Likewise, any sense that this would rescue individuals from their state of depravity was also absent from this work. Similarly there is no clear sense of how this might fit into any other part of his examination of the condition of prisons in England.[77]

By the start of the nineteenth century, Scottish legal theorists, alongside Paul, had also noted and welcomed the demise of shame punishments. Most prominent amongst these was the lawyer and historian Sir Archibald Alison (1792–1867).[78] Principle Seventeen of Chapter XVII in his *Practice of the Criminal Law of Scotland* first published in 1833, states that 'Whipping and the pillory are the only corporal pains, inferior to death, which are still in use; and of these the first is the only one which, from its frequency, is deserving of a place in a practical treatise of jurisprudence.'[79] Alison goes on to explain that in an attempt to curb the sudden surge in criminal offending which had become evident at the time, public whipping as a punishment had something of a resurgence in early nineteenth century Scotland, where it was often added to a sentence of transportation or imprisonment. This was most regularly the case in instances where a criminal had been particularly 'cruel' in carrying out their crime.[80] In this respect, the Scottish judicial system appears to have listened to George Onesiphorus Paul's calls for shame to be reserved for the most 'depraved' offenders, and indicates that some regimes did retain the use of shame-based punishments into the more modern era.

In contrast to the augmented use of scourging in Scotland, however, Alison describes how:

> The pillory is much less frequently inflicted now than formerly; and, indeed, there has been hardly an instance of its being inflicted for the last fifteen years. It is obviously an unjust and unequal punishment; being excessively severe to any convict who happens to be obnoxious to the populace, and proportionally light to those who are not the objects of such obloquy. It was much in use in former times; but it is to be hoped the good sense and justice of our Judges will be slow to revive a mode of punishment which subjects the prisoner to the passions of the rabble, as likely to exceed the dictates of justice in one case, as they fall behind them in another.[81]

Here Alison's comments present something of a dichotomy in contemporary legal thinking. On the one hand legal theorists welcomed the limited preservation of shame-based punishments for the most heinous criminals, but on the other hand, they were quick to point to the ineffectiveness of this type of penalty. Echoing the fears of Benjamin Rush of nearly 150 years earlier, Alison implies that punishments such as the pillory could send the wrong kind of message to the general populace. Moreover, he also states (just as Jeremy Bentham did) that the infliction of shame could often go amiss depending on the mood of the participants, and the process of punishment could thereafter descend into tumult and chaos, perpetuating and disseminating bad behaviour amongst the masses.

From this investigation of the works of a number of theoreticians, it is possible to recognise a number of general trends in progress. Although it could be argued that it is relatively rare for shame on its own to be discussed as an aspect of punishment it does find itself scrutinised in the context of punishment regimes as a whole. The role of shame in punishment, and arguably the wider society, was central to the late eighteenth century debate on the 'bloody code' and whether this regime was providing a system of justice that was fit for purpose. This rested not simply on humanitarian arguments, but increasingly drew in utilitarian ones that had commenced the debate with a desire to provide the best possible system to control and counter criminality. Most commentators criticised the piecemeal, arbitrary and irrational nature of the prevailing system of punishment, which almost all of them attacked for its production and dissemination of distinctly mixed messages. All punishment, their consensus argued, should be rationalised and modernised to actively serve society by bringing active credit to the notion of justice. These arguments fundamentally rested on aspects of enlightenment thought and its explanations about how the mind and the individual were more sophisticated than previous societies had accepted. Within these mounting arguments for modernization, was an assault upon the supposedly primitive emotion of shame, and its failure to be a rational component of punishment. Instead regulated and measured systems of punishment, generally involving forms of incarceration, were to be modern and judicious replacements for the unpredictability of shame.

This analysis, thus far, fits relatively well with conventional historiography outlining the history of punishment and penology. This suggests a move to quasi-codify the law and, whilst modernising it, to propose a rationalisation of punishment regimes. This had, by and large, moved from the exemplary to more private forms based largely on incarceration. The chronology sketched here would also partly coincide with the history Foucault outlines in his seminal work *Discipline and Punish*. This, as we are aware, noted a move away from the exemplary punishments to ones involving restraint and incarceration. As we know, Foucault was also at great pains to point out the illusory claims of the so-called humanitarian arguments for this modernization and change. As he suggested, the application of expert knowledge to create objects for gaze and study, and the growing element of surveillance within punishment, made it more effective but no less painful for those in receipt of it. Certainly by reading sections of the texts quoted in this chapter, it is possible to see how Foucault reached this conclusion. In places they speak eloquently of the torment and anguish the individual and their conscience may well have to endure within solitary confinement. Read in this particular way, we can also see how this was a clear movement away from the community's role in punishment, and Foucault's earlier point that so often punishment operated as a dialogue between the miscreant and their audience. Brought into the private sphere, it is easy to see how Foucault might construe this as an attack upon the subjectivity of the individual.

But as we have also seen, even within the texts of modernisers like Beccaria, Bentham and Hume, lie notable traces of shame conceived of as a potentially useful part of punishment. Whilst there was a repugnance against its cruder manifestations there was nonetheless a desire to make it more subtle and effective within a socially utilitarian system of punishments. There were also some texts which thought about the issue of shame and shame punishments somewhat differently. In some of these there is a precursor of more modern arguments that shame punishments have a role to play in a thoroughly modernised system. As we have seen, one commentator saw that shame was actually an enlightened and modern antidote to the tyranny and danger to society offered by the 'bloody code'. These authors argued that shame punishments were able to educate the citizen and prevent them from engaging upon a lifelong career in crime, or conversely, that degrading shame punishments should merely be reserved for the most depraved members of society. Although these equate to minor critiques and alternative versions of the modernization view of society and its attitude to crime and the criminal, it is worth noting how some of the more mainstream arguments contain counter tendencies to those outlined by Foucault's analysis. We should particularly note how writers like Bentham, deep within his text, still see an important and utilitarian role for the exemplary nature of punishment. In this model, shame punishments had gone, but some elements of shame had been thoroughly reintegrated into the modernised system.

Perhaps most importantly of all, Foucault's analysis of shame punishments and their passing focussed on the role of authority as the prime mover and broker in the whole culture of punishment and wider shame within society. As it was central to his theoretical approach, Foucault was arguably too ready to see this change as monolithic and accomplished within an impossibly short period of time. Shame continued to perform functions in many aspects of the law and behaviour that resulted in recourse to the law. Indeed it could be said that shame played an important part in individuals discovering and exhibiting their subjectivity and finding a voice they could use against authority which they found overbearing, spurious or oppressive. We can start to see this in action within examples contained in the chapters which follow.

Thus at the precise moment when the role of shame was scrutinised and debated against the enlightenment yardsticks of rationality and utility, we do not see an unequivocal triumph of modernity seeking to eradicate shame. Nor do we see an imperative to place society on the road to replacing this outmoded concept of shame with individualised guilt. Some saw shame as a rational and modern answer which would save English society from the injustice and tyrannies of the 'Bloody code'. Surprisingly, through writings which analysed the dynamics between individuals, institutions and ideas our influential thinkers display ways that shame itself came to be capable of surviving beyond the modernisation of punishment. Even humanitarians and utilitarians displayed an awareness of shame's value and ways in which it was (in Hume's words) 'appropriate'. Similarly they were conscious of how it could be incorporated into new systems that by this period explicitly evaluated the reactions of individuals to the punishment they received. Within attempts to reform and rehabilitate such individuals shame became a part of punishment chiefly though incarceration and its attendant apparatus. Thus shame was capable of surviving into the modernised world of rational and rehabilitative punishments yet, as we shall discover within the next two chapters, it could also appear inside the context of legal proceedings. These ensnared individuals in webs of expectation and competing behaviour, and arguably shame proved instrumental in the initiation and progress of these cases and their eventual outcomes.

6

The Everyday Life of a Wexford Parson: The Rev. William Hughes' Taste for Drink, Blasphemy, Indecent Exposure, Criminal Damage, Bestial Voyeurism and Field Sports

As we saw in the last chapter shame continued to exist after the reformers of punishment had processed and refined it within their utilitarian and humanitarian alternatives. It was obvious in the last chapter, that even in the post-Enlightenment period, shame still had a fundamental if not always acknowledged place in the philosophy of punishment, and the conduct of human social and class relationships. Shame had not been modernised, nor civilised out of existence, and the evidence of this chapter and the succeeding one suggest it became accommodated within the range of responses that individuals and groups had to the testing and trying situations which confronted them, particularly in areas of personal and individual conflict. Within a more complex world, shame still disciplined the behaviour of those who transgressed moral and community norms. However, as we shall see in these two chapters, both this definition of community and the ways in which shame would be brought to bear were changing.

It is probably safe to say that the Dublin Consistory Court of the late 1820s had never seen anything quite like the protracted and amazing case against the Reverend William Hughes. Certainly the proceedings which kept the court by turns enthralled, amazed and disgusted, were regularly declared by the protagonists to be beyond extraordinary. The case was not so much a cause célèbre, as an unbridled sensation which was painstakingly written up in a pamphlet stretching to almost a hundred pages. Nearly 180 years after the event, this can now be read by the curious at the British Library and its alternately hilarious and shocking contents constitute an ambivalent surprise awaiting any (un)fortunate reader.[1] This pamphlet is significant, since most of the other court and parish records about the case have not survived. It is also probably trustworthy, since it was produced by a newspaper reporter who had attended the case. Discernible bias seems substantially absent from the piece with the voice of the reporter similarly silent. The length and the level of (sometimes hair razing) detail it contains suggests a desire to reproduce all that had transpired and certainly, the author would have had his hands full merely to report the bare facts disclosed in detail. This was especially significant since the formal legal record of the case would obviously have contained some significant omissions, as we shall see.

Yet there is rather more beyond this ribald attempt to display clerical life as outrageously transcending anti-clerical accusation and wishful thinking. The life and apparent 'pursuits' of William Hughes allow modern readers a window onto many aspects of early nineteenth century shame in a rural context. Likewise the narrative's status as a painstakingly reported court case allows us clearly to see several discourses of shame at work, and to view the precise words and concepts individuals use to describe and respond to what they accepted as poor or unremittingly shameful behaviour. It also showcases how shame and disgust were articulated precisely, what measures of propriety individuals operated and how these were matched by ideas constructed by informal and official discourses. The incident also demonstrates for us some of Norbert Elias's 'thresholds of repugnance' in action and thus exposes us to the areas where the margins and limitations of civilisation were the subject of real debate. Lastly it answers, or addresses one of the chief tasks of cultural historians created for us by Robert Darnton's seminal suggestion that the reader's job was to 'get' the joke of the *Great Cat Massacre*.[2] In this instance, the case of William Hughes and his numerous escapades whether fictional or fact, allows us to understand (or 'get' in touch with) how shame operated simultaneously for an individual Church of Ireland clergyman, his community and the Ecclesiastical Court of his archdiocese. Within this discussion of shameful behaviour and allegedly shameful practices (and more importantly the defences of individual conduct offered by protagonists) emerges a series of ideals of behaviour and models of propriety that speak loudly about expectation and the gap between this and reality. This gap, and studying instances where it appears at its most blatant, is fundamentally important to unpacking the function of shame in past historical contexts and societies. It is also especially important here as we enter the period where it is traditionally argued shame was being supplanted by more modern conceptions of guilt.

The Reverend William M. Hughes a married and family man in his early 60s (at the time of the trial) had been Rector of Killinick in southern Wexford for some time. As was habitual in the Church of Ireland during this period, pluralism remained a problem demonstrated in this instance by Hughes also operating as vicar of another parish (Maglas) and retaining further curacies in no less than six other parishes.[3] Hughes had lived and worked in the vicinity of this part of Wexford since 1813, and this was undoubtedly long enough to gain him considerable (even raucous) notoriety amongst the local populace. The evidence of the case against him demonstrates that Hughes and his activities excited emotions ranging from considerable irritation, to unbridled revulsion through finally to utter disgust. Hughes, if the bulk of the population (and the charge sheet) were to be believed, was guilty of almost all of the possible moral misdemeanours that the polite and even impolite mind could conjure or imagine. These were compounded by his apparent serial repetition of such offences which allowed the prosecuting counsel to bring into court over 20 witnesses. Still worse for his reputation, Hughes refused to mend his ways, denied the charges, and his reoffending whilst the case had commenced against him, seemed to flout all conceptions of propriety further antagonising his community. In short, Hughes constituted a walking, talking personification of the supposedly far fetched anti-clerical accusations of two generations, as well as an especially convincing and potent advert for Irish disestablishment.

Yet the sheer mobilisation of the whole community to testify against Hughes raises questions about the case now, as it did nearly 180 years ago. What was the essence of Hughes's bad behaviour and why was he so relentlessly pursued by his parishioners? Was Hughes's behaviour really so appalling and if so why was he so dramatically out of touch with the standards expected of him by his parish and diocese? How could he have so manifestly misjudged his sporting companions or mistakenly imagined their taste for the profane and ribald? Or were there ulterior motives that led his community to fabricate evidence and testimony against him? If so this community's construction of a character of whom the diocese should be ashamed provides us with a clear contemporary image of unacceptable behaviour that demanded action, as well as both popular and official sanction. Unlike skimmington rides, charivari or rough music, this displeasure found its way directly into the court room, into witness statements and provides a whole panoply of articulate dissent and opinion that the historian really wished survived more often.

When the issue came to the Consistory Court, Hughes was charged with a scarcely credible and outrageously long litany of offences. He was charged with 'blasphemy, profane swearing, drunkenness, lechery and lewd and immoral practices', yet the detail of the case would bring still more apparent misbehaviour to light.[4] The case had certainly taken its time getting to the Consistory Court. The formal accusations had first seen the light of day in April 1825 when a citation against Hughes was filed. This initial attempt to entrap him however, fell foul of problems around the precise jurisdiction of the court. Hughes' parish was nominally in the Diocese of Ferns yet the citation carried the seal of the Diocese of Leighlin and Ferns. This procedural error enabled Hughes to successfully have the case annulled on this occasion.[5] When a subsequent suit was quickly lodged, Hughes now turned to contesting its validity within the court by lodging 24 separate objections to the charges, thereby arguing he was not compelled to answer it. This submission was overruled by the Surrogate Bishop of Ferns which pushed Hughes into an appeal to the higher Metropolitan Court of Dublin which was also overturned. An appeal above the Metropolitan Court to the High Court of Delegates was similarly unsuccessful, and when Hughes was once again ordered to 'join issue' in the case he was forced to change tactics yet again.[6] This time he obtained a Conditional Order from the King's Bench which prevented the Ecclesiastical Court from proceeding. Yet this temporary delay was to prove damaging to Hughes. When the King's Bench sat to consider the issue, it found in favour of the court and Hughes was saddled with the legal costs of this attempt to overturn the suit. Hughes now had no option but to 'join issue' and he lodged a long and intricate written defence which immediately raised objections from the prosecution. By now, wise to what it could only conclude was a sequence of delaying tactics and due to their growing desperation, the prosecution declared that this overblown defence was substantially aimed at protracting the proceedings still further.[7] When the judge concurred, the case was finally able to proceed to the Consistory Court and nearly four years of legal procrastination and procedural delay was at an end.[8] Eventually, when the case finally opened, witnesses appeared offering evidence against Hughes that stretched back as far as 1820. Moreover, the time lag in presenting and offering evidence against an individual across the divide of almost a decade offers us two possible yet equally tantalising conclusions. If the evidence offered against Hughes was carefully fabricated, then unbecoming pictures were being deliberately constructed, drawing on disgust and fears which were wrapped around an unpopular authority figure. If such events were true, it was significant proof positive that communities had extremely long memories. This fact alone in other historical contexts has often functioned as a species of popular sanction and justice which constrained the behaviour of authority figures throughout eighteenth and nineteenth century agrarian societies.[9]

For some, the concerted strategy of evasion adopted by Hughes seemed to signal that he was guilty or at least had much to hide. Many comments at the trial clearly indicate that this feeling was widespread, even if it was inevitably voiced most strongly by the prosecution camp.[10] At such a historical distance, the truth of this speculation is somewhat difficult to tease out; but from the subsequent charges and the lurid detail offered in the case it is safe to assume that Hughes was mortified that even the accusations would be associated with him. If guilty, he had considerable cause to feel ashamed. If innocent the desire to prevent his name being even falsely associated with the charges against him must have been almost overwhelming. So what did his parishioners accuse him of? As the case opened, the prosecution somewhat histrionically prepared the court for what was to follow. This was led by Dr George Moore M.P. who craved the indulgence of the court since he would divulge 'revolting and disgusting details', the detail of which left him almost lost for words. The charges were emphatically the worst he had seen in his career and the duty before him, even as the prosecutor was 'repugnant to his feelings'.[11]

The first charge offered against Hughes was that he would frequently lose his temper in a variety of situations and utter blasphemous profanities. On one occasion, Hughes had corrected an individual who had lost his place in the liturgy during divine service with an angry rebuke of 'Damn it – there it is!'[12] Similarly, whilst assisting a friend with an unruly horse in October 1823, he was observed to lose his temper with the animal exclaiming 'By God I would shoot him, if I had a pistol, by Heavens I would let his guts out, had I a knife.'[13] Hughes had also been observed throwing vitriol upon the partridge nets of one of his parishioners and when confronted with the crime threw up his hands crying 'I imprecate the vengeance of heaven, here and hereafter, may God afflict me with every disease in this life, and may perdition be my eternal lot, if I had act or part in the destruction of your nets.' When the accusation was persisted with, Hughes was reputed to have hung his head 'apparently overcome with shame, and stung with conscious remorse'.[14]

Further accusations followed Hughes when he indulged his penchant for hare coursing. This taste for field sports was to prove immensely costly for Hughes and his reputation, since many of the worst allegations against his behaviour turn around events which occurred during his quest to be a local sporting gentleman. When individual coursing events did not follow Hughes' expectations, his quick temper readily appeared as he rounded on his sporting companions. One individual deemed responsible for a disappointingly early kill received the rebuke 'it was all your fault, by the Holy Saviour if I was near you, I would teach you how to act.'[15] In the witness's testimony, Hughes later scourged this individual with the expression that 'he would rather see him and his whole family dead, than one of his dogs injured.'[16] Another, in Hughes' eyes, allowed a hare to escape to be greeted with 'God damn your soul, you blind rascal; by the Holy Saviour if I was alongside of you I would stretch you with this pole.'[17] Another, James Howlin, seemed to be a particular target of Hughes's wrath demonstrated by the latter's loss of temper when Howlin's dog was considered to be more proficient in the field. Howlin would later appear in other accusations levelled against Hughes and the defence would also proclaim the partisan nature of Howlin's testimony and his implication in a conspiracy against Hughes. Nonetheless, many witnesses were prepared to testify to the truth of these utterances with a prolific number especially willing to subscribe to the numerous hare coursing misdemeanours.

Hughes, according to the prosecution, and various witnesses from his community, also had a long and undistinguished career as a highly visible and embarrassing drunkard. The charges against him were numerous and were certainly enough for the court to use the term 'habitual' in describing them. Nonetheless, a significant number of specific incidents were singled out for consideration, many of which were associated with his sporting activities. On one occasion, whilst out coursing he was observed by Howlin to drink considerable quantities from a bottle he professed to always carry with him. When Hughes proceeded to have dinner with Howlin at a nearby farmhouse, he supplemented his meal with almost an entire bottle of sherry followed by a further three tumblers of whisky punch.[18] On another occasion, Howlin saw Hughes enter a public house in Cartnacuddy and consume a considerable quantity of beer mixed with whiskey and eggs which rendered him insensible.[19] Howlin had helped him from the premises whereupon he vomited on the road but recovered sufficiently to continue his pursuit of game whilst tippling from a Whisky bottle during the rest of the day – a scenario virtually repeated before Howlin on at least one other occasion.[20]

John Cooney's testimony largely concurred with Howlin's but he could be more specific. Whilst coursing with Hughes, Cooney observed the frequent tippling from the sporting whiskey bottle and the invariable retirement to a public house. At this establishment on this occasion, Cooney observed Hughes consume 'two quarts of beer and half a pint of whiskey mixed with two eggs beat up'. Invariably intoxication ensued with the Reverend narrowly escaping an accident on the road, since he was unable to operate the reins of his horse.[21] Hughes was unfortunate enough in this instance to meet another acquaintance, Thomas Furlong, who confirmed his intoxicated state and his precarious command of his horse adding that he was 'unable to express himself intelligibly to the deponent, with whom he attempted to enter into conversation'.[22] Furlong also recalled an earlier occasion when out shooting with Hughes, where the latter had declared that his poor performance with his gun had been due to the previous evening's alcoholic overindulgence. Furlong jovially offered Hughes a 'hair of the same hound' and his flask was gleefully accepted and Hughes continued to indulge himself from this throughout the rest of the day.[23] Howlin had also witnessed Hughes give a bellicose rendition of an obscene song 'Kate Martin', an incident later corroborated for another occasion by a soldier, Morgan Connors.[24] Hughes had reputedly lain slumped in a ditch whilst he raucously sang with Connors. This ballad may well have been a variation on the well known, vaguely risqué ballad Kate Kearney. This had a 'call and response' verse structure that might well have suited the befuddled clergyman and the soldier. The ballad is generally found as a variation of the following:

Kate Kearney
O Did you not hear of Kate Kearney,
She lives on the banks of Killarney
From the glance of her eye shun danger and fly,
For fatal's the glance of Kate Kearney;
For that eye is so modestly beaming,
You'd ne'er think of mischief she's dreaming.
Yet Oh I can tell how fatal's the spell,
That lurks in the eye of Kate Kearney.
Oh should you e'er meet this Kate Kearney
Who lives on the Banks of Killarney,
Beware of her smile for many a wile,
Lies hid in the smile of Kate Kearney;
Though she looks so bewitchingly simple,
There's mischief in every dimple,
And who dare inhale her mouth's spicy gale,
Must die by the breath of Kate Kearney.

ANSWER

O Yes I have seen this Kate Kearney,
Who lives near the lake of Killarney
From her love beaming eye what mortal can fly,
Unsubdued by the glance of Kate Kearney;
For that eye so bewitchingly beaming,
Assures me of mischief she's dreaming,
And I feel 'tis in vain to fly from the chain,
That binds me to lovely Kate Kearney.
At eve when I've met this Kate Kearney
On the flower mantled banks of Killarney
Her smile would impart thrilling joy to my heart,
As I gaz'd on the charming Kate Kearney;
On the banks of Killarney reclining,
My bosom to rapture resigning,
I've felt the keen smart of love's fatal dart,
And inhal'd the warm sigh of Kate Kearney.[25]

Beyond this, in quite matter of fact fashion, Hughes was further accused of frequenting unlicensed ale-houses in which he lodged for days and even sometimes weeks at a time.[26] Given the context, this last, almost throwaway accusation scarcely suggested a clergyman with a deeply felt vocation, or an individual devoted to the welfare of his flock; an impression which the prosecution would have clearly been at pains to emphasise. But the accusations which turned around drink took an even further vulgar and worrying turn. Stephen O'Connor recalled that on 22nd of January 1824, he had encountered Hughes on the main thoroughfare between Ferry Carrig Bridge and Wexford town. Hughes was visibly drunk and staggering about the road reeling from one side to the other in some distress. Still worse, he was caked in mud and had his breeches open displaying his genital area for all to observe. O'Connor then stated that he had seen three ladies on the footpath who had observed Hughes's condition in an initially shocked manner. When two of them had begun to laugh they were swiftly reproved by their 'matronly companion'.[27]

However, whilst the court might have been jolted by this testimony, nothing can quite have prepared them for the unseemly and astounding evidence which was to follow. The prosecuting counsel himself described imparting this information as 'a painful duty' to divulge a charge 'the details of which were of so repulsive a nature, he would, but cursorily, advert to part of the circumstances, as the disgusting particulars would be brought before the court, in the several depositions which would be read hereafter.'[28] Whilst Hughes had been hare coursing, he had introduced the assembled company to his starter terrier called 'Dick'. Dr Moore for the prosecution then described how the dog would bring a hare killed by the sportsmen back to the company. Hughes would then take the hare by the fore legs and hold the dead animal in position. This would then be the cue for 'Dick' to 'get upon the Hare, as upon a female of his own species, and make such motions as if he were in the act of sexual intercourse.' This was accompanied by Hughes expressing 'satisfaction' alongside the singing of lewd and obscene songs. Another deponent witnessed 'Dick's trick' on another occasion and declared that the obscene incident lasted for almost three minutes.[29] Still worse was to follow, since John Cooney witnessed an even worse exhibition by Hughes. The clergyman had taken up a dead hare and had craved the attention of the assembled individuals whereupon he:

> drew out the penis of the hare – using most obscene and indecent action, and making use of many lewd, obscene, and indecent words and gestures (more particularly described in the deposition, but unfit to appear in print), and that the said William Hughes continued this sport of lecherous and vicious conversation for a considerable time, in deponents presence, at which deponent, as well as others, were greatly ashamed and disgusted.[30]

But, unbelievably, still worse was to come, when Patrick Pitt gave evidence of his own unfortunate encounter with Hughes and his dog. On this occasion, whilst the dog was indulging himself with the hare, Hughes was alleged to have asked Pitt 'if he wanted a pup' presumably describing the proposed issue from the two animal's copulation. When the dog had, in Pitt's words 'satisfied the unnatural lust', Hughes took hold of the hare and tied a card to its leg. He was then said to have given the hare to Pitt with instructions to give it to the driver of the New Ross coach who was then to convey it '...for the Judge's dinner that day in Waterford'.[31]

Despite nearly 180 years having past, the impact of this testimony has scarcely dimmed and it revolted contemporaries as much as it affects the modern reader today. It is significant that such behaviour was manifestly portrayed as utterly alien to those present and to the witnesses, who were themselves supposedly familiar with the practices involved in hare coursing. Moreover, their testimony suggests that they were willing to declare that it did not belong even in raucous ultra masculine sporting company. If Hughes did perform the acts described, were they simply connected with alcoholic overindulgence? Certainly the evidence does not suggest this. If these events were a fabrication, where did the idea spring from? Had someone witnessed or practiced such abominable behaviour in the past, or was it a hunting custom of remote history now shunned? If this were so, it is worth asking where Hughes got his wildly inaccurate information about sporting behaviour and his presumption that his fellow sportsmen would be jovially impressed with his performance. Did hunting literature, travel literature or literature critical of Irish rural manners describe these events and practices? Was Hughes, 'slumming it' in the worst possible way, or did he make a woefully inadequate calculation of the apparent baseness of his companions, drawing fatefully upon species of stereotype and prejudice? Certainly the prosecution added fuel to the fire of this argument by stating that the defence appeared to be arguing that 'Mr Hughes, was a Gentleman of talent and address, who could adapt his demeanour to suit the society he was with; he therefore, when he felt it necessary, was cautious enough to lay a restraint on those propensities, which he could not but feel would disentitle him to mix with persons of distinction.'[32]

Although the full and possible answers to these questions are hard to confirm with the passage of time, some material from the rest of the trial gives us a picture of a community divided in various ways along class, ethnic and religious lines – all potential sources of misunderstanding, antagonism and accusation. Equally, the prosecution's precise ordering of the charges was itself significant, since they build from the profane and alcohol-related to a crescendo of the bestial. More importantly, the bestial behaviour is so extreme, that its credibility is only established through the court's acquaintance with the previous charges associated with possible profanity and alcoholism. In this, Hughes's flouting of expectations became a drama which built from lesser charges to a climax. The evidence offered by the prosecution against Hughes seems to create an undiluted picture of a blackguard priest unable to control his appetites and his behaviour once he had dramatically overindulged them. Only when we look at the evidence offered by the defence, do some tantalizing cracks start to appear in our picture of both the Reverend Hughes and the neighbourhood of Killinick. As we are aware, thoughts and feelings of shame, function as a species of deference to, and acknowledgement of, authority. Shame occurs because individuals are confronted with the disapproval of authority. In the Hughes case, it becomes evident that the accusation and counter accusation represented a struggle for this authority in which possession of the ability to shame was a valued prize. This in itself indicates the still vibrant presence of shame and its status as a tool related to the holding and exercise of cultural power.

Hughes's defence counsel Dr Thomas Staples immediately focussed upon the fact that it was reputation and character that were under attack from the allegations which, if proved, would render these 'utterly value-less'.[33] This clearly demonstrates how reputation functioned as a species of currency that allowed the individual to function and undertake duties within a community – indeed respected performance of such duties was arguably a method of adding to this currency. Hughes was utterly convinced that the 'fabricated' evidence against him was part of a conspiracy that had influential promoters. As his advocate outlined, this was engineered by Charles Walker, the son of the premier local landowner Thomas Walker, with whom he had had a considerably fiery relationship.

Hughes had antagonized the younger Walker in the sporting arena and had similarly clashed with him on the bench of magistrates where he had accused the clergyman of corrupt motives in denying a parti-cular individual a liquor license. This had supposedly occurred because the publican had refused Hughes the tithe payment due to him. Hughes retaliated with an inconclusive lawsuit, but this only antagonized Walker still further, inciting him to purchase land in the parish with the sole intention of hounding Hughes in his own vestry meetings.[34] The Bench had also been the arena for a profoundly damaging and public exchange between Hughes and Howlin. The latter had angrily pulled a chair away from Hughes as he was about to sit down. Such an apparently trivial (although visible) slight could mushroom in the local mind and its impact as a clear and ongoing grievance is evident in this case. Howlin himself would later claim that the incident had happened the other way round, with Hughes being the guilty party.[35] The defence also argued that fundamental differences over politics were also crucial in the matter. Walker had expressed himself in favour of Catholic Emancipation, whilst Hughes had stridently opposed the measure.[36] This latter opinion was also seen as the source of opposition to Hughes amongst the lower orders of Killinick and the surrounding area. Hughes had further incited the local populace through his apparently harsh treatment of a Catholic priest named Carroll who had come before him on a charge related to the murder of a child.[37]

Hughes's erstwhile sporting companion, James Howlin, had also brought a libel suit against Hughes in 1827 turning around an accusation that Howlin had been behind leaflets, or 'Scullys' which had embarrassed and obstructed Hughes in the collection of his tithes.[38] Both Howlin and Walker, according to the testimony of a Rev. Newland, were hell bent on destroying Hughes and fermented their plot against him in England, claiming they would 'proceed till they had stripped Impugnant of his gown.'[39] The essence of Hughes's defence was that some of the accus-ations could not be substantiated, and that some circumstantial evidence could be used to deny them. The charge levelled against him concerning his profane swearing, was countered by a claim that the one oath that he had used ('by the Holy Saviour') was of particularly Irish origin. The asser-tion was that an English educated clergyman would not use such an expression.[40] As for the charge of indecent exposure, the defence high-lighted the fact that the women concerned could not be produced. More-over, the story had not even circulated in rumour nor had it been the subject of local gossip. As the defence council argued, if the incident had been so shocking '...was their matronly companion such a prude as not even to whisper the scandal at cards, or at the tea-table.'[41]

As for the outrageous behaviour of the dog, the defence claimed that his infamous 'trick' had been acquired long before he came into the ownership of the Reverend Hughes. When the dog had performed his 'trick' Hughes himself had been appalled and had readily resorted to beating the animal as a means of ridding him of this habit. Moreover, Hughes was adamant that he failed to express '...any gratification at such, gambols, when put into practice by the unlucky cur.'[42] Yet the prosecution seized on this and asked not unreasonably, why a clergy-man should retain the possession of such an animal for a considerable period of time. The question remains a good one to this day, especially since earlier evidence suggested that other animals in the vicinity were of better hunting quality than 'Dick'.[43] Moreover, this picture drawn by the defence indicted Hughes in persistent, and more importantly ineffective, cruelty to an animal everyone considered unfortunate.

As was customary in most early nineteenth century court cases, the bulk of the evidence was character witness statements amassed on either side of the argument. It is here that we start to get the most revealing evid-ence of the community of Killinick and its behavioural expectations. It is also interesting that the dynamics of class, religion and ethnicity were also played by the defence to discredit the evidence of the opposition. This line of thinking from the defence suggested that the community's destabilised picture of morality would be restored by the side able to amass the greatest social 'respectability' behind its arguments – and argu-ably heap the most forms of shame upon its opponents. The evidence against Hughes was said to come from 11 illiterate peasants, whilst Cooney's testimony amounted to 'downright perjury'.[44] Moreover, Howlin's moral status was questioned since he was cited as bearing the 'appearance of a gentleman' yet 'does not betray the feelings of one'.[45] This allows us to consider how much the marshalling of respectability behind miscreants and their supporters functioned as a method of defusing organic and legal attempts to shame them in public.

Yet this character testimony also contains important clues for the historian about norms and ideals of behaviour. Hughes, in the mouths of his defenders, was constructed as something of a model priest and an example to the whole community. For the defence, Dr John Hamilton read a whole series of submitted depositions which established the benign and benevolent character of Hughes. John Noble declared him to be a man 'duly and properly attentive to his duties' and that his example 'induced his parishioners, friends and acquaintances to live well and Christian like.'[46] The testimony however went further to suggest that Hughes was more than a clergyman to his parishioners, since he was pre-pared to 'conciliate and cultivate the affections of the lower orders, by a profession of great zeal and interest in their cause, and in their relief from pretended grievances, and has thereby acquired a preponderating influence over said people.'[47] Hughes's advocate then produced depos-itions from further witnesses including an army captain and a Lieutenant-Colonel. The latter of these two, Lieutenant-Colonel Robert Johns expressed his approval of Hughes as an example for his son to follow if he should enter the church and he would thereby earn 'the esteem of (the) bishop'.[48] William Harvey denied any knowledge of Hughes's wrong-doings and gave a clear suggestion of a perfectly balanced individual that performed 'all the duties of a minister of the Gospel, parent, husband, friend, magistrate and member of society, with strict propriety.'[49] The Reverend Thomas Harding deposed that he had tried to persuade Howlin and Walker to desist from their vendetta against Hughes and further offered yet again that Hughes was an exemplary character:

> That he never knew the Impugnant to be a man of immoral habits, – that he considers him chaste, and pious, performing all the duties of public and private life, with strict propriety, and in exemplification, – and that the Impugnant has on divers Sunday evenings, before bedtime, of his own accord, read prayers – that he has at times heard the Impugnant, read a lecture in addition

to the church Liturgy, – that he believes this suit vindictive, and the result of a conspiracy, and believes Mr. James Howlin, is a partisan, from the circumstance, that he has come to London, to see deponent, as he believes, for the purpose of influencing his testimony in this cause, – that the Impugnant has always avoided excess in drinking, and has shunned vice, and immorality.[50]

The Reverend Ralph Boyde of Taghmon declared he had regularly dined with Hughes and 'never knew Impugnant to curse, or drink to excess, or act unbecoming a clergyman.'[51] The Archdeacon of Kildare, Charles Lindsay was more guarded expressing no knowledge of Hughes's behaviour in his parish, although he readily witnessed his behaviour at the houses of mutual friends. Lindsay was prepared to admit that he heard Hughes 'make use of expressions 'not strictly delicate'.[52] Further circumspect testimony came from the Reverend Henry Newland, the surrogate Bishop of Ferns, who clearly disapproved of sporting activities and declared that he could not deny that it was likely that Hughes had indulged in the drunken behaviour on the Ferry Carrig road.[53] Nonetheless he believed that it was possible that Hughes was the victim of a conspiracy.[54] The conspiratorial aspects of the charges were further reinforced by the testimony of three individuals Murphy, Woodcock and Davis who declared that they had all been approached by Walker and Howlin, or labourers in their employ, with a view to learning information about Hughes and his nefarious appetites.[55] Howlin also cuttingly suggested that Hughes's attempts to protract proceedings were liable to have a considerably untoward affect upon Mrs Hughes, regretting that 'any husband should reduce an unoffending wife to such misery.'[56]

The prosecution countered with the suggestion that these individuals were drawn from areas some distance from Hughes's own parish and that the defence had significantly neglected to contact and produce the gentry of the area around Killinick as character witnesses.[57] This was tantamount to devaluing this testimony because it did not represent Hughes's own community and implied that his reputation in the immediate vicinity was perhaps of an entirely different character. The prosecution then alleged that another individual, James Bowles, had been appointed as the local constable by Hughes as a means of buying his complicity and silence. Bowles and his father Thomas both denied the allegations of favouritism, although they admitted Hughes's role in enabling the younger Bowles to enter the local constabulary.[58]

The case had now dragged on for four days and the fifth day saw the prosecution and defence deliver their closing statements. Sir Henry Meredith speaking for Hughes reiterated the extant evidence of a conspiracy and protracted assault upon his client's character. In Meredith's words he had been 'called upon to vindicate his fame and character, or to hear a sentence worse than death itself.' Meredith also indicated that the shameful nature of the charges inevitably meant that if Hughes was found guilty he would suffer instant deprivation of his benefice; moreover no subsequent parish would entertain the idea of employing him.[59] The speech (which according to the record lasted three hours) then turned to justifying the obfuscation of Hughes and his advocates throughout the four year period leading up to the trial. This was clearly intended to short circuit the accusation that the delays had been intended to destroy or damage the case against Hughes. Meredith argued that his client could not expect justice from a 'country surrogate' who would apparently have been 'quite incompetent in a suit of such magnitude'.[60]

It was then the turn of the suit's promoter Charles Walker and his sidekick Howlin to be lambasted by Meredith who flew into a tirade. Howlin was described as:

> ...this young Napoleon in company with the promoter, the merriest harrier in all Wexford, rides through the whole country in search of evidence – they course, trace, hunt it through all its mazes, they ask the witnesses, 'is not Mr Hughes a drunkard? A curser, has he not a dog? The dirtiest creature alive, a disgrace to any person to keep' They threaten, they promise, and when they cannot prevail on those wretched people, to sell their souls, they tell them they shall be brought to a place, where they must tell the truth.[61]

Meredith also asked, not unreasonably, how witnesses could remember the precise words of impieties spoken almost a decade hence and was again scathing about the social standing of these witnesses. They were described as '...marksmen, labourers, wretched mendicants, poor illiterate creatures, acting under the tyranny of this young Napoleon, and the delusion of a junta of a conspiracy formed at Belmont.'[62] Warming to this particular theme, Meredith then emphasised the extraordinary good standing of Hughes's own character witnesses in a clear attempt to trump the truth and value of the prosecution case. Hughes had produced the mayor of Wexford alongside various magistrates and grand jurors. The mayor had described Hughes as 'a man whom the tongue of calumny had never assailed'.[63] In concluding, Meredith emphasised that the effect of the case had been to previously devalue Hughes's reputation even before the verdict had arrived. Mere association with the charges had meant that Hughes:

> ...has for years hung his head in shame; now he can look his brother clergy in the face, in confidence, that your judgement of acquittal, will restore him to that rank he has hitherto held in society, will heal the divisions, malice has excited in his parish, and prove the glad harbinger of that joy and comfort, too long absent from the bosom of his afflicted family.[64]

Interestingly, this issue of reputation was a theme taken up by the prosecution who wanted to damage Hughes no matter what. It was suggested by the prosecution that an acquittal would be manifestly less than a triumphant one, and that Hughes's own delaying tactics had contributed to this. Hughes in the prosecution's eyes was guilty of breaching the 42nd Canon of the Irish Church which declared:

> That no clergyman shall resort to taverns, or pot-houses, nor give themselves to drinking or riot, nor spend their time idly, by day or night, or play at any game unbecoming their function – but they shall, at all convenient times, study the Holy Scriptures; they are to endeavour to profit the church of God – to excel all others in purity of life, and be examples to the people, to live well and Christianly, under pain of ecclesiastical censures, to be inflicted with severity, according to the quality of their offences.[65]

The prosecution also countered the class-biased slander the defence had used upon the prosecution's witness depositions, noting British law 'tells us, not rank, dignity or station, can supply credibility to a witness: the oath of a peasant is as worthy of credit in a court of justice as that of a peer.'[66] Interestingly, the thrust of the prosecution's argument in this summing up then turned to highlighting what was irrefutably established fact that the defence had conceded during the course of the case. This was namely that Hughes was clearly addicted to his sporting activities and neglected his parish during the week – 'My Lords, on his own shewing, this is a melancholy picture of a clergyman of the establishment, and at a time when the church has so many assailants.'[67] Circumstantially was he also guilty of the profane singing that so enraged many of his sporting companions? The prosecution's allusion to this clearly demonstrated that 'thresholds of repugnance' had advanced to such an extent that such behaviour was now marginalised and its appearance in moral authority figures was simply not to be tolerated.

> The same lips which, on Sunday, give utterance to the divine precepts of a pure gospel, in the house of God, and attune themselves to hymns of praise before a Christian congregation, – are heard on Monday, under a hedge, endeavouring to captivate the rude ears of surrounding rustics, with songs of ribaldry, which, though productive of present mirth, are sure to leave behind them permanent contempt, and lasting abhorrence.[68]

The prosecution concluded by noting that Hughes's own witnesses (30 of them) merely commented upon his supposed character and fed the 'conspiracy' story. The court adjourned with the Archbishop declaring that the case was of such importance that judgement and sentence would be deferred to another occasion.[69] This resulted in a further delay whilst the Archbishop made up his mind and the court at last reconvened on the 13th of August 1829. The Archbishop was indisposed but sent a written judgement and sentence which the court eventually agreed to receive.

It was a double-edged verdict that probably pleased no-one. The suit offered by Walker was declared to be suspect and unreliable, yet enough had emerged about Hughes for him to be reprimanded and to be shamed in public. As the judgement declared (which is worth quoting in full):

> For a considerable portion of five years, he appears to have been wasting his time on what are termed field sports, in the eager pursuit of which he has been, for the most part attended, if not accompanied, by persons of the lowest description, who, as is usual on such occasions, were in the habit of partaking of spirituous liquors, and as is sufficiently proved, not without the appearance, at least of his example.

> What should be but a temporary relaxation (if it is becoming in a clergyman, to indulge in such field-sports at all) has been with him a principal employment, and seems to have become an engrossing passion. The consequence of these dissipating habits, discreditable to a Christian minister, must necessarily have caused

(though the Sunday service, does not appear to have been omitted,) that degree of neglect, towards his flock, for the rest of the week, and especially of the instruction of the young and ignorant persons of his parish, and of that ministration, to his sick and indigent parishioners, which is the duty of every pious and conscientious Pastor to afford. This too, in addition to the effect of his example on the people, and of the obstruction which must necessarily be thrown in the way of his spiritual studies, and the improvement of his professional knowledge.

I therefore, cannot avoid expressing my disapprobation, and censure of his past conduct, though it is not essential as in proof of the crimes alleged in the articles, and admonish him to be more circumspect in future, and to abandon those habits unbecoming to one of his order; and which, by casting over the circumstances communicated to the Promoter, a colour of probability, might have induced him to credit them as facts, instead of rejecting them as falsehoods and might have combined with other predisposing causes to lead him to institute the present suit. I now dismiss the Impugnant from this suit, without Costs.[70]

At last the case seemed over, but there was to be a significant quarrel over the verdict and what portion of it constituted the sentence to be entered on the record. The prosecution wanted the whole document to be declared the sentence – containing as it did the lengthy reproach of Hughes's sporting habits. The defence naturally merely wished the dismissal of the charges to constitute this. This disagreement provoked an 'animated discussion' which culminated in a request for the Archbishop to attend court and deliver his sentence in person.[71] This duly occurred, with the material admonishing Hughes for his sporting behaviour omitted from this verbal sentence. When the prosecution objected, a new phrase was at last inserted 'Impugnant in future to be more circumspect, and not to give too much of his time to field sports.'[72] This phrase was considerably milder than the original admonition given to Hughes and must have represented something of a victory for him, given the circumstances. At last the case was over, yet the window it opened for subsequent historians to gaze at an individual's, a community's and an institution's shame remains.

This episode produces fascinating insights for the historian of shame no matter which version of William Hughes behaviour represents the truth. If Hughes was guilty he spectacularly misjudged his behaviour and the reactions of his parishioners represented a vote of censure against a tiresome and unsavoury embarrassment. That the issue was constructed into a legal suit showed the interplay between community disapproval, political disagreement and personal enmity. Moreover this had the occasion of demonstrating the limits of acceptable behaviour and to 'get' the function of shame in this society in this particular instance. As we suggested earlier, why did Hughes imagine he would not be observed when serially the worse for wear from his drinking? Similarly, how could he have imagined that his behaviour with the bestial dog and the hare would be a source of amusement to his coarser sporting companions? The answers are suggestive of changing attitudes. Had Hughes heard of such behaviour and did he believe that sportsmen routinely practiced such jokes? Did he make a catastrophic error in his estimation of the bestial nature and tastes of the Irish rural populace? That the idea of performing the lewd tableau existed at all asks questions about thresholds of repugnance and their shifting limits. In this perhaps we should view ecclesiastical and other courts where moral issues were discussed as both arenas and enforcers of changing values. Thus they therefore appear, for cultural historians, as effective places to investigate the history of the promotion and endorsement of 'thresholds of repugnance'. They may also have exhibited a hubristic and purgative value – after all shame was on display in many dimensions of the Hughes case.

Not only was Hughes himself on trial, but his institution was confronted by an individual whose behaviour (if true) embodied many of the anti-clerical arguments against the Irish Church established by law. Certainly, the reaction of the church and the verdict showed a significant instinct for self-preservation and damage limitation. Whilst Hughes's specific crimes (the material of anti-clerical caricature) were dismissed, the Archbishop's judgement focussed upon what appeared to be the source of the shame generated around the Church of Ireland. If Hughes kept himself away from the sporting field the opportunity for certain accusations against him (and by implication all ministers of the church) simply would not arise. This highlights for us that increasingly over time, shame was used to punish and attack reputation, rather than the physical body. In this instance, this was true, not simply of Hughes himself, but of the Church of Ireland, the institution he and his 'ministry' represented. The importance of this issue of reputation also explains the tactics chosen by those who wished to eject Hughes from his benefice. By shaming an authority figure, the institution he represented was pressed into a form of investigation that was visible and provided a choreographed and stylised shaming ritual in the public gaze of the Consistory Court.

If, however, the accusations were false and the conspiracy against Hughes was a reality, it demonstrates the community politics of shaming conducted by ruthless and comparatively modern co-ordinated means. Even more tantalising is the implication that the portrait, nay caricature, of the neglectful parson was so readily and easily constructed. In the accusations that centred around drink, all the witnesses indicated what they considered to be both temperate and excessive consumption. Similarly, poor behaviour influenced by drink was also defined for the court, for the wider public and for posterity. This also indicated a gulf between Hughes and the ideals held by both the church and the defence witnesses. Whilst some accusations, if untrue, probably came from folk memory, the catalogue of offences Hughes was accused of bear a striking resemblance to the 42nd article of the Church of Ireland cited above. Hughes *did* frequent pot houses and he *did* indulge in unbecoming activities and his activities with his starter dog *did* perhaps constitute a species of riot. Hughes's community emphatically *did* know how to shame him and his behaviour through quoting and activating the laws of his own institution against him. All of this points to nineteenth century rural societies having a considerable armoury of discredit at their disposal. Rough music and charivari existed alongside the possibility of formally recorded legal action. But it was time, circumstances and context that would lead individuals and communities to choose how they could act together to decide the precise weapons they would use, and one of these available to them was shame. Eventually we might suggest this refined and measured use of shame to tarnish reputation was arguably more powerful than its previous manifestations in less structured, but more brutal, public forums.

Lastly, although this episode demonstrates a rural community seeking to use litigation in a comparatively modern manner (rather than exhibit the indignation involved in tithe and anti-clerical riots elsewhere) there remain elements of a highly traditional form of disciplinary action evident in this incident. It is rather striking how the Hughes case represents an emphatically gendered space. The case effectively turned around the proprieties and definition of masculine behaviour which the defendant was accused of flouting. Indeed the parade of witnesses brought against Hughes was determined to assert and uphold these codes through demonstrating the activities of a miscreant in their midst. Similarly, the sporting field, again a solely male arena, was the scene of clashes over masculine behaviour and its limits. Likewise where women do appear in the story they are almost stock caricatures which themselves elaborated upon and reinforced female codes of behaviour. Mrs Hughes appears fleetingly as the wronged innocent wife put upon by her husband's serial misdeeds.[73] The three women who confronted Hughes on the highway (who never appeared in court) are divided into the stern disapproving matron and the giggling teenage girls. Interestingly, the former is given the subsequently invented role of gossip in the case for the defence. Our only other 'woman' to appear in the incident is the mysteriously glamorous Kate Martin (Kearney) in the ballad sung by Hughes and the soldier. Kate Martin (Kearney) was the missing character in this drama, the wanton, siren like dispenser of extremely strong liquor, ready to lead men astray with her considerable charms and to inspire their drunken singing. Whilst these characters might have jumped from the London stage, they would also have been recognised by Pitt-Rivers in his seminal anthropological exploration of early twentieth century Mediterranean society and its shaming rituals. Whilst women were the cause and repository of virtue and shame, incidents around shame were ultimately negotiated by the men in such communities. Whilst early nineteenth century Wexford showed signs of modernity in its comprehension of the law, its gendered patterns of behaviour were still deeply rooted in much older practices.

This chapter has demonstrated how shame still had a crucial role to play in disciplining wayward authority figures and calling them to account. As such it was a tool grasped for by those who needed to reclaim power over their own trying circumstances. However we should especially note here how shame's applied use was sophisticated; with inflammatory stories, anecdotes and material stored up for use finally within the regulated arena of the courtroom. This was the place where, importantly by the first third of the nineteenth century, the complainants felt they would have their deepest and most potent effect. It allowed bystanders, far beyond the locality of Wexford, to witness the interplay of individuals and their behaviour with a series of institutions and their ideals all turning around the fundamental issue of shame. In the next chapter we will see shame arguably in a wholly modern guise, as it was brought to bear in the courtroom to discipline an uncivilised recourse to anachronistic and customary behaviour. We will also see how the widespread publicising of shame via the printed word could be taken a stage further, with the more developing powers of the press and the dissemination of news.

7

'The Woman in the Iron mask': From Low Life Picaresque to Bourgeois Tragedy – Matrimonial Violence and the Audiences for Shame

Our previous chapter showed us the acceptance of modern methods of shaming which turned around the successful censuring of reprehensible behaviour in a sophisticated public sphere. This was the course of action chosen by the people of Wexford in 1825. However the case discussed in this chapter dates from 1870. As such it introduces us to some further issues later in the century that undermine the idea of a linear, modernising, history of shame. Shame, by this point, had partly evolved to be carried out upon reputation (in the case of William Hughes). Yet, the case discussed in this chapter emphasises the application of shame upon the body, ironically in this case to preserve and perhaps even enhance public reputation. In this we discover that shame was also capable of being turned into public 'entertainment' to discuss wider cultural reputations.

The February 6th 1870 edition of *Reynolds's Newspaper* contains a phenomenally eye-catching story entitled 'The Woman in the Iron Mask' which recounts the essential details of a court case which had occurred a week previously in St Helier on the island of Jersey. The substance of the case concerned a man's seemingly barbaric cruelty through his decision to imprison his wife's head in an iron mask. However the case itself, as reported by *Reynolds* and other newspapers, demonstrates how the husband and wife protagonists found themselves caught between the demands and expectations of an older customary society and one more regulated by law and more codified forms of behaviour. The fact that an individual had been cruel to his wife, in a reckless and thoroughly visible manner, was extraordinary enough, but what made it an enthrallingly interesting story was its catchy title and a number of twists and turns in the narrative of the case. Most importantly of all, it grew in complexity as journalistic license rewrote the story for different newspaper outlets and audiences. For these outlets, the story's success relied on sensationalism, the interplay of the two protagonists and witnesses, narrative coherence and ultimately its very uniqueness. It is the last of these which hint that for these protagonists and for audiences, shame was central to how this story worked.

As we shall see, shame was portrayed and managed by these press reports on several levels and the impression of shame, and what was ultimately shameful, was closely massaged and highlighted by nuances within these reports. As such, they spoke to audiences about differing forms of behaviour and their gender, class and even regional connotations and significance. Ultimately, these suggest to us that exposing and portraying shame also became a genre of quasi-didactic entertainment that attached itself to the 'scandalous event', and this could be used to promulgate an increasingly formulaic set of values and expectations. It also tells us that the management of shame around matrimonial disharmony and violence was probably one of the most obvious points at which shame entered an individual's life. By 1870, the earlier mechanisms of discipline within marriage were a distant memory, although they were nonetheless in a state of flux during most of the nineteenth century.[1] The Scold's Bridle and similar disciplinary measures were no longer accepted and the whole notion of discipline within marriage had altered considerably. Moreover there is also a sense that the reading public of 1870 had been partly prepared for the Le Roi case, through two events of the previous year. The first of these was the publication of Trollope's novel *He Knew he was Right* which emphasised the whole issue of the male abuse of power within marriage.[2] The second of these was the extensive press reporting of the infamous Kelly versus Kelly case. This involved a redefinition of the legal concept of marital cruelty, asserting that physical violence was not an essential part of the definition, but that a threat to the wife's health was a sufficient ground for legally sanctioned separation.[3]

Let us commence with the facts that appear to be consistent when we view the case reports side-by-side. John Le Roi, a 60 year old watchmaker from St Helier, appeared before the magistrate on a charge of assault. The substance of the charge was that he had assaulted his wife by placing her head in an 'iron mask' which he had fashioned for the purpose. This consisted of a 'piece of rod iron about a quarter of an inch thick, formed into a ring, about eight or nine inches in diameter' further held together by 'vertical bars of strong hoop iron...The instrument opened with a hinge in the front, was fastened at the back by means of a padlock, and weighed three pounds. In the front part immediately opposite the mouth, a piece of iron hoop had been placed horizontally to prevent the wearer from getting anything up to her mouth.' This had been supplemented by detaining her in what was variously described as a 'cage' and a 'dungeon'.[4]

Mrs Le Roi had not willingly submitted to having her head confined in the mask and gave evidence that her husband had coerced her into her imprisonment. Moreover, it was also evident that Mr Le Roi had made careful and public preparation for this act, since he had clearly publicised his proposed course of action in the local neighbourhood. Although this seems strange it was also clear from the press reports, and Le Roi's attitude in court, that he believed that he had committed no crime, nor even transgressed any boundaries of propriety. He may even have been seeking popular consent for his actions, and if this was the case it would perhaps mirror earlier community punishments which required such consent for their operation. Le Roi testified that he had acted in good faith and that the restraint was in the best interests of his wife as it was essential to her well-being, her reputation and ultimately the future of their marriage. He admitted that his wife was an almost chronic alcoholic (although he scarcely needed to, since all the witnesses testified to the truth of this) and that he had been left with no alternative. His wife disappeared to the public house with the relentless purpose of rendering herself incapable. She had been confined to the local workhouse hospital on no less than five separate occasions, yet clearly no lasting resolution of her problems with alcohol had succeeded or even appeared possible. Similarly the 'cage' or 'dungeon' was a device resorted to by Le Roi in an attempt to prevent his wife leaving the marital home. On previous occasions when he had locked the doors she had made her escape to the public house through the windows.[5] In short, Le Roi was asking the court and the neighbourhood to believe that he was engaged upon damage limitation. He may even have felt justified in his actions had he been aware of instances where magistrates had incarcerated individuals for their own protection when inebriated.

In reply, the unfortunate Mrs Le Roi could only confess that she had, in all other respects, been a good wife to her husband and that her habit of intoxication was her only fault.[6] The fact that the violence and marital discord had come to court, led the magistrate to suggest that the couple separate. The husband was asked if he would consent to this and further undertake to provide his wife with a small, but regular, alimony payment. Upon the husband's agreement, the judge fined Mr Le Roi the sum of ten shillings and ordered confiscation of the 'Iron Mask'.[7]

Even an analysis of the bare facts of this case raises some extremely interesting questions about shame appearing at the fault lines between old and new conceptions of custom and law. Why did John Le Roi resort to fashioning his own physical restraint to curb his wife's unacceptable behaviour? Why did he believe his actions would be endorsed by his own community? Why did he also palpably deviate from orthodox legal solutions to his problems such as divorce or legal separation? What part did shame play in all of these proceedings and how was this negotiated? Lastly, when we look at the different versions of the story itself, we are compelled to ask questions about how shameful episodes were consumed by those who merely had access to the press reports. This invites us to think how shame could be cast into various genres including the didactic, the picaresque, the melodramatic and the farcical. Similarly, the case illuminates very interesting issues about the debate around public and private space and the ability of communities, through witness testimony, to take action against transgression in their midst.

John Le Roi had clearly found his wife's own behaviour shameful and must have felt considerable shame and humiliation at his wife's very public drunkenness. This situation was compounded by her incarceration in the St Helier Workhouse/Infirmary from which she was presumably released after an improvement in her condition. This pattern was unfortunately repeated on no less than five separate occasions with each presumably piling further pain and ignominy upon the husband. Thus shame clearly existed for John Le Roi in the local community's unwitting, or at least unplanned, surveillance of his wife's public drunkenness and inappropriate behaviour – further compounded by the fact that there appeared to be no end to it in sight. Thus John Le Roi must have created for himself a narrative and justification for his actions; one he may even have prepared himself to share with others in the community. In return he probably expected their respect, or at least their tacit sympathy. Given the regularity of his wife's intoxication, her five visits to the workhouse infirmary and her escape from the family home, Le Roi was, in his own mind, entirely justified in his attempts to use further draconian restraint. Whether the desperate nature of his position influenced his extreme choice of restraint is clearly a moot point. Very obviously, these actions would be highly visible to both friends and enemies in the local community, and he may have considered himself to be at his wits end. But it is also worth speculating whether Le Roi saw himself, or was even encouraged by some to see himself, as refashioning disciplinary practices within marriage. Did he imagine that the community might yet take notice of and adopt these practices and restore the respect that Le Roi perhaps imagined he had lost. Whatever the truth of the matter, Le Roi had clearly to balance the shame he felt when his wife and her behaviour let him down so spectacularly within his community, against accusations that his restraint of his wife had very obviously gone too far. Clearly, for a number of reasons, John Le Roi decided very definitely in favour of restraining his wife and her unruly behaviour.

Alternatively, we might prefer to take John Le Roi's protestations at face value. He scarcely appears to have been contrite, nor did he seem to recognise that his actions were either contrary to law or what was recognised as a standard of decent and civilised behaviour towards his own wife. If this second explanation is nearer to the truth, then we have stumbled upon an instance where attitudes to violence and sup-posed barbarism were in a state of flux or at least transition. This of course also applies to the tensions inherent in shame exposed in many of the chapters of this book. John Carter Wood has noticed that during the latter half of the nineteenth century, attitudes to previously accepted forms of violent behaviour changed quite dramatically. In particular, he notes a late nineteenth century 'discovery' of violence which would partly explain the community's reaction to John Le Roi's treatment of his wife.[8] Equally, however, Le Roi's behaviour would also explain the action of a husband seeking to save his family and reputation from shame and his willingness to employ whatever appeared to be the older disciplinary tools to hand, regardless of whether they met any prescribed standards of morality, manners or decorum. In this, his actions once more echo the conclusions of the anthropologists who studied shame cultures where women are the source of this emotion, but it is the social task of men to manage this within their families and the wider community.

However, John Le Roi's actions also strongly suggest a quite complex interaction between the agencies of protection and discipline. It could be argued, for instance, that Le Roi had sought a civilised and accept-able solution to his wife's ailments through confining her to the work-house on no less than five occasions. From Le Roi's point of view, it was arguably the failure of more modern conceptions of treating his wife's condition as an 'illness' that had repeatedly failed him and his family. These failures, Le Roi might have argued, were the cause of his desire to take the treatment of his wife into his own hands and see it once again as a disciplinary matter. Thus, this case does not simply suggest the state's invasion and intervention in matters an individual family considered private. It also suggests a resort to older, individual-ised forms of discipline when more modern agencies and solutions were found wanting. Yet John Le Roi could even be considered unfor-tunate in his timing, since the judicial decisions in the Kelly case had not simply altered the law, but had brought the whole issue of marital cruelty to the attention of society at large and reading publics in parti-cular. Husbands still had overarching authority, but it was an authority which required gracious and freely given consent. Moreover, such author-ity endorsed the principle of separate spheres, which the husband in the Kelly case had so dramatically overturned through his denial of his wife's right to manage her own household.[9]

So John Le Roi's high handed and disturbingly visible actions brought the wrath of the authorities down upon him, arguably intro-ducing him to further species of shame that he had scarcely bargained for. However, in cases of domestic breakdown and scandalously uncivilised behaviour, it is clear that press reports have the ability to show diverse types of shame to distinct audiences. In particular, the case against John Le Roi was used by different agencies of the press to tell significantly different narratives. Through the disclosure of certain information, and the omission of other information, it was possible to prepare and persuade audiences to draw certain inferences from what they were reading. Many assumptions drawn from these narratives turned on issues of nationality, locality, class and gender. Comparing these narratives of the Le Roi case suggests to us that the nineteenth century press may have played an important role in the formation, articulation and sustenance of values associated with cultures of shame.[10]

What is unequivocally striking about the majority of the press reports is that they cling to the eye catching title of 'The Woman in the Iron Mask' with which to stimulate (and titillate) their respective audiences. Moreover, the incongruous appearance of the word 'Woman', where the reader is expecting to read the title of Alexandre Duma's adventure novel, further serves to emphasise the shocking nature of her incarceration. This, however, appears to be but one important reference point for how local, regional and metropolitan newspapers chose to feature the story, with one interesting exception (see below). There were ostensibly four different press reports of the story, and each used the details of the case in subtly different ways.

The report in the London-based *Reynolds's Newspaper* was the most widely used and syndicated version. This also appeared in the

Birmingham Daily Post, the *Liverpool Mercury*, *Lloyds Weekly Newspaper*, the *Illustrated Police News* and in a paraphrased version in the *Pall Mall Gazette*.[11] This version chiefly portrayed the case as a picaresque piece of amusement that demonstrated the failure of civilisation to reach peripheral parts of the United Kingdom. After describing the mask in the detail outlined above, the report in *Reynolds's Newspaper* immediately introduced a note of farcical comedy to its report by suggesting that, after all Mr Le Roi's diligent work, the mask had been laughably 'ineffectual'. This was because Mrs Le Roi had found she could simply rotate the mask through a full circle so that the carefully prepared obstruction intended to be at the front was replaced by a large and obvious opening. *Reynolds's* went further to suggest that this had swiftly enabled her to take further intoxicating liquor, unbeknown to her husband.[12] Notably, this particular anecdote appears in neither of the other two reports from the local Jersey newspapers.

There is also considerable ambivalence in the *Reynolds's Newspaper* report about how Mrs Le Roi came to have the iron mask placed upon her head. The account describes John Le Roi placing the iron restraint upon her 'for the first time on Saturday, when she was in a kneeling posture'.[13] These words are woefully unclear about precisely whether Mrs Le Roi consented to wearing the mask. Although placing the heavy and unwieldy mask over her head may have necessitated John Le Roi lowering it from above, the implication painted by *Reynolds's* was the unmistakeable submission of the wife. John Le Roi's neighbours then encountered Mrs Le Roi wearing the mask and their actions ensured police intervention to restore a species of order.

The readership is then astounded by the revelation that John Le Roi had made no secret of the affair within the local community and 'had even asked one of the witnesses to allow him to use her head as a model!' These twin disclosures are revealing about the picture painted in *Reynolds's* of John Le Roi. The *Reynolds's Newspaper* account strongly suggests a man ignorant of civilised behaviour, indeed a man whose expectations come from another time and place. His mechanisms of propriety, revulsion and shame at his own proposed course of action seem, from the depiction, to be wholly absent. This portrayal also clearly suggests an antithesis between the protagonist and the readership. Le Roi is also seeking to gain assent for his actions by involving the community. They are allowed to see his wife restrained and, at an earlier stage, one of the local women is invited to model for the iron mask. *Reynolds's* interestingly does not include the woman's response, leaving ambivalence about the reactions of the community at this point. Clearly, the obvious revulsion felt by a local woman to such a suggestion could appear rhetorical through the use of the exclamation mark in the newspaper report. Yet Le Roi's expectation that a woman might genuinely consent to help him, alongside *Reynolds's* failure to disclose a refusal, leaves open the suggestion that a woman may indeed have modelled for the mask and that there was a degree of complicity with Le Roi from his community. When considered together, *Reynolds's* is portraying the cast and characters of this case as coming from a semi-civilised community, with standards of behaviour several stages removed from metropolitan London.

Reynolds's description of Mrs Le Roi's confinement at home suggested that a box had been turned into a cage. This particular image and its propriety was problematic, since one of the witnesses was ambivalent about what they had seen. Mrs Le Roi was described by this witness as having 'plenty of room in it and received no injury'. Nonetheless, the witness was still sufficiently shocked to declare '...it was not the place for women to be in.'[14] The confused nature of this particular snippet of information would fit with the idea that *Reynolds's Newspaper* is seeking to exoticise behaviour in this episode. When it came to consider the behaviour of Mrs Le Roi, *Reynolds's* focussed squarely upon her addiction to drink. Its report saw this as the primary cause of her husband's outlandish behaviour, stressing 'that he did not know what to do with her' and that she was 'incorrigible'. John Le Roi, the report continued, was driven by a wish 'to put a stop to her drinking'. This line of sympathy for the husband was further emphasized by the physical description of Mrs Le Roi who appeared 'half-besotted' and 'fluffy'.[15]

The *Reynolds's* report then draws swiftly to a close with the magistrate encouraging the couple to enter into a legal separation with the provision of five shillings a week by way of an allowance, alongside the ten shilling fine levied upon Mr. Le Roi.[16] The economy of detail used in this particular report was very important for the narrative it told. In effect, the story was stripped down, removing it of its complexities so that it could represent the picture of laughable, yet semi-barbarous, behaviour in the peripheries of the kingdom. Elements of the story resemble farce – the outlandish use of the mask itself and its comical ineffectiveness – which were the starting point in vividly conjuring up the scene for the reader. The request for a local woman to model the mask celebrated another clearly comic episode. John Le Roi's only half-hearted objection to the use of the cage and his staged 'nonchalance' all function as humorous elements. The emphasis is not on cruelty, but on the sheer oddity of the behaviour described, alongside a description of the lengths individuals will go to in order to avoid public shame. However, the exposition of the story also emphasises that, with ill-chosen words and actions, individuals could also heap shame upon themselves.

To sum up, the portrayal of the John Le Roi case in *Reynolds's Newspaper* emerges primarily as a curiosity demonstrating woefully ill-chosen, inept and anachronistic behaviour on the part of the uncivilised. As such, it sits comfortably with many of the other stories which the London press frequently carried associated with the Celtic fringe. Yet although this was a backward community, the message about its uncivilised nature was also strongly emphasised. Whilst the *Reynolds's* version sought to find humour in the story, its underlying message portrayed a sober rationale. This is perhaps further emphasised by the fact that the voice of the magistrate is heard less obviously than in the other accounts.

The *Illustrated Police News*, in addition to its use of the *Reynolds's* version of the story, also carried its own vividly striking portrayal of the case. The front cover of its February 12th issue for 1870 carried a pictorial image of the 'Woman in the Iron Mask' as one of its featured stories, alongside others on a 'Murder in Paris', the 'Escape of Two Young Ladies from a Boarding School' and an 'Extraordinary Adventure with a Bear'.[17] A close examination of this image suggests that the *Illustrated Police News* saw the incident rather simply as an horrific episode of male aggression. Whilst there is a beer or spirits bottle on the table, this is the only suggestion which corroborates John Le Roi's account of events. All the other images in the picture suggest incredible and sensational marital cruelty, or, perhaps mischievously, a 'new' way of disciplining wives. The respectably dressed John Le Roi is bent over with a dark malevolent look on his face whilst placing the mask in position over his hysterically struggling wife. This does not portray her as being in a drunken stupor, but instead the close to hand spilt mop-bucket and resting broom suggests her to be in the middle of domestic chores. The mask appears starkly in the centre of the image, whilst in the background is the cage with its bars and menacingly open doorway.

The second version of the story which appeared in the London papers was a less sensational narrative, which appeared in *The Times* on February 3rd 1870. Its intention to be more objective was signalled by its refusal to use the rephrased Alexandre Dumas title, in favour of the less sensational heading 'An Iron Mask for a Drunken Wife'. This version rather isolates John Le Roi and his actions. The attempt to get a woman from the local community to model for the mask is omitted and it is suggested that

THE WOMAN IN THE IRON MASK

'John Le Roi imprisoning his wife in the "Iron Mask" as depicted in the *Illustrated Police News*, 12 February 1870'

Mrs Le Roi actively 'contrived to let some of the neighbours see it on her head' and that this resulted in the swift summoning of the police.[18] All this portrayed a community that acted more decisively against Le Roi than the *Reynolds's* version was inclined to suggest. There was also slightly more speculation about Le Roi's motive in this account. Although his behaviour emerged from this version as unacceptable, *The Times* version was more inclined to indulge his search for a 'tough love' solution. For instance, the report has Le Roi arguing that he would not have treated his wife so harshly if he had known his actions were illegal. This commentary is swiftly followed by his wife's acknowledgement of the truth of Le Roi's testimony, and her agreement with the marital separation and settlement of five shillings a week.[19] The juxtaposition of these last two statements was inclined to suggest that John Le Roi was entitled to more sympathy than he would have received from readers of the *Reynolds's* account.[20]

The reports carried in the local newspapers give a much fuller account of the case than in the more obviously synoptic story carried by *Reynolds's Newspaper*. When we look at these, the case really begins to open out in some quite unexpected directions, with some intriguingly conflicting narrative paths. The report in the *Jersey Express* for example, displays some elements of *Reynolds's* interest in the sensationalist; yet we learn much more of the detail, and as result the case grows in complexity.[21] In this report, we learn definitively that John Le Roi is a Frenchman and the disclosure of this may have had a significant bearing on the response of the readership, and conceivably how he was treated in court.[22] The description of the 'Iron Mask' is identical to that carried by *Reynolds's Newspaper* with a note that the production of the mask in court caused a sensation. We also hear more pleas in mitigation of his behaviour from John Le Roi. He testified that Mrs Le Roi's alcoholism had got significantly out of hand, with her visiting the public house between eight or ten times a day on occasion, sometimes escaping through the windows to do so. Le Roi claimed that the mask 'could not possibly hurt his wife' and that his only wish 'was to put a stop to her drinking'.[23]

He finished his defence with the assertion that he did not know his actions were contrary to the law. From here, he laid the blame for his appearance in court upon the disturbance created by his neighbours who had called the police. With this, John Le Roi was asserting that his 'tough love' style solution was not harming his wife and that the emotive appearance of the mask, and his neighbours' reaction to it, were the true cause of his further misery. This explanation for Le Roi's behaviour is arguably given credence by the testimony of one witness Vingtenier Noel (Edouard in the deposition), who had come to the house after he had heard about Mrs Le Roi's confinement in the mask. When he entered the house, he insisted that it should be removed, but the next exchanges suggest that Le Roi did not comprehend the fact that Vingtenier Noel considered the use of the mask uncivilised and unacceptable. Completely missing the tone of Noel's command, John Le Roi continued his conversation in which he declared that the mask was 'not quite finished, as he intended to put some wire all around it to prevent his wife getting anything to her mouth'.[24] The policeman who apprehended John Le Roi, Centenier Le Livre, gave further evidence which perhaps emphasised the desperation of the husband. Le Livre testified that he had known the wife for some considerable time and was aware of her confinement in the hospital.[25]

At this point we hear, for the first time, the authentic voice of Mrs Le Roi. Although, the *Jersey Express* described her as having 'a half stupid and a bloated appearance', she gave testimony which called into question John Le Roi's account of his own behaviour and the history of their marriage. It is at this moment, that the story of the Le Roi's appears to have different pathways with different potential effects upon readerships. From hereon in, a history of marital abuse begins to emerge in the local press reportage, which immediately removes the humorous elements from the incident which appeared to be central to the more metropolitan and mainstream coverage of the case. Mrs Le Roi testified that the occasion of placing the mask on her head had involved John Le Roi kicking her and slapping her in the face. She also confirmed that she had been kneeling when he forced it upon her head; declaring that he had hurt her considerably. It is almost impossible to resist the conclusion that John Le Roi was intent upon shaming his wife, even if he thought his actions were for her own good!

From here, the report contains an interesting gender divide with two stories which emphasise the cruelty of the husband on one side, and the intolerably embarrassing condition of the wife on the other. The female witnesses, who emphasised the cruelty of John Le Roi, were allowed to speak first. A Mrs Barrett admitted that it was she who had involved the police after she had failed to persuade John Le Roi to remove the iron mask. This witness also told the court that the Le Roi's rowed continually and had done so for a considerable period of time. She then mentioned the wife's drinking habits, conceivably suggesting that they were linked with her unhappy domestic condition. This was followed by a list of the cruelties inflicted by John Le Roi which included flogging his wife with a whip and the use of the 'large box with iron bars to keep her in'.[26]

Another witness mentioned the incident in which John Le Roi had approached her to model for the mask. He had produced a pattern for it and requested her assistance in allowing him to use her face as the model for a workable instrument of confinement. The witness declared that she had refused, but this testimony again serves to corroborate both John Le Roi's desperation and his contention that his actions were both justified and lawful due to his wife's provocation. This witness had also seen Mrs Le Roi's confinement in the large box declaring that she was not uncomfortable in it, but she believed 'it was no place for her to be in'. This witness also corroborated the sorry story of Mrs Le Roi's inveterate drunkenness.[27]

The male witnesses told a story that was somewhat more sympathetic to John Le Roi. His own defending counsel, Advocate Bichard, declared that Le Roi had been under considerable strain since his wife's incapacity through drink had left him to tend to both family businesses (a grocer's and a watchmakers shop). Another witness, Abraham Ennis, declared that he had known Mrs Le Roi for some years and had been aware of her problems with drink for some considerable time. He further noted that he had 'not seen her ill treated by her husband, whom he knew to be a peaceable man.'[28]

Upon hearing this contradictory evidence, the magistrate (in this account of the story at least) weighed up the fault on both sides. He noted 'there is no doubt about the wife's drinking; but that's no reason why she should be treated in that manner'. He also reprimanded the wife for her drinking declaring 'if you continue to drink in this manner, it will be impossible for your husband to live with you.' In this version of the story, the separation was suggested by John Le Roi through his defence counsel, and he received in return a strong reprimand from the magistrate, suggesting that his wife's future misbehaviour would inevitably make him 'give her into the hands of the police' (presumably for some form of further incarceration). If this account is correct, then Le Roi's actions in promoting the settlement look like a species of plea bargaining. This was, in itself, conceivably related to the shame he felt at not only being in court, but also regarding the revelations about his conduct towards his wife over the longer period of their marriage.

Interestingly, the *Jersey Express's* account of the story portrays a divided community. John Le Roi is given a respectable occupation in this version and indeed his attempt to maintain his social and economic status is offered as a mitigating circumstance in his defence. Male witnesses simultaneously testified to the hopelessness of Mrs Le Roi's alcoholism and one of these also went out of his way to assert the good character of John Le Roi. However, the evidence of the female witnesses contradicted this account. It alluded to a history of marital mistreatment going back some years and perhaps even suggested that Mrs Le Roi's drinking may have been a consequence of her husband's mistreatment of her.

Arguably, this version of the story further heightens the issues of shame which centre around this incident. If John Le Roi was a respectable member of the petty bourgeoisie (as witnesses attested), then the shame he felt at his wife's behaviour turns this version of the story into a bourgeois tragedy for its readership. Since both partners in the marriage had achieved a degree of prosperity, as members of the local 'shopocracy', there had clearly once been at least economic stability in their relationship. That John Le Roi now had to, in some way, supervise and manage the work of both businesses, represented a fall from previous status for him. Their marriage, and their options for continuing or ending it, may have been further constrained by issues associated with inheritance, economic viability and religious/personal belief that made separation difficult. Moreover this makes Mrs Le Roi's drinking both less easy to explain and a further source of shame since her actions suggest her own reputation to be expendable, or of little value. If all, or any, of this heightened the shame for Le Roi, then his decision to use the dungeon and the iron mask becomes explicable, if inexcusable. The chance to hide and confine the source of his shame, whether or not he considered it to contain genuine risks, may well have considerably outweighed the damage his wife's behaviour was doing to his local reputation.

The fourth version of the story which comes from the *British Press and Jersey Times* contains probably the fullest account of the whole case, and again we learn still more detail which adds further to the story's complexity.[29] This account appeared anxious to suggest that the laws and practices of the Channel Islands functioned adequately. Similarly, it argued that the islands also actively endorsed civilised behaviour, and we might argue demonstrated relatively modern 'thresholds of repugnance'. In this version, John Le Roi's defending counsel Advocate Bichard stated that he himself had seen Mrs Le Roi intoxicated on a number of occasions, sometimes 'lying on the floor in a senseless state.'[30]

Yet in this version we also meet a rather more defiant Mrs Le Roi who sought to defend her behaviour as an individual and as a wife. She stated that she could produce witnesses who could prove that drink was her only fault and that she did this only 'occasionally'. This was confirmed by one witness who declared her to be 'as good as any wife could possibly be'. From here she herself gave testimony of the maltreatment dispensed to her by her husband. She confirmed that she had been kicked on various occasions and had received blows to the head 'in the most brutal manner'. Likewise, she testified that the iron mask had been placed upon her head when she had been 'in a senseless condition' – a series of events confirmed by another witness who also reiterated the catalogue of past abuse.[31]

The testimony of another neighbour, Mrs Dugdale, told again how the prisoner had been told to remove the iron mask from his wife and had been threatened with the intervention of the police if he failed to do so. At this point, we get an intriguing suggestion that John Le Roi was perhaps less than the respectable shopkeeper that the *Jersey Express* had described. Mrs Dugdale noted that when the police had been mentioned, John Le Roi had said 'that he did not care for the police; the police knew him and he knew them.' Quite what this referred to was unclear, but it might hint at some incident in the past where Le Roi had used violence against his wife or another individual which had required police intervention of some kind. In this particular account, the concluding remarks of the magistrate are quite informative. In his summing up, he used the words 'this novel plan of torture was not to be tolerated in this island or anywhere else. The husband was wrong in resorting to such cruel means.'[32]

Thus the tone and emphasis of the *British Press and Jersey Times'* account differs considerably from the picaresque humour at the expense of the primitive islanders displayed in *Reynolds's Newspaper*. This account shows the inhabitants of Jersey to be rational and civilised and to have used all possible means at their disposal to act in the unfortunate case of John Le Roi and his wife. They had noted the husband's scandalous treatment of his wife and testified to this in court. They had used persuasion in trying to stop John Le Roi from restraining his wife in the iron mask and, when he had refused to do this, they had swiftly contacted the authorities. Last of all, the *British Press and Jersey Times'* report of the magistrates summing up, emphasised that John Le Roi's actions were as unacceptable on the island of Jersey as they were anywhere else. This was not the uncivilised periphery – the community in the end understood the law and had highly developed behavioural expectations.

Posterity would probably argue that both John and Ann Le Roi were unquestionably damaged by the incidents which led to the breakdown of their marriage. Whatever the condition of their emotional relationship (which interestingly is never made clear) John Le Roi's actions and their subsequent appearance in court had done neither of them any favours. Whilst separation had been the result, they had both been publicly shamed through having their behaviour held up to the mirror of communal and social expectations – inevitably with very poor results for them both. Given the wretched psychological condition of Mrs Le Roi, and the day-to-day struggles of her husband, their future probably did not look especially bright. The husband, after being dragged through the courts was now bereft of any shred of domestic solace, not to mention help, in maintaining the prosperity that this bourgeois couple may once have enjoyed. The effect of this case upon the reputation of John Le Roi may have had a subsequent impact upon his standing in the community as well as the prosperity of his business. The wife, now alone and conceivably lacking any restraint upon her alcoholism, may have found herself in a deteriorating condition. Despite the law's intervention, it becomes difficult to consider that either party gained significantly from the separation.

There does, however, remain an important question to answer that may help us unlock the related issues of shame, of shock and the advancing 'thresholds of repugnance' which this case illuminates. Precisely why did John Le Roi choose the iron mask as a means of controlling his wife? This decision is open to a number of especially fruitful possible interpretations. It would clearly be fanciful to speculate upon the publishing history of Alexandre Dumas' classic, and still less viable to place the work in John Le Roi's sitting room without further evidence. But nonetheless, in other ways, the iron mask itself may have had some small, but wider, cultural footprint in late nineteenth century Jersey.

We know for certain that Mrs Le Roi was confined in the St Helier Workhouse on at least five separate occasions. Even by the latter part of the nineteenth century, the Scold's Bridle can be traced in the records of many poor law unions (notably in the Home Counties) and evidence is clear that it had ceased to be used as a shame punishment to control unruly women by that time. Individuals were imprisoned in the bridle and made to sit for an extended period of time in a prominently public site within the workhouse: a classic form of shame punishment as described in Chapter 2, prevalent in the early modern period. The antiquarian T.N. Brushfield writing in the 1860s was already describing the Scold's Bridle as a gruesome anachronism, equating it with forms of torture.[33] Brushfield noted the numerous examples of the instrument which survived in Chester and other places in the more modern era and states that they were frequently in the possession of workhouses or municipal authorities.[34]

Although most commentators agree that the heyday of this punishment and its use was over by 1850 we are left with intriguing speculations. Was the iron mask still in use in Jersey as late as the 1860s? Did John Le Roi see it in action, and consider it an appropriate 'tool' with which to conceivably tame his own wife? If this scenario has any basis in fact, it rather unravels the assertion that Jersey was obviously civilised as the magistrate in the Le Roi case had claimed. Perhaps John Le Roi witnessed its use, or heard tell of its use in workhouses, whilst visiting his unfortunate wife. It is at least plausible that John Le Roi may have heard of the practice, even as an expression of past disciplinary attitudes and regimes outlined in local history or folklore. If this last speculation is near to the truth, then John Le Roi was reinventing the past as a result of his desperation to recover his esteem within his own community. If his wife was allowed to be visibly drunk in the neighbourhood then this signalled her unhappiness, and her husband's unwillingness or failure to alter her behaviour patterns. There is also the possibility that Le Roi's economic status was threatened and he thus sought to defend his respectable middle-class status and position.

This may have added a further dimension to the shame felt by John Le Roi. Perhaps for Le Roi, the use of the iron mask was a strident symbol that he had addressed his sorry situation. Not only this, but it also demonstrated his capacity for resourcefulness and initiative. The success of this venture would also show his own wife's capacity to, literally, 'lose face' in the community. Mrs Le Roi would thus have gone about her community imprisoned in a visible symbol of her husband's reasserted authority – an authority shown to be more effective than the new institutions who claimed jurisdiction over her drink problem. If John Le Roi was still exasperated by his wife, why did he not simply continue to physically chastise her, since her injuries and the discipline of which they were a manifestation would be an altogether more private matter? We should remember that the neighbours who knew of the domestic violence, and testified to its existence in court, had not taken any action prior to the case being heard. There had been no rough music or skimmington ride to demonstrate criticism of his behaviour. Thus the use of the iron mask in this story becomes crucial, since it represented a significant leap forward for John Le Roi's disciplinary approach to his wife's behaviour. After all, he had tried to elicit the support of the community through his request that one of the other local women model for the mask and may even have sought to advertise his innovation within the community in his search for approval.

It is worth noting that Brushfield believed that the inception of the Scold's Bridle had occurred during the sixteenth century at 'a time when judges began to believe that a feeling of shame might be useful in preventing petty infringements of propriety.'[35] Writing in the 1860s, Brushfield clearly conveys the suggestion that the Scold's Bridle was known within nineteenth century folk memory to convey the feelings associated with shame.[36] Thus it is worth speculating whether John

Le Roi envisaged some shame component within the treatment of his wife. Could he yet 'shame' her out of her alcoholic behaviour if her fate was to be linked with carrying a classic, and antiquated, 'loss of face' stigma and shame punishment? This may even constitute a still worse outcome for Le Roi, if we consider he might have had the very best intentions in mind with a desire to genuinely affect the cure of his wife. Ironically he was using shame punishment in its purest form, for an individual's own good with a desire to bring about their reformation. Of course, it could also be argued that his actions were an extension of his craving to restore his lost power and ego with the urge to reassert his authority. Yet unwittingly this change of tactic, which brought the issue of discipline into the sight of the community, also allowed its members to finally speak out against a husband it had known to have been cruel for some time. Perhaps this suggests that the community itself was finally shamed into taking action when confronted by a no longer acceptable manifestation of older disciplinary practices.

If the St Helier Workhouse had used the Scold's Bridle against Mrs Le Roi, then John Le Roi's imitation of this behaviour also asks some interesting questions. If this remote possibility exists, then of course, it would alter our reading of John Le Roi's actions. If the Scold's Bridle and the deliberate use of it as a shame punishment had been used on Mrs Le Roi, then John Le Roi would arguably have been problematising the whole issue of discipline and who had the authority to administer it – institutions or individuals? If he was asserting his power to shame in the context of his own marriage, then John Le Roi would arguably have been engaged upon a rearguard attempt to reassert an older, dwindling patriarchal culture. He may even have considered that his assertion of older disciplinary measures would have regained him some esteem within his community, amongst an audience invited to replace pity with respect. Unfortunately, this ultimately may explain how the case against him unfolded in a manner which left him thought of as an uncivilised and barbaric outsider by newspaper readers in Jersey, London and further afield.

We also know that John Le Roi's experiment in 'tough love', or his organic assertion of patriarchal authority, was doomed to failure. His attempt to confine and manage his shame within the community transgressed the norms of his society and he himself became subject to the disciplinary practices of his age. The organic customary solution of patriarchal discipline was defeated by the intervention of a legal system which, in suggesting separation and divorce, concentrated upon a strategy which delivered humanised justice and supposedly minimised harm to both parties. It is also suggestive of a change in judicial attitudes which argued discordant and unhappy marriages should be allowed to end, rather than be forced to continue beyond the boundaries of civility. The Le Roi's separated, taking their individual shame and its causes with them. Yet they probably never knew how their marital discord and sensational behaviour became a text through which local and wider literate communities would discuss the nature of the 'barbarous other', and respond to it with everything from indignant shock to barely restrained hilarity.

This episode exemplifies another important passage in our history of the use of shame. Its many dimensions show shame to be thoroughly individualised within the psyche of those involved as well as suggesting the importance of an ever increasing circle of onlookers from those in Jersey to much further afield. Once again the modern context of the courtroom was the place where this particular drama was played out. The case shows how popular shame was coming to be seen as unacceptable (both within the community and by authorities) as custom increasingly came under the scrutiny of law and various judicial systems became more ambitious and efficient. Shameful behaviour (like Mr and Mrs Le Roi's) by this point in time, should in theory, be managed without recourse to popular punishments or other older remedies. Society could now claim that it was providing many more civilised alternatives. However, the fact that instances of uncivilised 'throwback' behaviour, like John Le Roi's, appeared as late as 1870 meant that this writ of improvement, civilisation and modernisation was unsatisfactory and incomplete. Shame and its possibilities remained a powerful part of the late nineteenth century subconscious and as such, it was still a viable and functioning tool. The commodification of shame in order to carry a multitude of messages enabled its impact to traverse vast distances and to be raw material for the assumptions and moral makeup of still wider audiences, far beyond the incident's participants. As we shall see in the next chapter, shame retained potency in the construction of norms and expectations of behaviour that fed critiques of even the highest in the land.

8
Writing 'Cuckold on the Forehead of a Dozen Husbands': Mid-Victorian Monarchy and the Construction of Bourgeois Shame

In our previous chapter, we noted both the longevity and creation of shame as a modern species of entertainment and how the arrival of newspapers gave this a rejuvenated public face. We also noted how shame potentially lay close to the surface and was capable of being revitalised when specific purposes demanded it. This occurred not only in relation to individual circumstances, but could also be embraced by much wider communities held together by political disposition, sentiment or even simply reading habits. The following chapter is a further example which questions the argument that shame as a phenomenon had no legitimate part in a modernising society. This example illustrates how the power of shame was invigorated by an attempt to mobilise and address the aspirations of the Victorian middle classes. This is a departure from orthodox views which sees the middle classes as associated with the spread of politeness and the triumph of decorum. As this unfolded through the 1870s to the 1890s, shame was given a 'public' face once again; but this time on an even larger scale than we have seen before in this book.

This chapter illuminates how some of the component parts of charivari, skimmington rides and rough music could be recast and validated in middle-class bourgeois forms during the Victorian era. As such, they acquired the same power and purposes as their plebeian counterparts, yet they also resonated through literate communities in a manner their plebeian precursors could scarcely have imagined. These modernised and urbanised shame performances and offered public forms of discipline for impropriety. They confronted immorality and misbehaviour, while seeking to establish moral authority over these transgressions. They also demonstrated where the boundaries of such behaviour lay and defended rights which were felt to be fundamentally under threat.

The authority of the new emerging middle classes was an emphatically contested area in the early nineteenth century. Dialogues which spoke of respectability and restraint were frequently manufactured into badges of identity which marked out separate territories and behaviour patterns. These functioned in ways similar to the norms which governed and policed earlier community sanctions. Middle-class radicalism also appropriated many of the customary culture's ideas associated with concepts of fairness, and eschewed their revolutionary potential for a more developed culture of stern criticism. This was particularly evident in the relationship that middle-class radicalism had with institutions which, from the 1850s onwards, appeared to be amongst its most potent enemies – namely the aristocracy, in alignment with the monarchy. This found its most vibrant and penetrating critique in the ideas associated with republicanism.[1] But what is especially interesting to note, is just how this radicalism's conception of monarchical and aristocratic offence resembled earlier protests that Edward Thompson labelled 'class struggle without class'.[2] These complained about assaults on established rights and used the armoury of customary protest to upbraid the transgressor, thereby demonstrating the legitimacy of existing relationships.[3] It is also worth noting, that other historians have seen the creation of domesticity as containing a covert middle-class manifesto which sought to replace absolutism with the individual and the family as agents of ultimate social authority.[4] Middle-class republicans, as this chapter demonstrates, still found some of these component parts of customary shame culture surprisingly useful and powerful, in journalism which sought to protect middle-class rights and values from a profligate monarchy and a resurgent aristocracy. Like any attempt to shame individuals and institutions this was aimed at harnessing the opinion of a wide national 'community' against a transgressor in its midst.

It has become almost a commonplace of the historiography of nineteenth century monarchy to suggest that public opinion – the adverse nature of which had almost led to its demise and ruin – was actually the phenomenon which ultimately saved and preserved it. So the story goes, Britain's modern constitutional monarchy was once under profound threat from public opinion, yet it was eventually able to regroup, manage and harness its possible assets. Some contemporaries saw this as the manifestation of false consciousness amongst the classes originally critical of monarchy and labelled it the triumph of display over deeper ideological commitment. This last judgement, in particular, has served as a specific indictment of England's republican radicals and their impotence. This, however, takes an overly narrow view of politics and perhaps overshadows the cultural change that monarchy's public display represented. Whatever power monarchy brought to bear to convince the crowd of its value and social resonance, the fact remains that in court circles, garnering favourable public opinion was considered an important and valuable activity. Once we accept this explanation, this surely suggests that we should view criticism of the Victorian monarchy away from the more obviously conventional political dialogues and instead, focus upon cultural and social critiques.

When we do this, it becomes possible to fit this criticism of monarchy into a much broader history of propriety, of standards of behaviour, of morality and of shame. This history also offers us some explanations about how and why criticism of the monarchy functioned successfully, why it took the shape it did and why it fell short of a recognisable political programme. It also becomes possible to view the effectiveness of republican techniques of criticism, accusations and slights alongside the calculated motives behind their use. These also emerge as more purposeful and dangerous than the 'obscene radicalism' or indelicate satire that preceded them.[5] Certainly, monarchy was targeted by political radicals as an institution ripe for reform or removal, but a much broader swathe of criticism ultimately made it capable of reforming itself. In this, monarchy was forced to release its grip on personal power and instead came to see itself as capable of being judged alongside duly accepted measures of value, utility and worth. As such, it became an institution functioning around expectations rather than a phenomenon that acted on caprice and personal fiat.

Through this process, monarchy became subject to the same standards of behavioural scrutiny as the other subjects of this book. Republicanism did not triumph through these episodes but overarching standards of behaviour and the pan-class reach of shame became manifest, sustained and potent. This reach was emphasised by the spectacular growth and sophistication of the mass media and this has already been the sub-plot for at least two studies of the Victorian monarchy.[6] Thus the audience for monarchy came to dictate the stories of behaviour it wished to see aired in the public sphere and outlined the boundaries of its own vision of morality and conduct. What was also especially important about these mid-Victorian episodes was how they exposed a blueprint for how the middle classes and the wider public sphere would manage scandal and shame, whilst experimenting with the mechanisms of their dissemination. This widening of the public sphere, and its exposure of what could and could not be spoken or written about, invented the modern science of media trial by journalism. Most importantly of all, it widened the audience for the debate about appropriate behaviour and community sanctions, as reading publics could hold strongly fashioned opinions about individuals or institutions they had never personally encountered. The media then, came to make shame rise to the surface to be even more accessible than ever. Shame was now potentially global, rather than restricted to errant individuals within disparate communities.

Frank Prochaska has already argued that an ideological coherence is wholly absent from the collection of ideas that might otherwise be described as republican. According to Prochaska, principles should be replaced in our historiography with a mixture of self-interest, thwarted ambition, and even envious malice.[7] This persuades us to remember that, compared with continental republican activism, the English republican obsession with the civil list and issues of propriety and expense, appears parochial and indicative of over-reverence for constitutional forms of behaviour. According to this historiography, Victorian republicanism belongs solely to a precise historical 'moment' when it effectively took centre stage with its persistent sharp criticism of the late 1860s and early 1870s. This is traditionally seen to dissipate under the inexorable tide of 'typhoid loyalism' associated with the illness of the Prince of Wales.[8] Likewise Sir Charles Dilke's 'cost of the Crown' speech produced an irresistible backlash which henceforth led him to advocate a more measured, theoretically classical republicanism, which effectively marked his retreat from public life.[9]

By contrast, the popular, more durable radicalism of Charles Bradlaugh appears misplaced and his undoubted oratorical gifts ill-used in his apparent obsession with the minutiae of Palace and monarchical expense. Contemporary with the Commune's power to unleash forces that wanted to reshape social, political and gender relationships throughout society, was Bradlaugh's seemingly one dimensional diatribe *The Impeachment of the House of Brunswick*. This appears, on the surface, to be a disappointing and ideologically naïve pamphlet, which merely criticises the moral behaviour of the monarchy alongside an exhaustive and dull checklist of reckless unjustified expense.[10] For the historian seeking great principle, coherent republican alternatives and the basis of a lasting radical tradition, there is an instinctive urge to look elsewhere.

However, we should now think more critically about the context of such criticism and not accept Prochaska's accusation of simple jealousy and malice so readily. Antony Taylor, through a close examination of *Reynolds's Newspaper,* has linked the phenomenon of anti-monarchism with the agenda of populism that has recently influenced the study of most pre-1900 radicalism.[11] There is now a case for widening our perception to consider how coherent moral criticism can be explored by placing it alongside the more recent developments in the historiography of monarchy and of the growth of the middle class. Taylor equally suggests how important it is to reclaim criticism of moral failings as 'a serious component of popular politics'. As he suggests:

> Analysis of the moral case against aristocracy demonstrates that radical journalists undermined the virtues of the aristocratic state by revealing it as profligate, dissipated, and self-destructive.[12]

By integrating these three areas and emphasising their connected cultural history, we can perceive the creation of a more gradualist and deliberately permeable conception of shame and cultural criticism. The significance of Queen Victoria's colonisation of the newly created middle classes was not lost at all on republicans during the third quarter of the nineteenth century. Indeed, a close reading of many republican texts, journalism and speeches suggests that republicans actively sought to undermine (ironically with the unconscious assistance of Queen Victoria herself) the rapprochement which the monarchy had enjoyed with this class. What becomes evident from this is that Queen Victoria, quite unwittingly, created the phenomenon of widespread public opinion about monarchy in Britain. From this, such opinion learned how to construct and manipulate a complex network of shame discourses and moral standards. Through this message, the power of these values could be simultaneously demonstrated as ideals and reinforced through the display of their unsavoury opposite.

Whilst our historiography finds it convenient to link values around moral propriety, commercial instinct and a disdain of aristocratic behaviours, it is worth remembering that such a system of values was also perceived to have potential pan-class appeal. This had followed eighteenth century developments in republicanism which, when combined with the contribution of Thomas Paine, had shifted the movement's centre of gravity. Emphasis upon the power of a ruling class, as opposed to the individual despotism of monarchs, had become apparent.[13] If public validation for virtuous and meritocratic aspirations could be nurtured and persuaded to thrive, then education for future citizenship would eventually triumph. However, this view of possible future aspirations also drew upon the ability to use communal sanctions and accusations, which had a long tradition.[14]

Whilst David Cannadine famously suggested that Victoria defined her age, there is now ample evidence to suggest that she may also have 'problematised' it for her subjects.[15] Adrienne Munich, for example, has demonstrated that so many of the traditional cultural truisms and tropes which were associated with Queen Victoria appear to be ambivalent once they are systematically unpacked. What is also abundantly clear, from Munich's analysis, is that the roles and images portrayed by Victoria were designed to be comforting and coherent when she represented one half of the foremost Victorian couple.[16] Here we might usefully recall Erving Goffman's suggestions about how individuals construct themselves socially and are thus constructed selves.[17] This arguably applies with particular resonance to the monarchy in the Victorian period. Victoria had to be monarch, wife and mother quite apart from her numerous constructed selves intended to woo and appease various audiences.

But after Albert's death, Victoria's various guises reflected anxieties about the capacity of the over mighty woman (Queen) to infantilise the men (subjects) in the vicinity.[18] Moreover the Queen's widowhood, at a comparatively young age, allowed more dangerous undercurrents of unrealised sexuality and a proto-ancestor of the 'Woman Question' to emerge in the person of Victoria herself. Her alleged romantic involvement with John Brown, according to Munich, further served to alienate the constituency which had earlier embraced the Queen's own Plantagenet and Anglo-Saxon 'invention of tradition'.[19] The phenomena of sexual innuendo, regularly evidenced in skimmington ride episodes, have even requested inclusion in this cultural history, through investigation of the double entendres intended in the title of the anti-monarchist pamphlet 'What does she do with it?'[20]

Our view of the early century middle class and the creation of its values has also been informed by the pioneering work of Davidoff and Hall who produced an analysis that was both theoretically aware and prepared to nuance hitherto unexplored areas of middle-class cultural creation. In particular, they illuminated the interplay between class and gender in the creation of the middle class.[21] These historians also noticed that the creation of this class involved defining what it found to be distasteful, abhorrent and shameful. They suggest that middle-class values of the second quarter of the nineteenth century involved an instinctive reaction against the mores of the court and its aristocratic associates:

> Aristocratic claims for leadership had long been based on lavish
> display and consumption while the middle-class stressed dom-

estic moderation. ...Court circles around the Prince Regent, the 'Fashionables' among whom high class prostitute openly appeared in public, also outraged provincial decorum. But so too did the London-based opponents of the Regent's lifestyle, the Dandies. This all male social clique had its own aesthetic, disdaining coarse womanizing, but was opposed to business pursuits or habits, ostentatiously even refusing to wear a watch, and spurning all domestic burdens. The Dandies set their mark on London Society with their fashionable elegance and concern with clothes, the antithesis of domesticated masculinity dedicated to business.[22]

Davidoff and Hall also emphasised the importance of dissent, non-conformity and certain species of evangelicalism which provided the theological background for the middle-class turn to seriousness.[23] Phenomena like the Queen Caroline affair were also seen as vital episodes in airing and articulating nascent ideals of domesticity. The Queen Caroline affair was a contest in which the power to shame was a specifically important prize, whilst victory by either party threatened to define the limits of acceptable behaviour to the wider community. Issues around the practice of virtue and the nature of corruption in action were made significant talking points by the middle-class audiences for this ideological battle.[24] This discovery of the rise, and growing popularity, of middle-class cultures for achievement and legitimation has also been augmented by newer studies which seek to investigate the more obviously political manifestation of these cultures.[25] However, elsewhere in this book we have also noticed the precarious nature of middle-class life, self-image and 'face'. Those striving to maintain social position and respectability were also those who profoundly understood the damaging nature of adverse opinion and the power of shame.

We also have ample evidence of the success of Queen Victoria's capture of middle-class hearts and minds, as well as pockets. Margaret Homans has also suggested how physical images of Queen Victoria were multiplied and circulated as a means of emphasising Victoria's middle-class affinity, whilst also endorsing the social and cultural practices of this class.[26] Part of Victoria's own feminisation of the monarchy, was also an explicit appeal to middle-class conceptions of duty and domesticity.[27] Albert radiated an especial appeal for the manufacturing and commercial classes, since he argued the philanthropic work of middle-class capitalists was 'a form of enlightened self-interest', which to other eyes, could appear to be a throwback to older forms of paternalism and the recognition of social responsibility.[28] In an age of free trade, the Prince Consort promoted a social economy in which the charitable enterprise, working with commercial interests, complemented state provision for the poor.[29] Yet, arguably, it also set up high standards of behaviour and courted expectations about how governors of the community should behave, and be expected to behave. In this, Albert set a standard for monarchy which would be hard to sustain.

So how did republican cultural ideas use contemporary understanding of the moral family, propriety and shame to try and control a phenomenon that historians tell us Victoria had harnessed so successfully in the previous generation? In order to accomplish the successful spread of middle-class republican ideas, would-be republicans had to achieve several related objectives. They had first to discredit Victoria's dutiful images of benign modernising domesticity that had so captivated the middle classes in the earlier part of her reign. Central to the success of this project, was publicity of the innate moral rationality of meritocracy in contrast to the irrational defence of the immorally inherited and to make this shameful.[30] Lastly, the middle classes had also to be persuaded that a sustainable meritocracy sprang naturally from precisely this moral rationality.[31] This also, as in many forms of communal action, was a method of wrestling authority away from social superiors who had abused it. Similarly, inverting moral authority with the reality of articulate and lasting grievances was also to have more sustained impact than conventional forms of rough music or misrule.

The currents of thought prevalent in republican journalism provide important insights into how they perceived and 'imagined' the middle class that they were seeking to invoke and mobilise as agents of shaming. Regular emphasis on the importance of wealth creation and the achievements of commerce contained a distinct echo of republicanism's paineite past. Similarly, the importance of achievement, meritocracy and promoting an enabling and visibly confident public sphere also had roots in this line of thinking.[32] However, unconnected with the earlier era was an ability to comment upon the actual gains such a civilisation had achieved for the England of the previous 30 years, and the resulting benefits to a latter day 'commonwealth'. This clearly had affinities with the Manchester School doctrines of Cobden and Bright, but also with the Positivism of Harrison and Beesly.[33] Where this loose collection of ideas had really moved on from Paine, was the nature of its interest in both individual property (and to a lesser extent communal property in the guise of institutions) as a foundation of civil society.[34] Whilst Bradlaugh considered the maldistribution of land to be a social evil, the defence of legitimately earned property loomed large in his thinking. Public institutions, clubs and societies – themselves products of middle-class endeavour and the evolution of 'trust', were also portrayed as a species of public good or even 'property'. Betrayal of trust and the apparent display of corrupt motives were also potentially powerful initiators of the urge to shame.

Demonstrating just how flimsy such rights and institutions actually were could be achieved through exposing how many of them, particularly in the realm of local government, rested not on written law but upon the gracious extension of privilege. Playing upon its psychological association with the language of arbitrariness, the notion of 'privilege' conveyed the fear of advantages withdrawn as easily as they had been extended.[35] This also linked such decisions with the idea of the often shameful behavioural choices of monarchy and aristocracy, rather than the rule of law or the realisation of 'rights'. Monarchy could easily become the present centred and recklessly hedonistic, risk addicted, criminal seeking immediate gratification without reasonable restraint. Those betrayed by their passions would be most readily exposed to the power of shame. This also came to further emphasise the contrast with middle-class thrift, sobriety and duty. Likewise, it was hoped that in suggesting how easily achievements could unravel, shame inspired criticism could suggest how progress away from an aristocratic society was by no means inevitable. This potentially played on middle-class anxiety and fear of their own social decline – classes that had been made could perhaps be readily unmade.

Yet shame was also a powerful tool which had the capacity to paralyse an individual, or it was hoped, an institution. From this point, showing monarchy as a rapacious and arbitrary invader of property and despoiler of achievement was a less than difficult task. This process importantly coincided with the first moral panics amongst the middle classes generated around criminal behaviour. R. Sindall has noted that the 'ticket of leave' scares of the late 1850s and the garrotting panics of the early 1860s had really emphasised how the power of the press and the written word could create middle-class anxiety and insecurity.[36]

As far as seeking to discredit the monarchy was concerned, republicans could justifiably have felt that the institution was doing their work for them during the 1860s. The death of Albert was quite clearly a watershed in this, since almost overnight the image of the perfect couple was irretrievably shattered. Victoria's own approach to mourning completely altered the character of the monarchy and its social behaviour. Reticence and reclusiveness replaced confidence and display as Victoria herself retreated from public life. Indeed from this point onwards, Queen Victoria and her family ceased to resemble the socially young, brash and upwardly mobile middle classes and instead began to resemble doomed, dissolute aristocratic relics. In her dress and demeanour, the Queen went, again almost overnight, from the merely dowdy to the dowager and seemingly cared little for her reputation, nor that of the monarchy itself.

Henceforth, those who sought a lead in fashion, philanthropy and most worryingly of all morality and behaviour from the monarchy were to be singularly disappointed. Moreover, Victoria's absence from public life crucially undermined middle-class conceptions of duty. The extraordinarily potent image of the vacant throne spoke squarely of neglect, but also appeared to betoken a lack of care and a form of indolence which had not clustered around the monarchy for more than a generation.[37] There was, of course, a global dimension to shame which would later see the republican Charles Bradlaugh offer critiques of both monarchy and aristocracy that indicted its shameful behaviour around issues of corruption.[38] Albert's death also began to focus attention upon monarchy as an institution and its potential future instability, embodied in the Prince of Wales, was a further source of considerable concern. 'Bertie', as contemporaries were well aware, was extraordinarily poor raw material for a future king. Monarchy had also to be portrayed as a brooding, slumbering cultural threat to middle-class values that might yet appeal over their heads to the still relatively unknown quantity of working-class opinion, for whom enfranchisement seemed only a matter of time.[39] In this we might again note the precariousness of middle-class achievement and status acquisition. Once the favour and support of the monarchy could be shown to be expedient, conditional or even occasionally ambivalent, then it was possible to encourage moral criticism and sow quasi-republican doubt.

Newspapers like the *National Reformer*, which first saw the light of day in the year before Prince Albert's death, was one of the important conduits through which these dialogues and shaming critiques flowed. It was immediately intent upon undoing the connection between monarchy's discourse of decorous family construction and true middle-class propriety. Amidst its expected political copy in its very first issues is, at first sight, an apparently strange series of articles on 'Love and Marriage' which later acquired the sobriquet 'The Way to Domestic Happiness'.[40] Throughout this collection of advice is a latter day blueprint for middle-class domestic ideology that Davidoff and Hall would readily have recognised from an earlier age. It outlines how a virtuous man might compile a checklist of middle-class domestic accomplishments that he desires from a prospective wife.[41] As a legitimate 'trade' for these accomplishments the *National Reformer* continued to emphasise the benevolent, yet potentially contractual, nature of its marriage ideal.

> In marriage, as in the market, I should expect to give value for value. I would, therefore, while looking round for a first rate woman, try to make myself and prove myself a first rate man.[42]

Further advice included a checklist of desires and circumstances that would make for a companionate and successful marriage. These included agreement upon religious issues and proximity of age between husband and wife wherever possible. Allusions to the dangerous moral and shameful practices of other classes were contained in the stern advice to avoid duels and lawsuits and to maintain a regime of economic propriety. All this functioned as a distinct riposte to the success of the Victorian monarchy's cult of domesticity, but even within such guidance was a powerful critique of Queen Victoria's own domestic arrangements, with the ribaldry and rough music only slightly submerged. In the nearest this advice gets to discussing sexual relations, the paper suggests that a degree of Malthusian abstinence was compatible with happiness, representing a significant contrast with the rapacious fertility of Victoria and Albert.[43]

Perhaps the most powerful attack upon monarchical domesticity was the *National Reformer's* objections to the marriage of close kin. In particular, the paper had distinct moral objections to the marriage of cousins declaring '... it is certain that first cousins have often ill-formed, unhealthy and insane children'.[44] The proximate references to royalty were confirmed with an alternative amusingly carnivalesque and pejorative picture of Albert's journey from the continent. The *National Reformer's* dialogue suggested 'It is the custom of breeders to bring animals from a distance to secure a superior offspring'.[45] The newspaper thus concluded in quite emphatic style 'We cannot, therefore, but pronounce the marriage of first cousins unwise and criminal.'[46] Interestingly, this had focussed upon marriage as a species of attack upon monarchy and its practices.[47] This introduced a spirit of lampoon, ridicule and a moral critique of incestuous impropriety that would not have looked out of place in a customary skimmington ride. However decorously it had achieved its goal, the *National Reformer* had questioned the propriety of allowing marriage within such a close degree and compared the individuals concerned to farmyard breeding stock.

Elsewhere, the *National Reformer* was particularly anxious to highlight popular expectations of the value of meritocracy and the quest for proper behaviour. On the 18th of June 1867, it quoted a letter from W.J. Linton, who declared that healthy morality required '... the abolition of the tyrannies of the rank and wealth, the abolition of all arbitrary distinctions and artificial disabilities calculated to prevent any individual from reaching the fullest growth and perfection of his or her nature.'[48] Even the issue of combating primogeniture could be linked to the earlier triumphs of the middle class, particularly the 1832 Reform Act.[49] Charles Bradlaugh, almost certainly as a result of his connexion with land reform, very clearly saw the entrenched nature of the aristocracy as a most significant threat to social, cultural and moral reform. He argued their behaviour was actively shameful since:

> ...those distinctions of rank and class which are the bane of English society.... the great source of inequality is the artificial distinctions of rank and social position created by the law.... The elevation of the aristocracy is thus the degradation of the people. It lowers the dignity of labour, and encourages the notion that a life of idleness and luxury is more to be respected than one of honest industry.[50]

Here shame was a potent method of inverting the accidental social order to produce a true aristocracy of virtue and labour. This also began to suggest that societies founded upon hereditary preferment and aristocratic connexion were inherently shameful and should be exposed to public glare at every opportunity.

H.V. Mayer in an article entitled 'Republic v Monarchy' pushed further with the idea that monarchy was inherently shameful and anti-meritocratic. He declared it to be a violation of the principle of representation and 'repugnant to justice', going as far as to describe it (with an interesting display of patriotic radicalism) as 'the popery of politics' – both sentiments that readily appear in older communal protests.[51] Warming to his theme, he argued that 'genius is not hereditary, talents are not transmissible. We do not recognise the hereditary principle in the bar, the church or the army, nor in any of the administrative departments of the state, from the first lord of the treasury downwards.'[52] Lecturing in New York in September 1873, Charles Bradlaugh emphasised that the power of English republicanism was that it persuaded the aristocracy to assent to social change that it would not otherwise concede. As though anti-monarchical rough music was ultimately capable of establishing shared communal values and propriety, yet that a vigilant public community may yet be called upon to police this.

Aristocracy's resurgence as a social and cultural force threatened the achievements of the public and private spheres and their recognition of class attainment. Far from securing the status of the middle classes, the culture of attainment was potentially at the mercy of the devious wiles of the monarchy and aristocracy. These attainments had only been possible while society had tolerated them, and the sheer breadth of these made them vulnerable once unconditional sympathy was withdrawn. This attempt to remind audiences of serial past misdemeanours, was one reason for various republican's use of the regular tactic of referring to the shortcomings of the Queen's immediate predecessors through satire and lampoon. Such references reinforced contemporary propriety, yet obviously reminded audiences of the link between past and present moral misdemeanours. Bradlaugh regularly used this descriptive tactic, notably in *George, Prince of Wales* and in sections of the *Impeachment*.[53]

The *National Reformer's* coverage of the Mordaunt Divorce scandal is itself illuminating in this regard. The Mordaunt divorce case was discussed through the writings of a correspondent to the paper, Ernest Wells, who was portrayed as a moral commentator wanting to uncover the so-called 'mysteries' of the case.[54] It was pictured as a spectacular melodrama with profound moral resonance in which monarchy had a distinct and shameful role in the destruction of the middle-class domestic narrative. It was an occasion upon which the sanctity of hearth, home and family had been systematically and rapaciously invaded by the heir to the throne. This individual's conduct was then exhibited for public condemnation and shame. The story follows a well-trodden path that in other times and circumstances generally ended in an episode of rough music. Wells picked up on the fact that Sir Charles Mordaunt had set the scene by telling his wife that '...the Prince of Wales was not fit company for her. That, in fact, the heir to the throne was not exactly a safe associate for one of his mother's subjects.'[55] The precise invasion of private space by the heir to the throne was conveyed by Wells' second mystery. He asked why Mordaunt had been persuaded by a servant to come down from his bed (upon which he was resting) to confront the Prince of Wales within his own house? This particular confrontation also carried a potent and resonant collision of the issues around marital propriety, authority, behaviour and shame.

Mordaunt was clearly exposed to profound shame and loss of face in this confrontation. His own wife had been (at the least on this particular occasion) consorting with the Prince and this was obvious to Mordaunt and the rest of the household. Yet Mordaunt was in an especially difficult position, since the Prince was an authority figure and profoundly difficult to challenge. But also, the 'trust' and propriety that Mordaunt had a right to expect from authority figures was being abused and debased. To any audience for this Mordaunt appeared potentially cuckolded, yet also intolerably found himself in a situation which rendered him almost powerless. Wells, citing the rituals of domestic custom, asked not unreasonably whether Mordaunt had questioned the Prince upon his business in his house. He then wanted to know whether Mordaunt had shown the Prince of Wales the door and why the heir to the throne left the premises in quite such a hurry. In this, Wells was also arguably creating printed, and widely circulated, rough music although in a variation upon traditional practice this was arguably created on Mordaunt's behalf. The status of this as a powerful narrative of contempt for society's institutions was confirmed by Wells' declaration of the third mystery. Here he asked why the Prince of Wales so carefully rehearsed his performance in the court with a particularly histrionic oath, something which undermined the status of law and the widely accepted apparatus of moral regulation. This in particular, was described by Wells as 'a bit of solemn burlesque introduced into a great tragedy'.[56]

Occasionally the *National Reformer* also used the forays of monarchy into the realm of civil society to unsettle the status and solidity of both institutions. In 1869, Charles Bradlaugh addressed the Prince of Wales as a fellow freemason and drew attention to the solemn nature of promises and vows to the institutions that were the lifeblood of such civil society. Reminding him that Masonic relationships depended explicitly on trust and a developed sense of honesty, Bradlaugh then set about shaming the Prince's behaviour, noting that he was sarcastically reassured that the Prince could clearly not have been:

> ...a runner after painted donzels, that he has not written cuckold on the forehead of a dozen husbands, that he is not deep in debt.... We know, brother, that you would never have voluntarily enrolled yourself in the world's grandest organisation, if you had been as these. It would have been perjury if you had done so.[57]

Similarly, writing in August 1874, George William Foote used the occasion of the Queen's fourth son Leopold's coming of age, for a calculated shaming attack upon the neglect of duty and apparently inherent laziness of monarchy. In doing so he also created quite compelling images of wrongdoing and inappropriate behaviour:

> So even the task of opening parliament has been too much for her weakness to undergo, although she can join in a reel with

scotch ghillies at her own house at Balmoral. There is indeed something eminently sacred about this widowed grief, this perpetual remembrance of the departed dead. And we may further congratulate ourselves upon maternal as well as wifely affection of our Queen, for we have unmistakable evidences of it in the persistent solicitude that she manifests for the material welfare of her children.[58]

In September 1874, Bradlaugh also spotted that the Conservative Government was attempting to raise money to fund the visit of the Prince of Wales to India and suspected that this may be used to pay off his debts.[59]

Republican moral criticism wished to alter expectations, opinions and cultural values at a much deeper level than the simply political. In undertaking this, it sought an alliance with the middle classes and aimed to demonstrate to them the fragility of their own position and earlier triumph. In judging the receptiveness of their audience, republicans sought to play simultaneously upon middle-class aspirations and fears enabled through the power of shame. An aristocratic looking monarchy, that might yet join an alliance with jingo and patriotic opinion against the middle classes, appeared to be a deadly and credible conspiracy against seriousness and moral propriety.[60]

Yet the popular and widely read observer Thomas Wright in the late 1860s and early 1870s directly addressed contemporary concerns about the nature of the coming politics in his *Our New Masters*.[61] Throughout, Wright was anxious to explain the rational ways of working men to the middle classes and to calm fears suggesting they understood both propriety and morality. Wright was also anxious to show how simplistic views of their behaviour were little more than an insult to working men. In suggesting this, he was drawing the sting from the pejorative epithet Robert Lowe had pronounced and had used as his starting point (he had famously described those enfranchised by the Reform Act of 1867 as 'our new masters'). In a measured attack upon the mischief perpetrated by the contemporary press, Wright advanced a wholly different picture of working-class attitudes to monarchy in the face of the illness of the Prince of Wales – the so-called 'typhoid loyalism'. Far from being a universal rush to embrace monarchy and ditch the republican aberration, Wright suggested that the wave of feeling which emanated from the working classes was a natural, and moral, response to a family drama which would have elicited sympathy in a household of any class. Sympathy existed here solely as feeling for a husband and father and the possibility of a family tragedy in the making.[62] This was also consciously asserting the universal qualities of Victorian 'manliness' rather than associating monarchy with a deeper moral prerogative.[63] This journalism also censured the monarchy's claim that its behaviour was special or exemplary and thus deserving of extra license or particularly elevated status.

The end of the 1860s and the start of the 1870s also problematised the correlation between femininity, domesticity and social propriety – denting middle-class confidence in this paradigm. Much republican journalism of this period was especially anxious to demonstrate how this was dissolving. As has already been mentioned, Queen Victoria's own emotional constancy as grieving widow was severely questioned by the rumour surrounding her relationship with John Brown. The shame inherent in the Mordaunt divorce scandal also brought the unimpeachable moral virtue of aristocratic women into question. *Reynolds's Newspaper*, in particular, was vitriolic about the moral behaviour of female members of the aristocracy. For instance, Lady Mordaunt's claim that all around her were behaving as she had done, led this paper (with deep censure and distaste) to describe the English aristocracy as 'living in a state of advanced Mormonism.'[64] Skilful reporting of the shamed misdemeanours of the Prince of Wales was also a method of associating monarchy's active inroads into civil society with a boorish Hanoverian masculinity. This in itself may have provided a tentative answer to the 'problems' Adrienne Munich suggests a feminised monarchy posed for those legitimating authority for themselves and others.

The Mordaunt divorce scandal was also significant in alerting newspapers to the power of public opinion. This was not simply about the behaviour of members of the aristocracy and monarchy, but it had also begun to tackle a much wider question. Many now believed, as indeed *Reynolds's* did, that a nation was judged according to the moral character of those who ruled it. As it suggested, the behaviour in question was a distinct return to 'the infamous Georgian era'. Moreover this should not be tolerated because 'the middle and humbler orders are the power of the nation, and they had spoken out.'[65] Even the philanthropic work of the monarchy, the phenomenon which so impresses Frank Prochaska, could at best be satirised or indeed at worst be viewed as cynical and instrumental. *Reynolds's* waspishly asked whether the rumour was true that an '"illustrious personage" was to be offered the chairmanship of the Magdalen hospital and the chair at the next meeting of the YMCA.'[66] In this respect, we should begin to remind ourselves that the level of royal charity work was starting to be less important than what the people actually thought about it and the motives for carrying it out.

From these small beginnings, republican critiques created a phenomenon of public opinion around the monarchy where thought and criticism of the institution and its uses increasingly became the norm. If monarchy could be shown to regularly ignore the middle-class methods of opinion formation (discussion, consultation with civil society and its institutions, the rule of law and sanctioned precedent) then it would face the new phenomenon of informed, articulate and powerful discourses of shame. Indeed, the numerous discussions about the antiquated nature of monarchy and how its image appeared as a result of the Royal Titles Bill of 1876, lend interesting evidence for this view. The Royal Titles Bill enabled the *National Reformer* to suggest that it implied the use and eventual abuse of 'despotic power'.[67]

Paradoxically, through arbitrary action, the monarchy had opened the door to wider criticism where public opinion would create a cultured articulate form of disrespect and the use of shame to prevent further despotic incursions. In an open letter to Disraeli, Charles Bradlaugh argued that the Royal Title and its alteration by Parliament, was capable of breaking the attitude of individuals to an individual title. That change would make it easier to alter such titles further for the advantage of the country.[68] As we know, the later remaking of monarchy enabled the institution to survive and prosper. But a notion that appearances and opinion about the institution and its value were fundamentally important was actively enshrined by this rejuvenation. Indeed, shame and the reaction to it actively enforced this revival. In 1879, George Standring's otherwise predictable tilt against monarchical expense ended by comparing monarchy to other institutions and demonstrating that such comparison made it liable to the intense scrutiny of public opinion.[69] The phenomenon of public opinion was arguably one attempt to create a rapprochement between classes not around economic dialogue, but around conceptions of virtue, propriety and merit that those participating in Edward Thompson's much earlier 'Moral Economy of the English Crowd' would recognise.[70] This potentially indicates the reinvention of shame as a form of social control, used by both authorities and the populace more widely, to reprimand wayward individuals within a community, even if the definition of this was becoming ever wider. By this point in the Victorian era shame was once again being used by the populace, and this time also by influential commentators, to 'control' those in positions of power and authority, whilst reminding them of their duty. Since it was now a potent media tool, and one also used by individuals to control the actions of others, shame still relied upon the power of scandal. Shame now functioned most spectacularly when the media was involved, since it had access to the widest possible audience. The portrayal of shame as scandal was most convincing when the individual(s) being shamed had some distance to fall and some reputations to lose (such as the Royal Family), since popular opinion was now widely in the public sphere rather than being localised.

Agnes Heller has suggested that the phenomenon of shame can only function where communities are small, where values are homogenous and where behaviour patterns are essentially rationalized.[71] The story of the Victorian monarchy and the function of bourgeois shame both appear to contradict the direction of these propositions. The essence of the republican critique, and its assault upon the behaviour of monarchy and aristocracy, regularly stressed their irrationality as social phenomena. Similarly, the focus upon middle-class values and their social power was a statement about a social grouping's desire for autonomy and for its views to triumph – clearly an assault upon homogeneity. Yet the attempts to transcend the inherent size of the political and critical community willing to consume monarchical 'shame' were partly successful. Critiques of monarchy and aristocracy did persuade individuals to think through their psychological standards of propriety and to judge these against the reputations of people they had never met. However, seen as a political programme, such judgement and censure was episodic and did not lead to the destruction of these institutions – ultimately the quick triumph that republicans hoped would be theirs by the end of the 1860s, never materialized. Yet if we see this as a community using shame to re-establish new and old norms and stabilise them, the situation looks rather different. The dialogue which turned monarchy into an institution was an act of exposing monarchy to the scrutiny of democracy, through the application of the cruder mechanism of shame. This does perhaps fit with Heller's suggestion that democratic societies utilise shame through a multitude of outlets.[72] Either way the recognition of shame's incorporation into modern social systems and forms of social negotiation appears unequivocal.

Issues about the monarchy were aired alongside wider issues about accountability. The construction of what the new essence of public opinion might mean was one facet of this.[73] How it might be shaped and shared between classes, and how false conceptions about the mass behaviour of those classes might be refuted, were fundamental to this process.[74] Importantly we can see the censure of royal behaviour and its immorality becoming a staple of popular culture with a wide readership and wider acceptance. Indeed we can see evidence that this stood a very good chance of being internalized by many audiences. To demonstrate the potential for this we might conclude by noting how precisely this censure and discourse of shame appears in one of Conan Doyle's Sherlock Holmes stories, *Scandal in Bohemia*, published in *The Strand Magazine* in 1891.[75]

In highlighting this we should note perhaps the success of shame critiques of monarchy in permeating popular and widely read fiction, showing how frequent airings and exposure of shameful behaviour amongst the elite could shape conscious and unconscious opinion. In this, monarchy was portrayed as corrupt, dishonest and trifling, with the capacity to behave scandalously to protect 'face'. This episode also foregrounds monarchy as a despoiler of the moral reputation of women; the last sources of shame and virtue in pre-modern society. All of these images remain uncomfortably close to the misdemeanors of the Prince of Wales. The earlier Mordaunt divorce scandal had been supplemented by the baccarat card game scandal (known as the Tranby Croft affair) which occurred nine months before the *Strand Magazine* published *Scandal in Bohemia*. The plot of *Scandal* also mirrors the behaviour of the Duke of Clarence who succeeded in retrieving two compromising letters from prostitutes, also in 1891. Although these facts about the latter story were hidden until 2002, it is certainly possible that rumours concerning this may have been contemporary public knowledge.

In *Scandal in Bohemia* Holmes fails to catch his artful and wily opponent finding he has been outwitted by an actress (Irene Adler), once photographed compromisingly with the future King of Bohemia. Holmes is rapidly enamored of her skill, cunning and industry and is easily persuaded to have immense respect and admiration for this honourable and resourceful woman. She has manifestly shown the middle-class virtues of intelligence and enterprise, for once above that of Holmes himself. This is an argument for the meritocratic respect of an individual which the unscrupulous King of Bohemia described as 'not on my level'. It is worth remembering that the King was one of only two clients who ever required Sherlock Holmes to break the law, in this case through an act of burglary. The respect for Irene Adler is heavily contrasted with the brooding disdain for the King of Bohemia who emerges as lazy, corrupt, shallow, self-seeking and a dishonourable and shameful womaniser. After being outwitted by Adler in what resembles a revisiting of the Mordaunt divorce scandal, Conan Doyle has Holmes declare:

'What a woman – oh, what a woman!' cried the King of Bohemia, when we had all three read this epistle. 'Did I not tell you how quick and resolute she was? Would she not have made an admirable queen? Is it not a pity that she was not on my level?'

'From what I have seen of the lady she seems indeed to be on a very different level to your Majesty,' said Holmes coldly. 'I am sorry that I have not been able to bring your Majesty's business to a more successful conclusion.' 'On the contrary, my dear sir,' cried the King; 'nothing could be more successful. I know that her word is inviolate. The photograph is now as safe as if it were in the fire.' 'I am glad to hear your Majesty say so.'

'I am immensely indebted to you. Pray tell me in what way I can reward you. This ring...' He slipped an emerald snake ring from his finger and held it out upon the palm of his hand.

'Your Majesty has something which I should value even more highly,' said Holmes. 'You have but to name it.' 'This photograph!' The King stared at him in amazement. 'Irene's photograph!' he cried. 'Certainly, if you wish it.'

'I thank your Majesty. Then there is no more to be done in the matter. I have the honour to wish you a very good-morning.' He bowed, and, turning away without observing the hand which the King had stretched out to him, he set off in my company for his chambers.

The popular character of Sherlock Holmes is here made to speak to a wide reading public about monarchy, notions of honour, dishonor and shameful behaviour. Holmes' reaction also portrays that meritocratic virtue (in the shape of Irene Adler) could be found in unexpected places. Whilst history tells us that the republican critique did not triumph as a political discourse, however, the calculated use of shame brought informal opinion and censure to bear on standards of propriety and behaviour.

The calculated application of shame as a method of indicting the behaviour of the highest in the land, at the end of the nineteenth century, simultaneously demonstrates both the longevity and the continued potency of cultures of shame. Moreover amongst developed reading and thinking publics a mode of censure once considered by some analysts to be primitive and associated with pre-modern society actively flourished in this modern period, and was systematically nurtured by some individuals and institutions for gain. Moreover its adaptability in the face of new media and its ability to accomplish new and complex social tasks meant that, far from being marginalised by modernity, shame had become an intrinsic component of it.

9
Conclusion: Reconciling Shame with Modernity

Shame exercised an important but hitherto unrecognised and little researched influence over British society between 1600 and 1900. The fears of social collapse predicated upon the disintegration of moral and behavioural codes that stalked society in the 1650s, the 1790s, the 1840s and 1860s, never properly materialised. Similarly, the swathe of vice and immorality uncovered by organisations as diverse as the Scottish Kirk and the Society for the Suppression of Vice, did not ultimately overwhelm society north or south of the border. Individuals, and their supposedly rapaciously destructive instincts for wanton misbehaviour, were ultimately held in check during this period. Whilst clearly many saw they had a vested interest in the maintenance of moral order, others decided to limit, curb or adapt their behaviour as a result of a number of social and psychological stimuli. Of all the so-called 'dark figures' in criminal and behavioural history this must surely be the largest, one of the most significant and quite possibly one of the most fascinating. Those who conformed, accepted authority or even actively used its tacit power to police themselves, their desires and their behaviour, are quite likely to leave very little trace on the historical record. Nonetheless, it remains the historian's job to uncover this history and to try and tell the story of personal responsibility, morality, public punishment and the history of society's gaze at the individual. It is also important to relate changes in these to the nature of social relations that developed over the time scale covered by this book. To do this, it has been necessary to concentrate upon particular places and incidents where the issue of shame, culpability and guilt broke the surface. Only by focussing upon and closely interrogating these incidents, is it possible for the historian to analyse the various and changing functions of shame in action over this extended chronological period.

Shame, as we have discovered, has been a fundamentally important, yet neglected aspect of the history of emotions and behaviour. However, as a marker within the history of crime and the history of culture, it is emphatically so much more than that. Shame is a fascinating prism through which the evolution of behavioural expectations and their relationship to modernity can be examined. The breadth of this volume cannot hope to map all the precise changes over this vast chronological terrain. However, it has produced a coherent history by identifying and outlining many of the central trends and the central themes which govern the history of shame. In particular, it showcases shame's frequent uninvited appearances in the lives of ordinary people, as well as the outlook of the authorities at a number of important historical moments over the three centuries between 1600 and 1900.

The examples of shame which have been analysed and unpacked in this book have benefited from a considerably close analysis, which has allowed us to draw conclusions from the interplay between individual protagonists and the many faceted representations of them. These have come from a number of public spheres, but most readily the courtroom and varieties of the printed media. What is striking from these examples is the sheer vitality of shame and its continuity. Conventional understandings (as suggested in the introduction) offer something of a linear model which sees shame dismissed from the public sphere, in favour of the more sophisticated and privately regulated phenomenon of guilt. In some respects, this historiography appears at first sight more plausible, because many modern objections to the implementation of shame see it as a barbaric, primitive (or arguably unconstitutionally cruel and excessive) tool of 'social control'.[1]

At the start of our period, shame was closely linked to the phenomenon of punishment. This, we discovered in relation to the case of the resurrected infanticidal mother Margaret Dickson, the summary customary punishments meted out to those who infringed the community's norms of behaviour, and obviously in the use of shame elements within punishments such as the pillory. In all of these instances, we noted that the use of shame had a distinctly retributive function. In other words, it was imperative that individuals were made to pay, and seen to be made to pay, for their crimes against God, against authority and against humankind and wider society. A particular feature of this was that communities themselves were given a variety of roles in the mechanisms for punishing the offender. This was deemed by such a society to have many demonstrable and lasting virtues. Allowing the public shaming of offenders brought issues of justice and atonement close to the personal experience of the individual, where it also emphasised shared values about the nature and scope of culpability.

Demonstrating the rage and anger of others was also an especially effective mechanism in impressing upon the offender that they were isolated from the society against which they had offended. The use of such shame was also exemplary and put individuals in contact with the result of moral infractions, with the hope of deterring them from these. In the course of making an example of individuals, society and community also very obviously had numerous opportunities to give demonstrations of what it deemed to be correct and upright moral behaviour, and to readily identify and precisely name offences which undermined order. These shame rituals also displayed that the community assented to the binding nature of moral prescription. This also justified and reinforced the power of governance within the primitive state; a state which arguably had no other realistically effective powers of persuasion or coercion. The state must also have been relieved and gratified to notice how the functioning of shame rituals and shame punishments was also a method of justifying and consenting to its governance and moral authority.

However, as we have noticed, even at this comparatively early period it was not always possible to control how discourses of shame were created or how they were utilised by individuals. Certainly it is possible to detect the long-term ideological incoherence within shame punishment coming under intense scrutiny as the eighteenth century progressed. For instance, we have the example of the shame heaped upon Maggie Dickson, when the popular trope of providential survival overwrote and effectively 'trumped' the dialogues about atonement, culpability and evil. Here the failure of Dickson to receive her just desserts manifested the ambiguity and unreliability of shame discourses and punishments. This also demonstrated that shame could equally be internalised by the onlookers around such incidents. Such unreliability and unpredictability was also a cornerstone of the chapter investigating the use of the pillory. As we noticed with some victims of the pillory, the retributive and exemplary nature of this punishment became unpredictable and sometimes lost its coherence. This was particularly notable when the authority which dispensed this punishment found itself confronted with the ideologically motivated dissident.

These people had developed more sophisticated psychological strengths which allowed them to devise and implement defences which preserved their own self, as well as the integrity of their actions. No longer was the pillory, and arguably any other form of shame punishment, entirely reliable and obviously beneficial to society as a whole. Moreover, many influential commentators were coming to doubt the value and effectiveness of such shame punishments. Importantly this was not simply as a consequence of a growing humanitarianism, but was also spawned by dialogues about the eighteenth century's search for greater efficiency and rationality around the business of both control and punishment.

The value of shame and shame punishments was fundamentally questioned by both prison and punishment reformers. It should be noted that shame came to be devalued and denigrated, primarily because it was unpredictable and because its effectiveness could not be easily calculated or measured. There then arose a greater appreciation of the importance of the timing, the duration and the location of punishment. This led some to believe shame punishments were ineffective because they were altogether too brief, and sometimes fortified the sufferer against the remorse which was deemed fundamental to the effectiveness of punishment. A similar species of thought came to believe that confinement away from the world and from other prisoners was far more likely to elicit guilt, atonement and redemption. However, as we also noticed, it would be far too easy to simply equate the idea of prison and punishment reform with the universal turn against the supposed barbarity of shame punishment. In places, shame was seamlessly incorporated into new regimes, or survived as an unacknowledged component within these. In other places the argument against shame punishment is an unexpected part of the late eighteenth century's criticism of its own 'Bloody Code' and the fact that this was very obviously no longer fit for purpose. For some reformers, tackling the 'Bloody Code' was far more important, whilst some found themselves arguing that the reintroduction and reinvention of systematic shame punishments would save society from the perils of a judicial system that was morally and procedurally bankrupt. Nonetheless, for all of these ideological positions, stigmatisation of the past and its practices as anachronistic became the key motif in the evaluation of older policing and punishment regimes.

Whilst we might describe this as the governing authorities witnessing, and experiencing, a crisis of shame and shame punishments, the findings of this book suggest we should be quite wary of accepting that a simple modernisation model (or indeed an alternative Foucauldian model of change) resulted from this. The feeling and reality of shame still governed social relations after this point and both found their way into the work and operation of institutions. Indeed, they may have been rejuvenated and reinvented by the cumulative social anxieties of the nineteenth century. In this respect, it was not simply the growth and development of the working-classes that was important, but also the development of middle-class aspirational cultures which craved respectability. In this area, we argue that shame became recast and modernised, not as a feeling of revulsion against poor conduct, but as a fear that went alongside a sense of social position, reputation and respectability. Conceivably, the nineteenth century bourgeois had a greater and deeper sense of shame than the peasant rustic of the previous three generations. Fear of debt, bankruptcy and the loss of social position stalked the drawing rooms of the middling sort and we can readily see this in action showcased in the later examples discussed in this book. Habits intended to deliver restraint, moderation and sobriety, became fundamental to middle-class bourgeois identity. All this further undermines the supposedly simple modernising transition from shame to guilt cultures. Respectability and guilt did not supplant shame, but on the contrary actively provided and stimulated situations in which the character of shame was of enhanced importance.

Within this paradigm, was an important alteration in the perception of time and the individual's approach to it. Some 30 years ago, Edward Thompson sketched out for us how the Industrial Revolution had brought the management of time to both industrial production and the lives of the urban working class.[2] Only latterly has the impact of this renewed approach to the culture of time been applied to the middle-classes and their formative years. Becoming middle class, involved planning for the future, forgoing consumption and restraining habits and appetites. Those who were unable or unwilling to do these last acts, were those who deserved opprobrium and marginalisation within this newly developing culture. In sum, such behaviour and short-term approaches to life became increasingly associated with transgression and with criminality. Such views have persisted with surprisingly little qualification. One commentator in the early 1990s was ready to note that:

> Those with low self-control find it difficult to invest in conventionality because they discount future rewards in favour of immediate pleasures. Since they have fewer investments in the

> future, persons with low self-control have much less at risk
> than those with greater self-control...they have less to lose.[3]

If we follow this hypothesis, then those whose planning or short-term approach to life in the emergent bourgeois society was unsuccessful, risked marginalisation or utter alienation. This left them in awkward situations where society would still be likely to shame them, or otherwise, their own sense of shame might well provoke them to extreme action.

Moreover, what our more modern case-studies in this book point to (for instance the example of the Rev. William Hughes, of John Le Roi and of the mid-century British monarchy) is the persistence of conceptions of shame, arguably heightened by new regimes of politeness, etiquette and intolerance. But significantly their shaming, in a modernised form, consisted of appearances in court or, in the case of the British monarchy, appearance in the metaphorical dock of public opinion. Once again, anachronism was an important trope within each of these proceedings, since it railed against the no longer acceptable behaviour of blackguard pluralist priests, brutal husbands prepared to use primitive punishment methods and the parasitism of Hanoverian 'throwback' princes. Each of these examples produced outrage and mirth: the twin reactions of a society that considers itself sophisticated, modern and civilised. What these particular chapters demonstrate is that the supposedly narrow and primitive feelings and responses engendered by shame could become thoroughly sophisticated and modernised. Their existence could be enriched and commodified for wider consumption and they also could also be associated with the workings, and criticisms of, the most modern of institutions.

Thus far in this volume, rather than shame being modernised out of existence, we have seen it become rather intimately involved in the changing nature of later nineteenth century social relationships. But we should remember that a host of agencies (from moral reformers to evangelicals) as well as some historians (such as John Carter Wood) suggest the arrival of a more civilised outlook which distanced social responses from violence and other uncivilised reactions.[4] So how did conceptions of civilised and modern society seek to marginalise the apparent influence and power of shame? As befits our approach in this book of using and unpacking the nuances of specific examples, the next section discusses precisely one of the instances in which this happened. This occurred at the end of the nineteenth century and acts as an illustration of how a wholly artificial and ideologically driven watershed in the history of shame was created. Specifically, it outlines an attempt to implement a version of modernisation that considered social development to be a process occurring in predetermined stages. Thus, this had clear conceptions of what ought to be considered primitive and uncivilised.

II

When Thomas Hardy wrote and published *The Mayor of Casterbridge* in the latter decades of the nineteenth century, he created two significant incidents where the plot of the novel turned in new directions.[5] When the leading protagonist, Michael Henchard, drunkenly sells his wife and young child at a hiring fair, Hardy invoked the custom of wife-sale, allowing it to have lasting and catastrophic consequences for those involved. Similarly, a later episode in the book portrays Henchard's ex-partner and now rival, Donald Farfrae, engaged in a romantic relationship with Henchard's former flame Lucetta, who he subsequently marries. Lucetta herself emerges as an individual distracted and obsessed by the maintenance of reputation and the potential for shame to unravel her position and status. This strongly influences her attitude to Henchard as she learns more about his past transgressions. The former relationship between Henchard and Lucetta is publicly disclosed upon the privacy of Lucetta's love letters being breached. As a result the two are portrayed by the local populace through a Skimmington ride, in which both are paraded through the streets in effigy tied together, back-to-back, upon a cart.[6] Confronting this display proves too much for the pregnant Lucetta who, unable to tolerate the shame and ridicule of the local populace, immediately swoons and dies from an epileptic seizure. Both episodes dramatically foreground the concept of shame and interweave this deliberately, and tellingly, into the plot of the novel. This incident probably constitutes an important way that late nineteenth century urban audiences gained their perceptions of how shame operated within rural society.

Certainly this novel has coloured popular perceptions of these two folk customs and arguably the wider perception of nineteenth century folk customs in general. Hardy is often portrayed, quite rightly, as an ardent historiciser and eulogiser of rural habits and behaviours that he readily assumed were headed for oblivion. Everything from gentle courtship rituals, through picturesque superstitions, to unfamiliarly stoical behaviour, were utilised as contextual description or intricate plot device. However, we should also note that Hardy is also the stern moralist, with the wife-sale episode in particular carrying a message that evangelical reformers would have applauded. Later anthropologists and (as we shall see) folklore scholars would confirm this message.

As the first cultural historians who looked at both Skimmington rides and wife-sale testified, Hardy described much older incidents rendering our understanding of them unhelpfully coloured by his portrayal. Henchard's sale of his wife is pictured as a drink fuelled episode which was shocking to onlookers and a cause of intense misery to his wife. Upon realising his tragic behaviour and its consequences, Henchard forswears alcohol for the rest of his life and the reader is emphatically left to feel the tide of shame that engulfs this central character. Nonetheless, E.P. Thompson and S.P. Menefee rescued wife-sale from this association with poor and reprehensible behaviour. They have successfully demonstrated that the majority of wife-sales were consensual affairs, quite regularly instigated by the wife, and they represented an exchange transaction in a society in which marriage remained for many an economic partnership. Within this conception, the money paid to a 'deserted' husband functioned as legitimate compensation for the loss of earning potential or economic activity undertaken by the wife within the domestic sphere.[7] Despite this, it would be untrue to argue that wife-sale became wholly legitimised through this historical discovery. Thompson also discussed cases from Devon and Yorkshire which clearly contained distinct elements of shaming which were evident in the proceedings, and the forlorn behaviour of the wife concerned.[8]

However, a central theme of the latter stages of Thompson's chapter indicates how the entire practice itself was viewed erroneously, as a shameful example of the barbarity of rural behaviour. Citing the attitudes of some folklorists, evangelical reformers, and indeed the subject's earlier historians, Thompson described the portrayal of 'formless animal promiscuity' as something of a 'lampoon'.[9] Although this criticism was largely inspired by the moralistic distaste of these commentators, Thompson was adamant that nineteenth century attempts to legislate against wife-sale, and remove it from popular view, amounted to assaults by vested interests upon the survival of informal plebeian culture.

The history and trajectory of the skimmington ride throughout the century was slightly different. The incident portrayed in *The Mayor of Casterbridge* involved the local villagers uncovering and displaying a supposedly illicit liaison between Henchard and Lucetta. As we are aware, historians have since spent considerable time demonstrating that the English 'Skimmington' or the 'Charivari' were all variants of the community expressing its disapproval of husbands who allowed themselves to be beaten or chastised by their wives. The skimmington (a type of ladle in this instance turned to an object of violence) was itself an extremely potent visual symbol of unregulated female power.[10] As we have discovered in Chapter 2, the ritual itself involved the participation of the whole neighbourhood and frequently included comedic dress or other symbols of inversion (such as being made to ride backwards). All these expressed the community's displeasure at a male in its midst unable to establish or uphold gender and communal norms. In turn, the male victim of this ritual is often considered to be an individual 'shamed' twice by the ignominy of receiving female aggression, and the hostile mocking of his local community.

Thompson, in particular, viewed the two phenomena (wife-sale and 'rough music' or skimmington rides) as stylised forms of behaviour that had been overwritten by subsequent interpretation, and such exclusion to be driven by a civilising model and mission. Wife-sale had received the condescension of bourgeois society's ideal of companionate marriage and legally sanctioned divorce. Alongside this, feminist critiques of the practice emphasised its status as a display of masculine social and economic power against a largely defenceless victim. Thompson saw the conventional modernising interpretations and the later feminist ones, as robbing late eighteenth century, Regency and Victorian plebeians of their autonomy. Wife-sale's status as popular divorce was a visible display of such individuals' managing their own domestic, economic and emotional arrangements without the interference of external authority. Menefee's work in this area also served to confirm that whilst such sales were not governed by law or authority, the writ of degrees of custom, and contemporary understanding of them, ran deeply into these practices.[11]

When he considered the impact of skimmington rides and 'rough music', Thompson again pointed to their deeper association with resistance, the defence of rights and the defence of customary practices against violation and innovation. This interpretation owed its lineage to Thompson's previously noted assertion of an historical attempt to draw the political sting from such events. This was characterised as modernising condescension and the denial of autonomy to the working classes. It also fitted his agenda of a so-called 'class struggle without class' operating in the late eighteenth century, but arguably surviving still in supposedly pre-industrial contexts thereafter. This largely explains the appearance of pieces on customary right alongside a reassertion of the 'class struggle without class' thesis in *Customs in Common*.[12]

In his introduction to this work, Thompson noted how the historic-isation practiced upon folk customs seemed intent upon robbing them of any genuinely functional place within modern society. This made them obviously picturesque, notable, curious and separate incidents, yet importantly it denied them their attendant (and sometimes threatening) wider meanings.

> Thus folklore at its very origin carried this sense of patronising distance, of subordination.... As one folklorist wrote at the end of the nineteenth century, his object was to describe:
>
> > The old customs which still linger on in the obscure nooks and corners of our native land, or which have survived the march of progress in our busy city's life.[13]
>
> To such collectors we are indebted for careful descriptions of well-dressings or rush bearings or harvest homes or, indeed, late examples of skimmington ridings. But what was lost, in considering (plural) customs as discrete survivals, was any strong sense of custom in the singular (although with many forms of expression), custom not as post anything but as *sui generis* – as ambience, mentalité, and as a whole vocabulary of discourse, of legitimation and of expectation.[14]

After Hardy, the generation of folklorists who investigated wife-sale and the skimmington ride worked as archetypal archaeologists and rescue workers who tried to piece together the last vestiges of what they determinedly perceived to be dying customs. What directly inspired their work is sometimes an opaque mystery, yet trying to piece this together from guesswork and their catalogued conclusions, represents a chance to see in action a conscious attempt to actively eclipse forms of shame and their presence. The language and idioms used to delineate what they saw as anachronism, the changing context in which they wrote, alongside their mores and expectations, all give us clues as to the ways in which society perceived it had 'modernised' beyond shame.

Thompson had already noticed that it was also over-simplistic to view modernisation as the process whereby polite official forms of action supplanted the organic and informal. 'Rough music' and skimmington rides slowly transformed themselves during the nineteenth century into the communal censure of wife beaters and otherwise violent husbands. Yet Thompson persuasively suggests this was in response to specific strains that were the products of this particular social and economic context. Specifically, gender relations altered so that more traditional structures characterised by patriarchal society were becoming questioned. At the same time, geographical mobility may have removed women from the protection offered by male kin and thus made them vulnerable.[15] In this respect, the informal adaptation of forms of resistance and policing seem to have actually predated official attempts to tackle the problem at hand – a phenomenon evident in instances and circumstances described elsewhere in this volume.

In some respects, the most intriguing suggestion we get from Thompson is the idea that the existence of 'rough music' and skimmington rides represented contexts and instances where people strongly believed that some part of the law still belonged to them; another assertion that was obviously inconvenient for modernisation. Tellingly, Thompson is not romantic about this in the slightest, noting that this gave scope for the indulgence of irrational prejudice. From this perspective, the state came to intervene to protect individuals from the self. However, there was also an increasing importance of the private, and the opportunities it offered for negotiating and mitigating personal, sexual and familial problems, without risking exposure to the public humiliation of shame.

Moreover, in considering these attempts to marginalise practices, Martin Ingram has reminded us that we have always been in danger of overstressing the class dichotomy that labelled the skimmington ride as a 'rough' pursuit. Instead, he has emphasised that it so often expressed shared, rather than conflicting values.[16] This was evident in Chapter 2 where often shaming rituals were an officially sanctioned prelude to a court case. In explaining this, Ingram focussed upon the informal way in which such customary action supplemented the legal status of individuals and communities. These types of activities may have come to the fore where orthodox legal solutions appeared to be vague or ambiguous. As we also saw in Chapter 2 shame rituals increasingly existed where authority was absent and where justice was yet to be centralised and visible. This is, in part, explains why it appears that church ministers so regularly get involved in these types of rituals when the decline of church authority occurred in other spheres. Much of this could also be observed within the imagery of both skimmington rides and 'rough music', where horse-borne onlookers signified authority alongside the rest of the event's capacity for disorder and anarchy. This was also likely to be tolerated in a society which had evolved many fewer institutions and regulatory mechanisms, compared to the later nineteenth century. Very often such customs were also aimed at restoring different varieties of governance and demonstrated '...a system of collective values which were stronger than the vagaries of individuals.'[17] Usefully, Ingram has also suggested there may be a 'dark figure' in reverse operating around the issue of skimmington rides, charivari and 'rough music'. He states that suggesting the possible commonplace nature of such occurrences, may lead to their underreporting. By this assertion, Ingram may have altered the context for our study of the phenomena. If this contention carries any grain of truth, then the study and investigation of these supposed folk relics was a more regular and obvious occurrence than the folklorists actually let on. This suggests the possibility (but only possibility) that contemporaries spoke less about skimmington, charivari and 'rough music' than they did about what Thompson dismissed as 'well-dressings or rush bearings or harvest homes.'[18] Alternatively if underreporting has any basis in fact then folklorists may possibly have underreported to portray such customs as dying out, suggesting their reportage had more of a modernisation mission than many have realised.

A significant contribution to the historiography of interpersonal shaming, albeit for a slightly earlier period, has examined the phenomenon of public insult and legal remedies for those insulted.[19] As we have seen, Robert Shoemaker has suggested that individuals became less inclined to insult individuals, or to question their reputation within the public sphere, from the early nineteenth century onwards. He also noticed that part of this changed as a result of the rising prominence of both slander and libel. According to Shoemaker both of these appear to have been a consequence of developing cultures of politeness; a phenomenon which occurred at precisely the same time as London's citizens were absenting themselves from wider responsibilities for preserving order.[20] This, arguably, contradicts the findings of Ingram since it suggests covert and private criticism moved indoors, leaving 'rough music' to become a wholly plebeian pursuit.

> The power of collectivities such as neighbourhoods, guilds and crowds to shape individual reputations and behaviour was undermined, to be replaced by other forces: by new collectivities such as voluntary societies and class, by the printed word and by individual self-examination. Londoners still worried about their reputations, but their frames of reference had changed.[21]

This is portrayed as an almost inevitable product of modernity's onset, with everything from improvement in street management and cleaning, to the sophisticated burgeoning market in print culture having a modernising influence. Shoemaker argues particularly that this new world of print was where reputations were discussed. The power and importance of print is scarcely in dispute, yet within this analysis he would appear to offer a far too neat and cursory closure of the issue of shame.[22] Taken together, his conclusions suggest a marked feeling of repugnance against old practices, alongside the adoption of print culture as a method of mediating reputation. This, however, implies that shame wholly disappeared from the realm of punishment and that politeness ensured that print culture was the sole forum in which reputation was successfully negotiated away from more primitive concepts of shame. An analysis of the material included in Chapters 5, 6, 7, 8 and this chapter, would cast considerable doubt upon the sweeping nature of this conclusion. As we have shown, shame lived on as a concept that was still important within more rational regimes of punishment and in the conduct of social and interpersonal relations. Print culture also provided more means and ways for older versions of shame to survive and mutate, displaying distinct elements of both old and new practices.

The idea of legislation and the state 'catching up' with organic customary policing of social problems remains an important consideration. In their chronologically extended study of abstract justice, wife beating and charivari, Russell P. Dobash and Rebecca Emerson Dobash noted that the coming of effective legislation which formalised wife beating as a crime was a phenomenon specific to the second half of the nineteenth century.[23] The 1850s saw legislation to protect women and children from aggravated assaults culminating in the Matrimonial Causes Act of 1857. This was augmented by a similarly titled act in 1878 and a landmark case in 1891 (*Regina v Jackson*) which established that husbands could no longer physically restrict their wife's freedom.[24] This may, in part, go some way to explaining the waning importance of skimmington rides and 'rough music' as a loss of function, occurring as legislative action and formal authority began to police the 'gap' that the shaming ritual had previously occupied. This may have eclipsed shame's importance in this area, but this did not stop its appearance elsewhere as our latter chapters have demonstrated.

We can see further evidence of a modernising disdainful attitude towards the shame inherent in 'rough music' and skimmington rides amongst the writings of late nineteenth century folklorists and collectors, within their anthologies, articles and manuals. Writing in 1959 for instance, Violet Alford re-assessed the phenomenon of 'rough music' with obviously new eyes, rejecting the views of the previous generation of modernisers and 'well brought up people' who 'preferred to pronounce it dead and gone.'[25] Alford clearly displays respect for the defiance of such customs which had resisted '...church edicts, penances, threat of excommunication...civil imprisonments, fines.'[26] Yet her survey of many other folk customs, within this article, also point to some intriguing clues about why widespread knowledge of many such customs may have waned in the late nineteenth century and wholly disappeared in the twentieth. In surveying the customs associated with marriage throughout Europe, Alford noticed that there were a host of them associated with lampooning the unmarried state or assisting with the perceived infertility of young wives after a year of marriage.[27] The maintenance of such customs in their pure form required a uniformity of behaviour that was hard to sustain in the twentieth century. Perhaps on a more mundane level, the continuation of such customs required levels of local knowledge and surveillance that were simply beyond individuals and communities with an increasing range of other preoccupations. But this speaks about the occasions and instances of shame moving away from their earlier location but not explicitly about their disappearance. Whilst many may have lost their interest and desire to police morality within their neighbourhood, they were by now exposed to a range of media that still discussed such matters and sought to encourage moral judgements.

Other writers about folklore more obviously show elements of condescension and disdain, or display an acute awareness of it at work. In his important article, which tried to observe folkloric evidence within social protest (arguably the mirror image project of that which preoccupied E.P. Thompson), A.W. Smith noted how the earlier folklore scholars and researchers had operated with a crude class bias within their work:

> It is a nice point to consider whether these early folklorists were more impressed by the familiarity of what they observed among the savages or by the proven barbarity of their peasant compatriots. One thing however is very plain, the pioneers of serious folklore collected their material by leaning across a great chasm that divided the learned from the vulgar and the master from the servant.[28]

Certainly it is possible to see elsewhere how far folklorists worked with an in-built condescension. Writing in 1904, Andrew Lang noted that the modern method of folklore studies involved looking at the 'irrational and anomalous' in one's own culture and deciphering it by looking at its purpose within other less advanced cultures. He suggested the folklorist's method should be 'to compare the seemingly meaningless customs or manners of civilised races with the similar customs and manners which exist among the uncivilised and still retain their meaning.'[29] These key phrases strongly suggest an assumption that the very nature of the subject was the process of looking at practices that had been discarded or left behind. Some folklorists openly adopted and espoused a developmental and modernising approach to their study of supposedly lost and backward cultures. In places they exhibited an attachment to a species of social Darwinism which simultaneously steered and gave ideological justification to this approach. Writing in 1930, Alexander Krappe was prepared to envisage the folk customs of any contemporary era as being representative of a stage of development comparable to those previously recognised in other societies. He also proclaimed the assumed backwardness of rural societies where 'rural populations are still addicted to beliefs and practices long since given up by the bulk of the city population.'[30] In this, we can hear echoes of early twentieth century anthropologists and indeed the 'figurations' (or stages) that Norbert Elias argued societies inevitably passed through.[31]

Charlotte Burne, a one-time president of the Folklore Society, was capable of being equally, if not more, dismissive in her influential *Handbook of Folklore*. This work's opening pages declare folklore to be the comprehension of the beliefs, customs and stories of 'backward peoples' or the 'uncultured classes of more advanced peoples.' They were also not so much sanctioned by 'positive law or authentic history' but by 'habit and tradition'.[32] In other words, what E.P. Thompson might see as an analysis which consciously and deliberately drew the sting from such customs as skimmington rides or wife-sale. Burne also described the idea of such customs from 'the lower culture' as 'eccentric' and requiring the indulgence of the observer who should realise they are 'sensible and reasonable from the point of view of the folk who practice them'.[33] Burne's list of folklore customs were, interestingly, all affirmative and did not contain any rites or procedures for negotiating problems, challenges or difficulties.[34] This looks like a further attempt to note the success of a modernising project that produced more civilised methods of defusing conflict, leaving the remnant of custom to appear as anodyne and picturesque.

Nonetheless, even within the world of the folklore scholar we are given warnings that make us guard against the complacency that accepts the entire passing of local community shaming. Writing in 1979, Theo

Brown generalised about how the rural community interloper, a more regularly conspicuous individual during the course of the twentieth century, would remain fair game for the customary backlash of the community. In particular the Non-conformist minister or others who excelled or 'got above themselves' (such as one unfortunate rector's overzealous wife described in the article) would find themselves on the receiving end of community opprobrium. However, what was really striking in Brown's analysis was his perception of continuities of behaviour:

> Any remote villages in Britain, where the population is sustained between a handful of families, whose names can be seen in the earliest registers, extremely inbred, may present a smiling welcome to the summer visitors, but, at home, amongst themselves, they speak their own language, hold on to their thousand year beliefs and prejudices and family vendettas, and all combine to freeze out the meddling outsider.[35]

Thus this gives us a clear impression of early twentieth century society believing it was modern and that it had eradicated most forms of barbaric behaviour forever. Through its attempts to study such behaviour, it had developed a vocabulary of curiosity layered with condescension. This enabled it to convince audiences that primitive feelings, such as shame, had been removed along with their unwanted and unwarranted systems of cruelty. The impact of these arguments almost ensured the marginalisation of shame as a concept since it became associated with this archetype of the primitive and anachronistic.

III

Whilst considerable efforts were made during the twentieth century to further distance society from shame and remove its psychological shadow, this was scarcely the end of the story. As we have seen shame could be reinvented and recast within new media and new idioms. It remained as a cultural possibility for individuals and institutions to draw on as required. Whilst this reflected its existence after the nineteenth century had debated its role in punishment this very same debate would be revisited, albeit with somewhat different conclusions. From the perspective of the twenty-first century, it is true that enough evidence has surfaced to suggest that the idea of shame as a tool society might yet use again, has become somewhat fashionable in recent years. Some of the modern theorising about shame and its place in punishments has sprung from legal thinking, but also from its application in psychotherapy.[36] Recent legal speculation has stepped away from the purer modernisation arguments to suggest that shame punishments have an inherently educational function, and these views appear to have interesting theoretical allies. For this branch of modernisation theory, shame was a necessary stage in social development, yet one which still resonates in contemporary society with the commonplace shaping of the individual's behavioural choices. As Stephen Mennell and John Goudsblom noted in their reply to a critique of Elias:

> Can it be denied that in every known society, each member undergoes an individual, lifetime, civilising process? In the social scientific literature this is more usually referred to as 'socialisation', 'enculturation', or 'personality formation'.[37]

Even the contemporary construction of legislation against outcast groups in the West, has taken on a specifically shame-based dimension. Indeed it is still more interesting that some of this springs from community initiatives that are themselves slightly distrustful of governmental will and its ability to protect that community. The enactment of 'Megan's law', for example, which gave communities the right to know the whereabouts of convicted paedophiles within their neighbourhood, represents a classic contemporary demonstration of this in action.[38] This legislation conveyed a firm message to the individual concerned, that they were the subject of surveillance and thus 'imprisoned' within community norms and standards. Similarly, many of the tendencies in legal thinking, which from time to time advocate retributive and restorative justice in its various guises, owes much to this central core of theories and practices.[39]

Many of the reasons for this may themselves strongly suggest the importance of studying the history of shame and the changing circumstances which give rise to it. Paradoxically, many theorists suggest that shame may actually have become more potentially potent to a contemporary society that displays little or no conception of either embarrassment or dishonour. Initially this is perhaps because, as a clear consequence of modernity, aspects of superstition, fear and the power of communally expected standards of behaviour were themselves described as primitive. These were incompatible with the creation of the modern autonomous enlightened individual – the sort of figure we expect to result from Elias's 'Civilising Process'. Yet, some who feel that modernity has either stalled or unravelled have pointed to what is considered to be the western twenty-first century's re-acquisition of its carnivalesque darker ages. In re-visiting the poor habits of our collective past, so it is argued, we are apt to indulge in humour associated with the bathroom and the bedroom and as a result, have become the unfortunate progenitors of a de-civilising process.[40] We should also consider the possibility that such arguments about the re-emergence of shame are sometimes allied to the description of a post-modern society. This might be because shame can be characterised as a method of forsaking the primacy of fact and rationality in favour of an interest in narrative and spectacle.

Alongside such developments, there is also a series of arguments that point to what might be described as a contemporary crisis in conventional penal thinking. American academics have been bold enough to openly resurrect, and in some cases actively champion, the discussion of shame punishments and their efficacy. The arguments usually commence with a statement that society is well aware that its conventional approach to punishing offenders has substantially failed, and that newer (or perhaps older) initiatives should be given serious consideration. Typical of these is the suggestion by James Whitman that:

> ...there are surely very few people who believe any longer that prisons serve as 'penitentiaries' of the kind they were intended to be, as places of monastic isolation where the quiet, persistent voice of the offenders conscience would teach him to know guilt.... perhaps, if we were all believing Christians, we might accept the view of guilt as an emotion experienced only in isolation.[41]

These suggestions are also frequently augmented by the assumption that once the ineffective nature of incarceration is admitted, then American society should also accept that it is uneconomic to punish in this manner.[42] There is also a quasi-theological slant to these arguments which is sometimes, paradoxically, blended with legal theorists who see the law as a more obvious series of discourses than mechanisms. Whilst the first has leant towards biblical precedent, the second has posited the genuine role and function of revenge in the judicial process. Both these groups criticise the comparative sloth of the legal system and the, only gradual, impact that results from the punishment of incarceration or deprivation of money or property.

But shame is also becoming a coherent component of assaults upon new individuals who threaten contemporary conceptions of 'commonwealth'. In addition, it is becoming an important method of targeting the unacceptable, once again where the writ of policing and law is arguably at its weakest. The call for regulation of the banking and financial sector reminds us of how the pillory was used to punish those whose actions constituted an assault upon the confidence needed by the social and economic system. Similarly, the use of websites containing hastily snapped photographs taken by women to shame individuals guilty of minor sexual assaults on the London Underground, is an area beyond conventional policing. Individuals have also been seen attempting to sell their unwanted and wayward wives on internet auction sites. Although the intervention of authority, or self-censorship, makes such individuals ultimately withdraw from this action, these are people whose frustration and shame uncontrollably went public in a manner Maggie Dickson, William Hughes and John Le Roi would recognise. Whilst it might be tempting to suggest that these reactions suggest a laudable rediscovery of concepts of community, this book also warns us that they step back to a time before society held sober and rational debates about the role and function of punishment. The opportunity to use new media in old ways has always been a feature of social relations, whilst the confidence that deep-seated reaction and feelings around conflict were wholly marginalised by modernity looks substantially misplaced.

The confluence of these factors also suggests a further reason for wanting to place shame more firmly back in the later history of social relations. Some archaeologists have noted how the late twentieth century fashion for explaining changes became dominated by ideas of gradual acculturation. In this, explanations that focussed upon conflict or conquest were dismissed as anachronistic, primitive and old fashioned. Likewise evidence of ancient acts of destruction and iconoclasm could be unwittingly hidden by the overenthusiastic reconstruction of artefacts to their original state before such acts occurred.[43] We might see a close analogy in the historiography of behaviour and those who have suggested a teleological development of this towards a state of modernity. Much study of eighteenth century behaviour has focussed upon the development of etiquette and manners, with conclusions which have reinforced the portrayal of a relentless modernising shift towards an emphasis upon cultures of decorum and politeness. This is something we might also observe in late nineteenth century folklorists and their concentration upon affirmative and consensual customs, avoiding coverage of those messier episodes where conflict was confronted and mitigated. Such conclusions have also clearly been aided and abetted by the central thrust of Elias's 'Civilising Process' of which this is a clear and distinct echo. Whilst our assertions about conflict and shame do not wholly unravel the essential direction of this historiography, we strongly hope that mapping the longevity of shame and our conclusions about it have significantly problematised the oversimplified versions of this story, and have substantially altered its chronology. Shame remained potent throughout the nineteenth century and it persisted to regularly trump politeness and its expectations.

If our questioning of the teleological models is to be complete it is also desirable to speculate on what Foucault and Foucauldians would make of this recent shift away from the eighteenth century's invention of surveillance. Much of their philosophical criticism has fallen upon the army of experts who, in the episteme of surveillance, won the battle of discourses to decide what should happen to the criminal and the crime. The contemporary push towards more summary and immediate justice, more closely related to the idea of local revenge, would perhaps have considerable appeal to Foucauldians as philosophers. Subjectivity and individualised approaches to the individual crime and criminal would, to their delight, restore a world lost before the prisoner became an object in the hands of the pathologising specialists.

The findings included here point towards problems and anomalies with both of these neat teleologies whether applied to the past or the present. They also, for the first time, give us important glimpses of the other side of this equation. If politeness triumphed (even temporarily) as so many historians tell us, it was faced with a powerful series of alternative possibilities and this volume constitutes a sustained argument that these should be appreciated and further investigated. These possibilities were a place where people were sometimes stoically resistant to modernising tendencies and these numerous acts crave and demand their own history to be told.

Notes

Chapter 1

1 S.J. Rasmussen (2007) 'Continuing Commentary – Revitalizing Shame: Some Reflections on Changing Idioms of Shame – Expressions of Disgrace and Dishonour in the Narratives of Turkish Women Living in Denmark', *Culture and Psychology*, 13, p. 233.
2 T.J. Scheff (1988) 'Shame and Conformity: The Deference-Emotion System', *American Sociological Review*, 53, 3, pp. 397–8.
3 K. Riezler (1943) 'Comment on the Social Psychology of Shame', *The American Journal of Sociology*, 48, 4, pp. 457–65.
4 Joseph Arch (1986) *From Plough Tail to Parliament: An Autobiography* (London: Cresset Library), pp. 18–19 [Bodleian Library (BOD): 2288 e. 1492].
5 Ibid, pp. 19–20.
6 W.I. Miller (1993) *Humiliation and Other Essays on Honor, Social Discomfort, and Violence* (Ithaca and London: Cornell University Press), p. 134.
7 Ibid, p. 137.
8 T.J. Scheff (1988) 'Shame and Conformity', p. 396.
9 Ibid, p. 399. See also T.J. Scheff (2000) 'Shame and the Social Bond: A Sociological Theory', *Sociological Theory*, 18, 1, pp. 87–9.
10 S.P. Garvey (1988) 'Can Shaming Punishments Educate?', *University of Chicago Law Review*, 65, 4, p. 766.
11 Scheff, 'Shame and the Social Bond', p. 92
12 W.I. Miller (1993) *Humiliation and Other Essays*, p. 178.
13 See J. Delumeau (1990) *Sin and Fear: The Emergence of Western Guilt Culture: 13th–18th Centuries* [translated by Eric Nicholson] (New York: St. Martin's Press).
14 See P. Collinson (1967) *The Elizabethan Puritan Movement* (Oxford: Clarendon Press).
15 P. Oppenheimer (1997) *An Intelligent Person's Guide to Modern Guilt* (London: Duckworth), p. 64.
16 W.I. Miller (1993) *Humiliation and Other Essays*, p. 199.
17 See A. Heller (1995) *The Power of Shame* (London: RKP).
18 See for instance respectively G.K. Paster (1993) *The Body Embarrassed: Drama and the Disciplines of Shame in Early Modern England* (Ithaca: Cornell University Press); I. Gibson (1978) *The English Vice: Beating, Sex and Shame in Victorian England and After* (London: Duckworth); P. Moore (2005) *Beyond Shame: Reclaiming the Abandoned History of Radical Gay Sexuality* (Boston, Mass.: Beacon Press); B. Heimannsberg and C.J. Schmidt (1993) (eds) *The Collective Silence: German Identity and the Legacy of Shame* (San Francisco: Jossey-Bass); R. Leys (2007) *From Guilt to Shame: Auschwitz and After* (Princeton, N.J. and Woodstock: Princeton University Press); J. Kenneally (2007) *The Honour and the Shame* (London: Headline Review); and A.C. Bailey (2005) *African Voices of the Atlantic Slave Trade: Beyond the Silence and the Shame* (Boston, Mass.: Beacon Press).

19   See for instance A. Clark (1987) *Women's Silence, Men's Violence: Sexual Assault in England, 1770–1845* (London and New York: Pandora); J. Bourke (2008) *Rape: A History from 1860 to the Present Day* (London: Virago); B.R. Burg (2007) *Boys at Sea: Sodomy, Indecency and the Courts Martial in Nelson's Navy* (Basingstoke: Palgrave Macmillan); T. Newburn and E.A. Stanko (1994) *Just Boys Doing Business? Men, Masculinities and Crime* (London: Routledge); E.A. Stanko (1990) *Everyday Violence: How Women and Men Experience Sexual and Physical Danger* (London: Pandora); J. Bailey (2003) *Unquiet Lives: Marriage and Marriage Breakdown in England, 1660–1800* (Cambridge: Cambridge University Press); S. D'Cruze (1998) *Crimes of Outrage: Sex, Violence and Victorian Working Women* (DeKalb: Northern Illinois University Press) and S. D'Cruze (2000) *Everyday Violence in Britain, 1850–1950: Gender and Class* (Harlow: Longman).

20   For further discussion see J. Bailey (2010) 'Cruelty and Adultery: Offences against the Institution of Marriage' and K. Stevenson (2010) '"Most Intimate Violations": Contextualising the Crime of Rape', both in A.M. Kilday and D.S. Nash (eds) *Histories of Crime: Britain 1600–2000* (Basingstoke: Palgrave Macmillan), pp. 39–59 and 80–99 respectively.

21   See for instance N. Zemon Davis (1971) 'The Reasons of Misrule: Youth Groups and Charivaris in Sixteenth-Century France', *Past and Present*, 50, pp. 41–75; S.P. Frank (1987) 'Popular Justice and Culture among the Russian Peasantry, 1870–1900', *Russian Review*, 46, 3, pp. 239–65; L.T. Johnson (1990) 'Charivari/Shivaree: A European Folk Ritual on American Plains', *Journal of Interdisciplinary History*, 20, 3, pp. 371–87 and M. McKnight (2005) 'Charivaris, Cowbellions and Sheet Iron Bands: Nineteenth-Century Rough Music in New Orleans', *American Music*, 23, 4, pp. 407–25.

22   See especially E.P. Thompson (1991) *Customs in Common* (London: Penguin), pp. 467–538; E.P. Thompson (1992) 'Rough Music Reconsidered', *Folklore*, 103, 1, pp. 3–26; M. Ingram (1984) 'Ridings, Rough Music and the "Reform of Popular Culture"', *Past and Present*, 105, pp. 79–113 and M. Ingram (1995) '"Scolding Women Cucked or Washed": A Crisis in Gender Relations in Early Modern England', in J. Kermode and G. Walker (eds) *Women, Crime and the Courts in Early Modern England* (Chapel Hill, North Carolina and London: The University of North Carolina Press), pp. 48–80.

23   For further discussion see E.P. Thompson (1991) *Customs in Common*, p. 469.

24   For further discussion of the types of 'offences' or 'bad behaviour' that could result in instances of 'rough music' see E.P. Thompson (1992) 'Rough Music Reconsidered', especially pp. 10–17; M. Ingram (1984) 'Ridings, Rough Music and the "Reform of Popular Culture"', pp. 87–92; V. Alford (1959) 'Rough Music or Charivari', *Folklore*, 70, pp. 506–7 and D.E. Underdown (1985) 'The Taming of the Scold: The Enforcement of Patriarchal Authority in Early Modern England', in A. Fletcher and J. Stevenson (eds) *Order and Disorder in Early Modern England* (Cambridge: Cambridge University Press), pp. 116–36.

25   For further discussion see E.P. Thompson (1992) 'Rough Music Reconsidered', p. 10.

26   M. Foucault (1991, third edition) *Discipline and Punish: The Birth of the Prison* (translated from the French by Alan Sheridan) (Harmondsworth: Penguin).

27   See for instance M.B. Merback (1999) *The Thief, The Cross and The Wheel: Pain and the Spectacle of Punishment in Medieval and Renaissance Europe* (London:

Reaktion Books), chapters three and four and R. McGowen (1987) 'The Body and Punishment in Eighteenth-Century England', *Journal of Modern History*, 59, pp. 651–79.

28 For further discussion see M.B. Merback (1999) *The Thief, The Cross and The Wheel*, chapters three and four; R. McGowen (1987) 'The Body and Punishment', pp. 651–79 and V.A.C. Gatrell (1994) *The Hanging Tree: Execution and the English People, 1770–1868* (Oxford: Oxford University Press), part one.

29 M.B. Merback (1999) *The Thief, The Cross and The Wheel*, p. 126.

30 See V.A.C. Gatrell (1994) *The Hanging Tree*, p. 261.

31 Ibid, p. 262.

32 Ibid, p. 263.

33 Perhaps one reason for this was that those who wanted to investigate the range of emotions caused by guilt, shame and humiliation so often found them most graphically exposed and investigated in fictional literature. See Paul Oppenheimer, *An Intelligent Person's Guide to Modern Guilt* at note 14 above. This uses the works of Kafka, T.S. Elliot, P.B. Shelley and Shakespeare as stories with which to investigate shame. These all contain variations upon the soliloquy which is a time honoured method of conveying the interior emotions and feelings of the individual.

34 T.J. Scheff (1988) 'Shame and Conformity', p. 402.

35 See Norbert Elias (2000) *The Civilizing Process* [translated by E. Jephcott] (Oxford: Wiley Blackwell).

36 W.I. Miller (1993) *Humiliation and Other Essays*, pp. 200–1.

37 See for instance the works contained in A.P. Donajgrodski (1977) (ed.) *Social Control in Nineteenth Century Britain* (London: Croom Helm).

38 Miller noticed in a 1991 newspaper sidebar a particularly poignant story. It was a report of a Chinese couple whose wedding gift to a nephew was half the value of that given by other relatives. On being utterly unable to endure this shame they committed suicide – the husband hanged himself and his wife drowned herself in a vat. Miller noticed that the Reuters report emphasised the unusual nature of the incident and played it for quasi-comic value. The remoteness of the situation, the small sums of money involved and the manner of the wife's demise provided comic elements in constructing a primitive tableau that could function as western self-congratulation. Shame here was made comic remote and exotic. See W.I. Miller (1993) *Humiliation and Other Essays*, p. 40.

39 The Erving Goffman works relevant here are (1959) *The Presentation of Self in Everyday Life* (London: Penguin); (1963) *Stigma: Notes on the Management of Spoiled Identity* (Harmondsworth: Penguin); (1963) *Behaviour in Public Places: Notes on the Social Organisation of Gatherings* (New York: Free Press) and (1967) *Interaction Ritual: Essays on Face-to Face Behaviour* (Princeton, N.J. and Oxford: Princeton University Press).

40 E. Goffman (1959) *The Presentation of Self*, p. 160.

41 Goffman characterises the tools that might be used to negotiate experience through such devices as 'taking turns' in social interaction, the use of 'possessional' territory and material 'personal effects', as well as the ability to control what is said about oneself in open conversation – the so-called 'information preserve'. See E. Goffman (1971) *Relations in Public: Microstudies of the Public Order* (Harmondsworth: Penguin), pp. 62–94.

42 See Jürgen Habermas (1962) [trans. 1989] *The Structural Transformation of the Public Sphere: An Inquiry into a category of Bourgeois Society* (Cambridge: Polity).
43 See respectively H. Berry (2001) 'Rethinking Politeness in Eighteenth-Century England: Moll King's Coffee House and the Significance of 'Flash Talk', *Royal Historical Society Transactions*, XI, pp. 65–81; P. Langford (2002) 'The Uses of Eighteenth Century Politeness', *Royal Historical Society Transactions*, XII, pp. 311–31 and E. Foyster, 'Creating a Veil of Silence? Politeness and Marital Violence in the English Household', *Royal Historical Society Transactions*, XII, pp. 395–415.
44 See endnotes 10 and 11 for classic statements of this definition.

Chapter 2

1 For further discussion of officially sanctioned punishments involving the use of shame in Britain during the early modern period and beyond, see for instance V.A.C. Gatrell (1994) *The Hanging Tree: Execution and the English People, 1770–1868* (Oxford: Oxford University Press); D. Garland (1985) *Punishment and Welfare: A History of Penal Strategies* (Aldershot: Gower); R. McGowen (1986) 'A Powerful Sympathy: Terror, The Prison, and Humanitarian Reform in Early Nineteenth Century Britain', *Journal of British Studies*, 25, 3, pp. 312–34; R. McGowen (1987) 'The Body and Punishment in Eighteenth Century England', *Journal of Modern History*, 59, pp. 651–79; R. McGowen (1999) 'From Pillory to Gallows: The Punishment of Forgery in the Age of the Financial Revolution', *Past and Present*, 165, pp. 107–40 and G. Ryley Scott (1968) *Flagellation: A History of Corporal Punishment in Its Historical, Anthropological and Sociological Aspects* (London: Tallis P.).
2 For further discussion of the nature and extent of 'charivari' see E.P. Thompson (1991) *Customs in Common* (London: Penguin), pp. 467–538.
3 See for instance the references to community shaming rituals in works such as John Webster (2009, new edition) *The Duchess of Malfi* (Oxford: Oxford Paperbacks) and Thomas Hardy (2007, new edition) *The Mayor of Casterbridge* (London: Penguin). For further discussion of the relationship between drama and the type of community rituals referred to in this chapter see J.J. MacAloon (1984) *Rite, Drama, Festival, Spectacle: Rehearsals Toward a Theory of Cultural Performance* (Philadelphia, Pennsylvania: Institute for the Study of Human Issues), especially Part I.
4 M. Ingram (1984) 'Ridings, Rough Music and the "Reform of Popular Culture" in Early Modern England', *Past and Present*, 105, p. 81.
5 For further discussion see for instance N. Zemon Davis (1971) 'The Reasons of Misrule: Youth Groups and Charivaris in Sixteenth-Century France', *Past and Present*, 50, pp. 41–75.
6 For further discussion see for instance L.T. Johnson (1990) 'Charivari/Shivaree: A European Folk Ritual on American Plains', *Journal of Interdisciplinary History*, 20, 3, pp. 371–87 and M. McKnight (2005) 'Charivaris, Cowbellions and Sheet Iron Bands: Nineteenth-Century Rough Music in New Orleans', *American Music*, 23, 4, pp. 407–25.
7 For further discussion see S.P. Frank (1987) 'Popular Justice and Culture among the Russian Peasantry, 1870–1900', *Russian Review*, 46, 3, pp. 239–65.

8   For further discussion see for instance E.P. Thompson (1991) *Customs in Common*, pp. 467–538; E.P. Thompson (1992) 'Rough Music Reconsidered', *Folklore*, 103, 1, pp. 3–26; M. Ingram (1984) 'Ridings, Rough Music and the "Reform of Popular Culture"', pp. 79–113 and M. Ingram (1995) '"Scolding Women Cucked or Washed": A Crisis in Gender Relations in Early Modern England', in J. Kermode and G. Walker (eds) *Women, Crime and the Courts in Early Modern England* (Chapel Hill, North Carolina and London: The University of North Carolina Press), pp. 48–80.

9   E.P. Thompson (1992) 'Rough Music Reconsidered', p. 3.

10 E.P. Thompson (1991) *Customs in Common*, p. 469.

11 See for instance ibid, especially the examples in notes 4–8 on p. 517 and other commentary on pp. 516–30 and P.M. Gorsky (1994) 'James Tuckfield's "Ride": Combination and Social Drama in Early Nineteenth-Century Bristol', *Social History*, 19, 3, pp. 319–38.

12 For further discussion of the types of 'offences' or 'bad behaviour' that could result in instances of 'rough music' see E.P. Thompson (1992) 'Rough Music Reconsidered', especially pp. 10–17; M. Ingram (1984) 'Ridings, Rough Music and the "Reform of Popular Culture"', pp. 87–92; V. Alford (1959) 'Rough Music or Charivari', *Folklore*, 70, pp. 506–7; D. Rollinson (1981) 'Property, Ideology and Popular Culture in a Gloucestershire Village, 1660–1740', *Past and Present*, 93, pp. 70–97; J.R. Kent (1983) '"Folk Justice" and Royal Justice in Early Seventeenth-Century England: A "Charivari" in the Midlands', *Midland History*, 8, pp. 70–85; D.E. Underdown (1985) 'The Taming of the Scold: The Enforcement of Patriarchal Authority in Early Modern England', in A. Fletcher and J. Stevenson (eds) *Order and Disorder in Early Modern England* (Cambridge: Cambridge University Press), pp. 116–36.

13 D.E. Underdown (1985) 'The Taming of the Scold', p. 117. For further discussion see also J.A. Sharpe (1986) 'Plebeian Marriage in Stuart England: Some Evidence from Popular Literature', *Transactions of the Royal Historical Society*, 36, pp. 69–90.

14 For further discussion see D.E. Underdown (1985) 'The Taming of the Scold', pp. 110–21 and L.E. Boose (1991) 'Scolding Brides and Bridling Scolds: Taming the Woman's Unruly Member', *Shakespeare Quarterly*, 42, 4, p. 195.

15 For further discussion and elaboration see S. Forsdyke (2008) 'Street Theatre and Popular Justice in Ancient Greece: Shaming, Stoning and Starving Offenders Inside and Outside the Courts', *Past and Present*, 201, pp. 3–50 and pp. 19–20 in particular.

16 Ibid, p. 23.

17 For further discussion see for instance E.P. Thompson (1991) *Customs in Common*, p. 478 and J.R. Kent (1983) '"Folk Justice" and Royal Justice in Early Seventeenth-Century England', p. 74.

18 More serious sexual offences, such as sodomy, bestiality or rape would be indicted in a criminal court. On occasion, accusations regarding these offences could also be accompanied by 'rough music'. See for instance D. Rollinson (1981) 'Property, Ideology and Popular Culture', pp. 70–97.

19 See E.P. Thompson (1991) *Customs in Common*, p. 482.

20 V. Alford (1959) 'Rough Music or Charivari', p. 505.

21 For further discussion see E.P. Thompson (1992) 'Rough Music Reconsidered', p. 10.

22 For further discussion and examples see M. Ingram (1984) 'Ridings, Rough Music and the "Reform of Popular Culture"', pp. 104–13.

23 Even in instances where women were the intended target of 'rough music', they were regularly displaced in the ritual and replaced by male relations, see D.E. Underdown (1985) 'The Taming of the Scold', p. 129 and p. 133.

24 See for instance ibid, p. 129.

25 M. Robinson (1985) (ed.) *The Concise Scots Dictionary* (Aberdeen: Aberdeen University Press), p. 61.

26 Ibid, p. 61.

27 See L.E. Boose (1991) 'Scolding Brides and Bridling Scolds', pp. 196–7.

28 For descriptions of the nature of this punishment in England see W. Andrews (1991) *Old Time Punishments* (New York: Dorset Press), pp. 42–50 and T.N. Brushfield (1864) 'On Obsolete Punishments, with Particular Reference to those of Cheshire: Part I – The Brank or Scold's Bridle', *Journal of the Archaeological Society of Chester*, 2, pp. 42–3.

29 For further discussion on the origins and initial implementation of the branks see T.N. Brushfield (1864) 'On Obsolete Punishments: Part I', pp. 35–6 and especially J.G. Harrison (1998) 'Women and the Branks in Stirling c.1600 to 1730', *Scottish Economic and Social History*, 18, pp. 114–31.

30 See for instance the evidence presented in this chapter and also J.G. Harrison (1998) 'Women and the Branks in Stirling', p. 115. In England, the punishment was similarly gendered and the sole preserve of women, see T.N. Brushfield (1864) 'On Obsolete Punishments: Part I', p. 46.

31 For further illustration of the wide variety of offences for which women could receive public punishment in Scotland see Rev. C. Rogers (1884) *Social Life in Scotland From Early to Recent Times*, Volume II (Edinburgh: William Paterson), pp. 35–7, 64–5; 230–4 and 240–6.

32 Mitchell Library (Glasgow): Burgh Records of Glasgow, G 941.435 REN.

33 R. Renwick, Sir J. Lindsay and G. Eyre-Todd (1931) *History of Glasgow: Volume II – From The Reformation to the Revolution*, Chapter XVI – Life in the Burgh in the Reign of James VI (Glasgow: Jackson, Wylie and Co.), p. 161.

34 National Archives of Scotland (NAS), Kirk Session Records (CH): CH 2/122/3.

35 NAS, Sheriff Court Records (SC): SC 20/5/1.

36 NAS: SC 62/10/13 and SC 62/10/14.

37 NAS, Justiciary Court Records (JC): JC 26/143-145/2601-2721.

38 For further discussion of these 'courts of immorality' see Rev. C. Rogers (1884) *Social Life in Scotland*, pp. 250–1.

39 For further discussion of the process of branking see L.E. Boose (1991) 'Scolding Brides and Bridling Scolds', pp. 205–8; J.G. Harrison (1998) 'Women and the Branks in Stirling', pp. 116–17 and T.N. Brushfield (1864) 'On Obsolete Punishments: Part I', especially p. 33.

40 E.J. Guthrie (1994) *Old Scottish Customs: Local and General* (London and Glasgow: Llanerch Publishers), p. 53.

41 For further discussion and elaboration on the nature and construction of branks, including reference to the more brutal Scottish examples in existence see D. Wilson (1851) *The Archaeology and Prehistoric Annals of Scotland* (Edinburgh: Sutherland and Knox), pp. 692–94; D. Wilson (1863) *Prehistoric Annals of Scotland* (London and Cambridge: Macmillan and Co.), p. 520; T.N. Brushfield (1864) 'On Obsolete Punishments: Part I', pp. 33–48;

L.E. Boose (1991) 'Scolding Brides and Bridling Scolds', pp. 205–10 and W. Andrews (1991) *Old Time Punishments*, pp. 38–64.

42　M. Ingram (1995) '"Scolding Women Cucked or Washed"', p. 58. But see also evidence in Chapter 8 of this book that may qualify this.

43　For further discussion see T.N. Brushfield (1864) 'On Obsolete Punishments: Part I', p. 36 and p. 46 respectively.

44　Most of the data accrued in this respect (some 80 per cent) related to sentencing orders found in Burgh Records and Kirk Session Records. The remainder related to Bills of Complaint in the Sheriff Court and the Justiciary Court, where victims entered petitions seeking the court's assurance of their future protection within a given community or parish. Sources were analysed through five-year sampling surveys based on locations in the north, south, east and west of the country (where records survived), in order to provide a national picture of the type of communal shaming punishments in existence. This survey revealed more than 300 pertinent instances of communal shaming of one form or another.

45　See J.G. Harrison (1998) 'Women and the Branks in Stirling', p. 114.

46　For further description and elaboration on the cucking-stool or ducking-stool as a shaming punishment see T.N. Brushfield (1864) 'On Obsolete Punishments, with Particular Reference to those of Cheshire: Part II – The Cucking-Stool and Allied Punishments', *Journal of the Archaeological Society of Chester*, 2, pp. 203–34; L.E. Boose (1991) 'Scolding Brides and Bridling Scolds', pp. 185–9 and W. Andrews (1991) *Old Time Punishments*, pp. 1–37.

47　NAS: JC 26/1037-1041.

48　For further discussion of the process of ducking see the references in note 46 above.

49　See for instance M. Ingram (1995) '"Scolding Women Cucked or Washed"', pp. 61–2.

50　E.J. Guthrie (1994) *Old Scottish Customs*, p. 53.

51　See J.G. Harrison (1998) 'Women and the Branks in Stirling', p. 118.

52　C. Larner (1984) *Witchcraft and Religion: The Politics of Popular Belief* (Oxford: Blackwell) [edited and with a foreword by A. Macfarlane], p. 86 cited in M. Ingram (1995) '"Scolding Women Cucked or Washed"', p. 66.

53　This conclusion is based on a survey of the source material listed above in note 44 in relation to misdemeanours committed by men between 1600 and 1900 across Scotland. Although far less likely than women to be publicly punished for indiscretions of a minor nature, when sentencing did occur, the majority of men (77%) were sentenced to the 'govis' or pillory.

54　For further discussion of the gender differences related to shame punishments see L.E. Boose (1991) 'Scolding Brides and Bridling Scolds', pp. 189–90.

55　For further discussion see A-M. Kilday (2007) *Women and Violent Crime in Enlightenment Scotland* (Woodbridge, Suffolk: Boydell Press), pp. 147–57.

56　See for instance the discussion in E.P. Thompson (1991) *Customs in Common*, pp. 467–72.

57　For further discussion see especially D.E. Underdown (1985) 'The Taming of the Scold', p. 127 and p. 134.

58　For further description of the process see M. Ingram (1984) 'Ridings, Rough Music and the "Reform of Popular Culture"', p. 86; E.P. Thompson (1991) *Customs in Common*, pp. 469–77; B.H. Cunnington (1930) '"A Skimmington" in 1618', *Folklore*, 41, 3, pp. 287–90 and D.G.C. Allan (1952) 'The Rising in the West, 1628–1631', *The Economic History Review*, 5, 1, p. 76.

59 See for example the description in E.P. Thompson (1991) *Customs in Common*, pp. 469–77 and M. Ingram (1984) 'Ridings, Rough Music and the "Reform of Popular Culture"', p. 102.

60 For further discussion see V. Alford (1959) 'Rough Music or Charivari', p. 507.

61 For further discussion see R. Mellinkoff (1973) 'Riding Backwards: Theme of Humiliation and Symbol of Evil', *Viator: Medieval and Renaissance Studies*, 4, pp. 153–76. For further discussion on the impact of this type of punishment upon its victims see E.P. Thompson (1991) *Customs in Common*, p. 488 and A. Fletcher (1994) 'Men's Dilemma: The Future of Patriarchy in England 1560–1660', *Transactions of the Royal Historical Society*, Sixth Series, 4, pp. 77–8.

62 See for instance J.R. Kent (1983) '"Folk Justice" and Royal Justice in Early Seventeenth-Century England', p. 74.

63 For further discussion and elaboration of the process of 'riding the stang' see E.P. Thompson (1991) *Customs in Common*, pp. 471–5; E.C. Cawte (1963) 'Parsons Who Rode the Stang', *Folklore*, 74, 2, p. 399; W. Andrews (1991) *Old Time Punishments*, pp. 180–8; E.W. Pettifer (1992 reprint) *Punishments of Former Days* (Winchester: Waterside Press), pp. 169–70 and for a detailed example see R. De Bruce Trotter (1901) *Galloway Gossip or the Southern Albanich: 80 Years Ago* (Dumfries: Courier and Herald), pp. 439–43 [Bodleian Library: 27005 e.19].

64 For further discussion and detail on the process of 'Ceffyl Pren' see E.P. Thompson (1991) *Customs in Common*, p. 471 and pp. 520–4 and especially S. Carter Hall (1860) *Tenby: Its History, Antiquities, Scenery, Traditions and Customs* (Tenby: Mason), pp. 137–41 [National Library of Wales (NLW): Dyb2005A978]; C. Redwood (1839) *History of the Vale of Glamorgan: Scenes and Tales among the Welsh* (London: Saunders and Otley), pp. 271–95 [NLW: Wb3403] and R.A.N. Jones (1991) 'Women, Community and Collective Action: The "Ceffyl Pren" Tradition', in A.V. John (ed.) *Our Mother's Land: Chapters in Welsh Women's History, 1830–1939* (Cardiff: University of Wales Press), pp. 17–41. We are very grateful to Dr Katherine Watson for providing us with the latter reference.

65 For further discussion of the types of offences for which skimmington-type punishments could result see E.P. Thompson (1992) 'Rough Music Reconsidered', especially pp. 11–18; E.P. Thompson (1991) *Customs in Common*, pp. 493–530; M. Ingram (1984) 'Ridings, Rough Music and the "Reform of Popular Culture"', p. 87 and pp. 89–92; D.E. Underdown (1985) 'The Taming of the Scold', p. 132 and V. Alford (1959) 'Rough Music or Charivari', p. 506.

66 For further discussion see D.E. Underdown (1985) 'The Taming of the Scold', p. 131 and E.P. Thompson (1992) 'Rough Music Reconsidered', especially pp. 7–8.

67 For further discussion of the longevity of skimmington-type punishments across the United Kingdom see especially E.P. Thompson (1991) *Customs in Common*, pp. 467–538.

68 See V. Alford (1959) 'Rough Music or Charivari', p. 508.

69 The sources used in the Scottish study are outlined in note 44 above. There were 136 cases of 'stang-riding' uncovered in this analysis. For examples of this

punishment across England and not just in the south see E.P. Thompson (1992) 'Rough Music Reconsidered', pp. 3–26 and E.P. Thompson (1991) *Customs in Common*, pp. 467–538.

70 This was the case in *all* of the examples referred to in note 69 above.
71 For further discussion of the male domination of English skimmington rides see D.E. Underdown (1985) 'The Taming of the Scold', p. 129 and p. 133.
72 More than 65 per cent of the 'stang-riding' punishments uncovered in relation to Scotland 1600–1900 related to rural areas. For further discussion of the link between 'Ceffyl Pren' and rural areas see S. Carter Hall (1860) *Tenby*, pp. 137–41 and C. Redwood (1839) *History of the Vale of Glamorgan*, pp. 271–95.
73 See E.P. Thompson (1991) *Customs in Common*, p. 530.
74 See *The Carmarthen Journal*, 6th April 1838 [NLW: Microfilm De. 22.]
75 For further discussion of the 'legitimising notion' associated with skimmington rides, 'stang-rides' and 'Ceffyl Pren' see E.P. Thompson (1992) 'Rough Music Reconsidered', p. 8; V. Alford (1959) 'Rough Music or Charivari', p. 507 and p. 511 and also M. Ingram (1984) 'Ridings, Rough Music and the "Reform of Popular Culture"', p. 93.
76 Although many more Scottish men were sentenced to the govis or pillory for their indiscretions, nearly a third of the men sentenced to communal shame punishments were ordered to 'ride the stang'. For an example of how men were treated in this process see the case recounted in R. De Bruce Trotter (1901) *Galloway Gossip*, pp. 439–43.
77 According to the evidence at hand, repeated instances of 'riding the stang' were not very common in Scotland, but there were 11 instances recorded in the source materials used for this study. Usually the level of violence and abuse escalated when it was necessary to repeat the punishment, much in the same way as the Jane Davies case reported above.
78 There are no instances of these kinds of practices in the Scottish evidence uncovered for this study, and with the exception of effigy use on occasion, the Welsh examples also minimise the dramatic content of 'Ceffyl Pren'. See for instance the references found in note 64 above.
79 For further discussion see for instance M. Todd (2002) *The Culture of Protestantism in Early Modern Scotland* (New Haven, Connecticut and London: Yale University Press).
80 See the information in note 44 above.
81 The Regality Court was a jurisdiction in Scotland in the early modern period which dealt chiefly with minor acts of inter-personal violence. For further discussion on this jurisdiction see A-M. Kilday (2007) *Women and Violent Crime*, pp. 28–9.
82 For the full record see 'Petition for a Toleration to the Stang, With the Proceedings of the Regality Court of Huntly Thereon MDCCXXXIV', in (1834) *Miscellany of the Maitland Club Consisting of Original Papers and Other Documents Illustrative of the History and Literature of Scotland Volume I* (Edinburgh: H. & J. Pillans), pp. 486–93.
83 See J.G. Harrison (1998) 'Women and the Branks in Stirling', p. 118 and p. 130 note 8.
84 For some discussion of the decline of communal public shaming punishments in Britain see E.P. Thompson (1991) *Customs in Common*, pp. 524–31.

Chapter 3

1 See for instance A-M. Kilday (2007) *Women and Violent Crime in Enlightenment Scotland* (Woodbridge, Suffolk: The Boydell Press), p. 75; A-M. Kilday (2008) '"Monsters of the Vilest Kind": Infanticidal Women and Attitudes towards their Criminality in Eighteenth-Century Scotland', *Family and Community History*, 11, 2, pp. 100–15; M. Jackson (1996) *New-Born Child Murder: Women, Illegitimacy and the Courts in Eighteenth-Century England* (Manchester: Manchester University Press), pp. 4, 31, 35, 48 and pp. 111–17 and 124–5; P.C. Hoffer and N.E.C. Hull (1984) *Murdering Mothers: Infanticide in England and New England, 1558–1803* (New York: New York University Press), pp. 157–8; K. Wrightson (1982) 'Infanticide in European History', *Criminal Justice History*, III, pp. 5–8 and U. Rublack (1999) *The Crimes of Women in Early Modern Germany* (Oxford: Clarendon Press), pp. 163–4.

2 See for instance A-M. Kilday (2007) *Women and Violent Crime*, p. 75; A-M. Kilday (2008) '"Monsters of the Vilest Kind"', p. 103; J.R. Ruff (2001) *Violence in Early Modern Europe* (Cambridge: Cambridge University Press), pp. 149–50 and R.W. Malcolmson (1977) 'Infanticide in the Eighteenth Century', in J.S. Cockburn (ed.) *Crime in England, 1550–1800* (London: Methuen), pp. 192–4 and 202–6.

3 See R. Mitchison and L. Leneman (1989) *Sexuality and Social Control: Scotland, 1660–1780* (Oxford: Basil Blackwell), p. 9. For further discussion see K.M. Boyd (1980) *Scottish Church Attitudes to Sex, Marriage and the Family, 1850–1914* (Edinburgh: Donald).

4 See for instance R.W. Malcolmson (1977) 'Infanticide in the Eighteenth Century', pp. 189–90, and especially M. Francus (1997) 'Monstrous Mothers, Monstrous Societies: Infanticide and the Rule of Law in Restoration and Eighteenth-century England', *Eighteenth-Century Life*, XXI, pp. 133–56.

5 For further discussion of the communal nature of infanticide investigations see A-M. Kilday (2008) '"Monsters of the Vilest Kind"', pp. 103–4; A-M. Kilday and K.D. Watson, 'Infanticide, Religion and Community in the British Isles, 1720–1920: Introduction', *Family and Community History*, 11, 2, pp. 88–91; S.M. Butler (2007) 'A Case of Indifference? Child Murder in Late Medieval England', *Journal of Women's History*, XIX, pp. 59–82; M. Jackson (1996) *New-Born Child Murder*, 60–83 and D.A. Symonds (1997) *Weep Not For Me: Women, Ballads and Infanticide in Early Modern Scotland* (University Park, PA: Pennsylvania State University Press), pp. 69–87.

6 For further discussion of the role of religious authorities in infanticide investigations see A-M. Kilday (2007) *Women and Violent Crime*, p. 63; A-M. Kilday (2008) '"Monsters of the Vilest Kind"', pp. 103–4; A-M. Kilday and K.D. Watson, 'Infanticide, Religion and Community', pp. 91–2 and M. Jackson (1996) *New-Born Child Murder*, p. 64.

7 See for instance the cases compiled in the mid-eighteenth century against Margaret Rob (National Archives of Scotland [NAS], Justiciary Court Records (JC): JC 11/11) and Jean Miln (NAS: JC 11/12).

8 For further discussion of the suggestion that detected Scottish infanticide rates may be higher than elsewhere due to the prevailing climate of scrutiny see A-M. Kilday (2008) '"Monsters of the Vilest Kind"', pp. 102–4;

A-M. Kilday and K.D. Watson, 'Infanticide, Religion and Community', p. 90 and A-M. Kilday (1998) 'Women and Crime in South-west Scotland: A Study of the Justiciary Records, 1750–1815' (Unpublished PhD thesis, University of Strathclyde), chapter six.

9 See A-M. Kilday (2007) *Women and Violent Crime*, p. 63. Aggravated punishments for infanticide (particularly when carried out with violence) were also prevalent elsewhere in Europe in the early modern period. For example, child killers were ordered to be drowned, beheaded, impaled or burned in various European courts from the late sixteenth century onwards: see J.R. Ruff (2001) *Violence in Early Modern Europe, 1500–1800*, p. 153.

10 See for instance the sentence delivered against David Edwards who was convicted of murder and robbery at the South Circuit Court in 1758. After execution, his body was to be hung in chains on the gibbet, to rot in public view [NAS: JC 12/9]. Similarly, in 1765, Alexander Provan was sentenced at the West Circuit Court for the murder of his wife. He was to have his right hand cut off prior to his execution and then once his body had been cut down from the gibbet, he was to be publicly dissected and anatomised by a medical professional [NAS: JC 13/15].

11 This conclusion is based on the findings of an exhaustive study into the early modern crime-related broadside literature held in the National Library of Scotland, see A-M. Kilday (2008) '"Monsters of the Vilest Kind"', pp. 100–15.

12 Parricide was an alternative legal appellation for the crime of child murder in early modern Scottish courtrooms, see D. Hume (1797, 1844 edition, 1986 reprint) *Commentaries on the Laws of Scotland, Respecting Crimes* (Edinburgh: The Law Society of Scotland), I, p. 291. The indictment papers for the trial of Margaret Dickson can be found at NAS: JC 3/12/115-174.

13 For further discussion of how infanticide suspects were investigated see M. Jackson (1996) *New-Born Child Murder*, chapter three.

14 See for instance (1724) *A Warning to the Wicked, or Margaret Dickson's Welcome to the Gibbet* (National Library of Scotland (NLS), Broadside Collection (NLSBC): RB1.106/96); (Undated) *Particulars of the Life, Trial, Character, and Behaviour of Margaret Dickson* (NLSBC: APS.4.98); *The Caledonian Mercury*, 6th August 1724 (NLS: Mf N. 776 No, 679 4051) or M. MacLaurin (1774) *Arguments and Decision in Remarkable Cases Before the High Court of Justiciary and other Supreme Courts in Scotland* (Edinburgh: J. Bell), no. 37, pp. 71–2.

15 For further details see NAS: JC 26/108/1263/5.

16 For further discussion of the potential medical rationales for infanticide see R. Smith (1982) 'Defining Murder and Madness: An Introduction to Medico-legal Belief in the Case of Mary Ann Brough, 1854', in R.A. Jones and H. Kuklich (eds) *Knowledge and Society: Studies in the Sociology of Culture Past and Present*, vol. 4 (Greenwich, CN and London: JAI Press Inc), pp. 173–225; T. Ward (1999) 'The Sad Subject of Infanticide: Law, Medicine and Child Murder', *Social and Legal Studies*, VIII, pp. 163–80; H. Marland (2004) *Dangerous Motherhood: Insanity and Childbirth in Victorian Britain* (Basingstoke: Palgrave Macmillan) and D. Rabin (2002) 'Bodies of Evidence, States of Mind: Infanticide, Emotion and Sensibility in Eighteenth-Century England' (pp. 73–92), H. Marland (2002) 'Getting Away With Murder? Puerperal Insanity, Infanticide and the Defence Plea' (pp. 168–92), and C. Quinn (2002) 'Images and

Impulses: Representations of Puerperal Insanity and Infanticide in Late Victorian England' (pp. 193–215), all M. Jackson (ed.) *Infanticide: Historical Perspectives on Child Murder and Concealment, 1550–2000* (Aldershot: Ashgate).

17   For further discussion of the nature and content of infanticide legislation in Scotland compared to England see A-M. Kilday (2010) 'Desperate Measures or Cruel Intentions: Infanticide in Britain since 1600', in A-M. Kilday and D.S. Nash (eds) *Histories of Crime 1600–2000* (Basingstoke: Palgrave Macmillan), pp. 60–79.

18   See NAS: JC 3/12/171-172.

19   The papers from the official jury verdict of this case can be found at NAS: JC 26/108/1264/2.

20   See NAS: JC 3/12/115-174 and JC 26/108/1263/4.

21   For further discussion of the use of still-birth as a defence strategy in infanticide trials see M. Jackson (1996) *New-Born Child Murder*, chapter four.

22   See the references in notes 1 and 2 above.

23   See the references in note 8 above.

24   See A-M. Kilday (2007) *Women and Violent Crime*, p. 70; M. Jackson (1996) *New-Born Child Murder*, pp. 29–30 and 43–4; J.R. Ruff (2001) *Violence in Early Modern Europe*, p. 149 and J.R. Dickinson and J.A. Sharpe (2002) 'Infanticide in Early Modern England: The Court of Great Sessions at Chester, 1650–1800', in M. Jackson (ed.) *Infanticide*, pp. 41–2.

25   For further discussion of the crime of 'exposure' see F. McLynn (1989) *Crime and Punishment in Eighteenth-Century England* (London: Routledge), p. 112; R.W. Malcolmson (1977) 'Infanticide in the Eighteenth Century', p. 188 and A-M. Kilday (2007) *Women and Violent Crime*, pp. 73–4.

26   For further discussion on infant neglect resulting in homicide see O. Pollak (1950) *The Criminality of Women* (Philadelphia: University of Pennsylvania Press), pp. 19–20; L. Rose (1986) *The Massacre of the Innocents: Infanticide in Britain 1800–1939* (London: Routledge and Kegan Paul), pp. 82–4 and A-M. Kilday (2007) *Women and Violent Crime*, pp. 66–70 and pp. 73–4.

27   For further discussion see A-M. Kilday (2007) *Women and Violent Crime*, pp. 66–70.

28   See for instance S.X. Radbill (1968) 'A History of Child Abuse and Infanticide', in R.E. Helfer and C.H. Kempe (eds) *The Battered Child* (Chicago: University of Chicago Press), p. 9; R.W. Malcolmson (1977) 'Infanticide in the Eighteenth Century', p. 195; K. Wrightson (1975) 'Infanticide in Earlier Seventeenth-Century England', *Local Population Studies*, XV, p. 15; J. Kelly (1992) 'Infanticide in Eighteenth-Century Ireland', *Irish Economic and Social History*, XIX, p. 18 and R.H. Helmholz (1987) 'Infanticide in the Province of Canterbury during the Fifteenth Century', in R.H. Helmholz (ed.) *Canon Law and the Law of England* (London: Hambledon), p. 160.

29   L. Gowing (1997) 'Secret Births and Infanticide in Seventeenth-Century England', *Past and Present*, CLVI, p. 106.

30   For further discussion see A-M. Kilday (2007) *Women and Violent Crime*, pp. 73–8.

31   No evidence of violence was referred to by any of the witnesses for the prosecution, including Alexander Scot (Doctor of Medicine) and Ann Pringle (Midwife), both of whom specifically examined the infant's remains. See NAS: JC 7/12/68-69 and JC 3/12/170-172.

32 For more detailed discussion of the legal defences offered for Maggie Dickson see NAS: JC 7/12/62-64 and JC 3/12/146-150.

33 NAS: JC 3/12/150.

34 NAS: JC 3/12/143 and JC3 /12/145.

35 See NAS: JC 3/12/171-172.

36 The 'Letters of Exculpation' can be found at NAS: JC 26/108/1263/7b where Elizabeth Moscrop, Easter Moscrop and William Boll were charged to appear before the court to give testimony in defence of Margaret Dickson. However, as is clear from NAS: JC 3/12/173 and JC 7/12/70, none of the three were actually called to give evidence.

37 For instance see NAS: JC 3/12/147 and JC 7/12/62.

38 See the references in note 14 above.

39 See NAS: JC 26/108/1263/4.

40 For further discussion of the purpose and function of gallows speeches see J.A. Sharpe (1985) '"Last Dying Speeches": Religion, Ideology and Public Execution in Seventeenth Century England', *Past and Present*, CVII, pp. 144–67; R.A. Bosco (1978) 'Lectures at the Pillory: The Early American Execution Sermon', *American Quarterly Review*, XXX, pp. 156–76; P. Lake and M. Questier (1996) 'Agency, Appropriation and Rhetoric Under the Gallows: Puritans, Romanists and the State in Early Modern England', *Past and Present*, CLIII, pp. 64–107; T. Laqueur (1989) 'Crowds, Carnivals and the State in English Executions, 1604–1868', in A. Beier, D. Cannadine and J. Rosenheim (eds) *The First Modern Society: Essays in English History in Honour of Lawrence Stone* (Cambridge: Cambridge University Press), pp. 305–55; P. Lake (1994) 'Deeds Against Nature: Cheap Print, Protestantism and Murder in Early Seventeenth-Century England', in K. Sharpe and P. Lake (eds) *Culture and Politics in Early Stuart England* (Basingstoke: Macmillan), pp. 257–83; L.B. Faller (1976) 'In Contrast to Defoe: The Rev. Paul Lorrain, Historian of Crime', *The Huntington Library Quarterly*, XL, pp. 59–78 and J. Kelly (2001) *Gallows Speeches form Eighteenth-Century Ireland* (Dublin: Four Courts Press), especially pp. 11–70.

41 C. Emsley (1996, second edition) *Crime and Society in England 1750–1900* (London: Longman), p. 259. See also J.A. Sharpe, '"Last Dying Speeches"', pp. 145–7.

42 R. McGowen (1986) 'A Powerful Sympathy: Terror, the Prison, and Humanitarian Reform in Early Nineteenth Century Britain', *Journal of British Studies*, XXV, p. 316.

43 At the Scottish Justiciary Court, it was actually part of the judge's sentence pronounced against a convicted individual, that his or her execution should take place on a market day. See A-M. Kilday (1998) 'Women and Crime in South-west Scotland', chapter six.

44 J. Bland (1984) *The Common Hangman: English and Scottish Hangmen Before the Abolition of Public Executions* (Essex: I. Henry Publications), p. 110. A crowd of 75,000 witnessed an execution in Glasgow as late as 1841, see N. Adams (1996) *Scotland's Chronicles of Blood: Torture and Execution in Bygone Times* (London: Robert Hale), p. 122. For England, the largest crowd at Tyburn appears to have numbered 80,000, see F. McLynn (1989) *Crime and Punishment*, p. 266.

45 For evidence of this in Scotland see N. Adams (1993) *Hangman's Brae: Crime and Punishment in and around Bygone Aberdeen* (Banchory, Kincardineshire:

Tolbooth), pp. 62–3. For the English experience see J.A. Sharpe (1985) '"Last Dying Speeches"', pp. 144–67.

46 See J.A. Sharpe (1983) *Crime in Seventeenth Century England – A County Study* (Cambridge: Cambridge University Press), p. 142. This was certainly true in Maggie Dickson's case as various publications document the presence of her friends and family at the foot of the gallows. See for instance W. Jackson (1795) *The New and Complete Newgate Calendar* (London: Alexander Hogg Publisher), II (XV), p. 155 and R. Chambers (1828) *The Picture of Scotland* (Edinburgh: William Tait Publisher), II, p. 106.

47 For further discussion see J.R. Ruff (1984) *Crime, Justice and the Public Order in Old Regime France: The Sènèchaussèes of Libourne and Bazas, 1696–1789* (London and Dover, N.H.: Croom Helm), p. 60 and P. Spierenburg (1984) *The Spectacle of Suffering – Executions and the Evolution of Repression: From a Pre-Industrial Metropolis to the European Experience* (Cambridge: Cambridge University Press).

48 For further discussion see M. Foucault (1991, third edition) *Discipline and Punish: The Birth of the Prison* (translated from the French by Alan Sheridan) (Harmondsworth: Penguin), part one, chapters one and two.

49 For further discussion see N. Adams (1993) *Hangman's Brae*, p. 19 and T.M. Tod [with additional material by W. Nelson] (1985) *Scottish Crime and Punishment: Scots Black Kalendar – 100 Years of Murder and Execution* (Newtongrange: Lang Syne Publishing), p. 6.

50 For further discussion of these speeches, see the references in note 40 above.

51 J.A. Sharpe (1985) '"Last Dying Speeches"', p. 150.

52 See N. Adams (1993) *Hangman's Brae*, p. 19 and N. Adams (1996) *Scotland's Chronicles of Blood*, p. 120.

53 J.A. Sharpe (1985) '"Last Dying Speeches"', p. 163.

54 See F. McLynn (1989) *Crime and Punishment*, p. 269.

55 For descriptions of the similarities of executions in Scotland and England see N. Adams (1993) *Hangman's Brae*, p. 19 and F. McLynn (1989) *Crime and Punishment*, p. 269.

56 J.A. Sharpe (1985) '"Last Dying Speeches"', p. 149.

57 See N. Adams (1996) *Scotland's Chronicles of Blood*, p. 101.

58 (1724) *The Last Speech, Confession and Warning of Margaret Dickson, who was Execute in the Grass-Mercat of Edinburgh, for the Unnatural Murder of her Own Child, on Wednesday the 2ᵈ of September 1724* (NLSBC: Mf. G. 0639/46).

59 (1724) *The Last Speech, Confession and Warning of Margaret Dickson*, p. 1.

60 Ibid, pp. 1–2.

61 Ibid, p. 2.

62 Ibid, p. 3.

63 Ibid, p. 4.

64 For further discussion of the potential mythologising associated with gallows speeches and their related literature see L.B. Faller (1987) *Turned to Account: The Forms and Functions of Criminal Biography in Late Seventeenth- and Early Eighteenth-Century England* (Cambridge: Cambridge University Press) and A-M. Kilday (2008) '"Monsters of the Vilest Kind"', pp. 108–11.

65 For more detailed accounts of Maggie Dickson's survival see (1724) *News from Musselburgh: Giving a Faithful Narrative of the Wonderful Restoration of Margaret Dickson to Life, Who Was Execute in the Grass-Market of Edinburgh,*

the *2ᵈ of September, 1724* (NLSBC: RB.1.179 [91]); *The Caledonian Mercury*, 8th September 1724 (NLS: Mf N. 776 No, 693 4135) and R. Chambers (1861) *Domestic Annals of Scotland: From the Revolution to the Rebellion of 1745* (Edinburgh and London: W. and R. Chambers), III, pp. 500–2.

66 For further discussion of reanimation after hanging in the early modern period, with specific cases given as examples (including that of Maggie Dickson) see R. Chambers (ed.) (1879) *The Book of Days: A Miscellany of Popular Antiquities in Association with the Calendar* (Philadelphia: J.B. Lippincott and Co.), I, p. 824 and (1861) *Notes and Queries: A Medium of Inter-Communication for Literary Men, Artists, Antiquaries, Genealogists, Etc.* (London: Bell and Daldy), Second Series, XI, January–June, 1861, p. 395.

67 See for instance the accounts of the Maggie Dickson story in (1727) *The Last Speech and Dying Words of John Dalgleish, Hangman of Edinburgh* (NLSBC: L.C. Fol. 74 [039]); J. Grant (1890) *Old and New Edinburgh: Its History, Its People and Its Places* (London: Cassell and Co.), IV, p. 231; Sir J. Sinclair (ed.) (1975) *The Statistical Account of Scotland, 1791–1799: Volume II – The Lothians* (Wakefield: EP Publishing), p. 312; W. Jackson (1795) *The New and Complete Newgate Calendar*, pp. 153–6 and J. MacLaurin (1774) *Arguments and Decisions In Remarkable Cases Before the High Court of Justiciary, and Other Supreme Courts, in Scotland* (Edinburgh: J. Bell), pp. 71–2 as well as the accounts cited in notes 68–9 below.

68 *The Caledonian Mercury*, 8th September 1724 (NLS: Mf N. 776 No, 693 4135).

69 R. Chambers (1828) *The Picture of Scotland*, II, pp. 106–7. See also (1724) *News from Musselburgh: Giving a Faithful Narrative of the Wonderful Restoration of Margaret Dickson to Life, Who Was Execute in the Grass-Market of Edinburgh, the 2ᵈ of September, 1724* (NLSBC: RB.1.179 [91]).

70 Maggie Dickson's fame has certainly endured. A cursory search of the internet, for instance, will reveal that she has been the subject of several theatre productions; her case is referred to in the literary classic *The Heart of Midlothian* (Sir W. Scott, *The Heart of Midlothian* [Boston: Estes and Lauriat], Note Q); she has an entry in the Oxford Dictionary of National Biography (Oxford University Press, 2004, [http://www.oxforddnb.com/view/article/57792]) and there is a public house in the Grassmarket in Edinburgh which bears her name.

71 See for instance A. Pennecuik (1787) 'The Merry Wives of Musselburgh's Welcome to Meg Dickson', in A. Pennecuik (ed.) *A Collection of Scots Poems on Several Occasions by Alexander Pennecuik, Gentleman and Others* (Glasgow: Alexander Buchanan, Publisher), pp. 10–17 and various pieces of correspondence printed in *The Caledonian Mercury*, September 1724–July 1725 (NLS: Mf N. 776).

72 W. Jackson (1795) *The New and Complete Newgate Calendar*, p. 156. See also (1813) *Particulars of the Life, Trial, Character and Behaviour of Margaret Dickson* (NLSBC: APS.4.98.8).

73 See, for example, *The Caledonian Mercury*, 10th September 1724 (NLS: Mf N. 776 No, 694 4141).

74 See for instance the papers filed in NAS: JC 26/108/1266/7-12 and also W. Jackson (1795) *The New and Complete Newgate Calendar*, p. 156.

75 (1724) *A Warning to the Wicked, or, Margaret Dickson's Welcome to the Gibbet* (NLSBC: RB.1.106 [96]).

76 See for instance R. Chambers (1828) *The Picture of Scotland*, II, p. 107 and Sir J. Sinclair (ed.) (1975) *The Statistical Account of Scotland, 1791–1799: Volume II – The Lothians*, p. 312.
77 (1728) *Margaret Dickson's Penitential Confession* (NLSBC: RY.III.a.10 [076]).
78 See for example W. Jackson (1795) *The New and Complete Newgate Calendar*, p. 156; J. MacLaurin (1774) *Arguments and Decisions In Remarkable Cases*, pp. 71–2; R. Chambers (1861) *Domestic Annals of Scotland*, III, p. 502 and (1868) *The Life of Calcraft: An Account of the Executions in Scotland for the Past 200 Years* (NLSBC: L.C.Fol.73 [132]).

Chapter 4

1 This occurred under 1 Victoria Cap XXIII.
2 See G. Rudé (1959) 'The London "Mob" of the Eighteenth Century', *Historical Journal*, II, 1, pp. 1–18; R.B. Rose (1960) 'The Priestley Riots of 1791', *Past and Present*, 18, pp. 68–88 and J.L. Fitts (1973) 'Newcastle's Mob', *Albion*, V, 1, pp. 41–9.
3 Frank McLynn argues that the chief aim of the related punishment of public flogging was 'the inculcation of shame'. See F. McLynn (1989) *Crime and Punishment in Eighteenth Century England* (London: Routledge), p. 281.
4 See examples below in notes 7, 12, 17 and 20.
5 Robert Shoemaker notes that Londoners of this period were comfortable with a 'prominent role in public street life which also conferred legitimacy upon their actions: R. Shoemaker (2004) 'Streets of Shame? The Crowd and Public Punishments in London, 1700–1820', in S. Devereux and P. Griffiths (eds) *Penal Practice and Culture, 1500–1900* (Basingstoke: Palgrave Macmillan), pp. 232–57 at p. 235.
6 (1885) 'Elizabeth I: Volume 152: May 1590', *Calendar of State Papers, Relating to Ireland, of the Reigns of Henry VIII, Edward VI, Mary and Elizabeth* (London: Longman Green), pp. 337–49 [Bodleian Library (BOD): Upper RR (K.5.57)].
7 (1888) 'Middlesex Sessions Rolls: 1632', *Middlesex County Records: Volume 3: 1625–67* (London), pp. 41–9 [Accessed at British History On-line: http://www. british-history.ac.uk /source.aspx?pubid=553].
8 (1905) 'Sessions Books: 1696', *Middlesex County Records: Calendar of Sessions Books 1689–1709* (London), pp. 143–62 [Accessed at British History On-line: http://www.british-history.ac.uk/source.aspx?pubid=550] and (1905) 'Sessions Books: 1702', *Middlesex County Records: Calendar of Sessions Books 1689–1709*, pp. 235–53.
9 (1913) 'William III: October 1696', *Calendar of State Papers, Domestic Series of the Reign of William and Mary* (London: HMSO), pp. 407–28 [BOD: Upper RR (K.5.42)].
10 (1964) 'James II – Volume 2: November 1686', *Calendar of State Papers, Domestic Series, James II* (London: HMSO), pp. 293–313 [BOD: Upper RR (K.5.42)].
11 H.O. Warrant Book 6, p. 232 in (1900) 'William and Mary: December 1691', *Calendar of State Papers, Domestic Series of the Reign of William and Mary* (London: HMSO) pp. 21–80 and (1888) 'Middlesex Sessions Rolls: 1632', *Middlesex County Records: Volume 3: 1625–67*, pp. 41–9.

12 (1892) 'Middlesex Sessions Rolls: 1685', *Middlesex County Records: Volume 4: 1667–88* (London), pp. 260–8 [Accessed at British History On-line: http://www.british-history.ac.uk /source.aspx?pubid=554].

13 (1938) 'General Index: S, T, U, V' and 'Charles II: December 1683', *Calendar of State Papers, Domestic Series, of the Reign of Charles II* (London: Longman Green), pp. 486–504 [BOD: Upper RR (K.5.42)] and *State Papers Domestic* (hereafter *S.P. Dom*) 'Petition Entry Book', 2, p. 192 in (1895) 'William and Mary: February 1690', *Calendar of State Papers, Domestic Series of the Reign of William and Mary* (London: HMSO) pp. 441–86.

14 (1892) 'Middlesex Sessions Rolls: 1684', *Middlesex County Records: Volume 4: 1667–88*, pp. 230–59.

15 '...as of all and every other person or persons deposed or sworn in any action, matter, or cause, and the said perjurors so found to punish by pillory nailing or cutting off ears, wearing of papers, or otherwise according to the discretion of the said Chief Commissioner and Council.' See (1877) 'Elizabeth I: Volume 135: July 1588', *Calendar of State Papers, Relating to Ireland, of the Reigns of Henry VIII, Edward VI, Mary and Elizabeth* (London: Longman Green), pp. 548–86.

16 (1937) 'Sessions, 1615: 5th and 6th October', *County of Middlesex: Calendar to the Sessions Records: New Series, Volume 3: 1615–16* (London), pp. 24–72 [Accessed at British History On-line: http://www.british-history.ac.uk/source.aspx? pubid=567].

17 (1941) 'Preface', *County of Middlesex: Calendar to the Sessions Records: New Series, Volume 4: 1616–18* (London), pp. vii–xv [Accessed at British History On-line: http://www.british-history.ac.uk/source.aspx?pubid=568].

18 See for Example the trial of John Stein October 1802: *Old Bailey Proceedings Online* (www.oldbaileyonline.org, 13 March 2009) t18021027-149 and (1892) 'Middlesex Sessions Rolls: 1685', *Middlesex County Records: Volume 4: 1667–88*, pp. 283–300.

19 (1892) 'Middlesex Sessions Rolls: 1685', *Middlesex County Records: Volume 4: 1667–88*, pp. 283–300.

20 Ibid.

21 See respectively *Old Bailey Proceedings Online* (www.oldbaileyonline.org, 13 March 2009) t17150223-3: February 1715.

22 See ibid, t17251013-61: October 1725.

23 For material on this see D.S. Nash (2007) *Blasphemy in the Christian World: A History* (Oxford: Oxford University Press), especially chapter two.

24 For an extended discussion this link based on English evidence see D.S. Nash (2008) '"To Prostitute Morality, Libel Religion and Undermine Government": Blasphemy and the Strange Persistence of Providence in Britain since the Seventeenth Century', *Journal of Religious History*, 32, 4, pp. 439–56. See also D. Manning (2008) 'Anti Providentialism in Late Stuart England: A Case Study of the "Stage Debate"', *Journal of Religious History*, 32, 4, pp. 422–38.

25 D. Postles (2003) 'Penance and the Market Place: A Reformation Dialogue with the Medieval Church (c. 1250–1600)', *Journal of Ecclesiastical History*, 54, 3, pp. 441–68.

26 M.R. Baelde (1935) *Studiën over Godslastering* (Den Haag: Nijhof), pp. 109–10 and G. Schwerhoff (2005) *Zungen wie Schwerter, Blasphemie in alteuropäischen Gesellschaften 1200–1650* (Konstanz Verlag: UvK), p. 144. See also R. Van

Dülmen (1990) *Theatre of Horror: Crime and Punishment in Early Modern Germany* [translated by Elisabeth Neu] (Oxford: Polity Press). As Van Dülmen, suggests 'it was crucial that all punishments and combinations of punishments were carried out in public ... holding up to the delinquent a mirror of dishonesty reflecting the norms of the society from which he or she was on the verge of being expelled.' (p. 56).

27   See M. Flynn (1995) 'Blasphemy and the Play of Anger in Sixteenth Century Spain', *Past and Present*, 149, 1, pp. 29–56.

28   See S-M. Olli (2008) 'Blasphemy in Early Modern Sweden – An Untold Story', *Journal of Religious History*, 32, 4, pp. 457–70.

29   C. Parker (1997) 'The Moral Agency and Moral Autonomy of Church Folk in the Dutch Reformed Church of Delft 1580–1620', *Journal of Ecclesiastical History*, 48, 1, pp. 44–70; J.R. Watt (1989) 'The Reception of the Reformation in Valangin, Switzerland, 1547–1588', *Sixteenth Century Journal*, 20, 1, pp. 98–104 and S.C. Karant-Nunn (1994) 'Neoclericalism and Anticlericalism in Saxony 1555–1675', *Journal of Interdisciplinary History*, XXIV, 4, pp. 615–37.

30   A. Soman (1976) 'Press, Pulpit and Censorship in France before Richelieu', *Proceedings of the American Philosophical Society*, 120, 6, pp. 439–63.

31   See D. Postles (2003) 'Penance and the Market Place', p. 445.

32   (1933) 'Charles II: May 1683: January–June' and *S.P. Dom.*, Car. II, 422, no. 59 in *Calendar of State Papers, Domestic Series, of the Reign of Charles II* (London: Longman Green), pp. 222–84.

33   (1913) 'William III: March 1696', *Calendar of State Papers, Domestic Series of the Reign of William and Mary*, pp. 63–113.

34   (1866) 'Charles II – Volume 199: May 1–8, 1667', *Calendar of State Papers, Domestic Series, of the Reign of Charles II* (London: Longman Green), pp. 67–84.

35   See D. Lawton (1993) *Blasphemy* (London: Harvester) for a discussion of the ribald public performances of Thomas Sedley and the blasphemy of Sussanah Fowles and how this was related to insanity. The latter individual received a sentence of exhibition (three times) in the pillory. See pp. 23–36 for Sedley and pp. 17–23 for Fowles.

36   (1933) 'William III: December 1698', *Calendar of State Papers, Domestic Series of the Reign of William and Mary* (London: HMSO), pp. 423–41.

37   Ibid. Endorsed, R. Jan. 1698–9. 3 pp: *State Papers*, 32, 15, ff. 277–8 [Accessed at British History On-line: http://www.british-history.ac.uk/report.aspx?compid= 57960&strquer y= Pillory sentence for blasphemy].

38   Ibid.

39   (1937) 'William III: July 1700', *Calendar of State Papers, Domestic Series of the Reign of William and Mary* (London: HMSO), pp. 78–101 and *State Papers*, 44, 238, p. 439 [Accessed at British History On-line: http://www.british-history.ac.uk/report.aspx?compid=58086& strquery=Capt.Rigby].

40   (1960) 'James II: Volume 1: May 1685', *Calendar of State Papers, Domestic Series of the Reign of William and Mary* (London: HMSO), pp. 143–74.

41   *Old Bailey Proceedings Online* (www.oldbaileyonline.org, 16 March 2009) t16770117-1: January 1677.

42   Many differing accounts record his name either as 'Nayler' or 'Naylor'.

43   See L. Levy (1993) *Blasphemy, Verbal Offense Against the Sacred from Moses to Salman Rushdie* (New York: Knopf), pp. 103–11.

44 Ibid, pp. 174–80.
45 Ibid.
46 See D.S. Nash (2007) *Blasphemy in the Christian World*, pp. 118–24.
47 T. Burton (1828) 'The Diary of Thomas Burton: 18 December 1656', in J.T. Rutt (ed.) *Diary of Thomas Burton Esquire, Volume 1: July 1653–April 1657* (London: Colburn), pp. 168–75 [British Library (BL): W18/1815 DSC].
48 Ibid.
49 Ibid.
50 (1915) 'Preface', *Calendar of State Papers, Domestic Series, of the Reign of Charles II* (London: Longman Green), pp. vii–lxxiii.
51 D. Defoe (1703) *The Shortest-Way with the Dissenters; Or, Proposals for the Establishment of the Church* (London) [BOD: 4° T 20 (7) Jur.].
52 J.R. Moore (1939) *Defoe in the Pillory: A New Interpretation* [Humanities Series No. 1] (Bloomington, Indiana: Indiana University Publications), pp. 2–32. Moore notes the numerous works in which Defoe had attacked and vilified those who later became his opponents.
53 D. Defoe (1703) *A Hymn to the Pillory* (London: H. Hills) [BOD: G. Pamph. 1282 (9)].
54 Ibid.
55 Ibid.
56 Ibid.
57 Frank McLynn argues the pillory had become volatile during the eighteenth century and several instances (in 1732 and again in 1756) are mentioned when individuals died as a result of action against them during the course of their punishment. The sentence was routinely attended by sheriffs' men whose presence was intended to preserve orderly reactions and some level of safety for the accused. F. McLynn (1989) *Crime and Punishment*, pp. 283–5. Robert Shoemaker concurs with this gradual disappearance of the pillory in the eighteenth century, but notes the growth of doubts about its deterrent effectiveness or its appropriate or civilised nature. These occurred alongside changes in the use of public space and the decline in paternalist social and employment structures, which undermined the effectiveness of communal forms of punishment. See Robert Shoemaker (2004) *The London Mob: Violence and Order in Eighteenth Century London* (London: Hambledon and London) and R. Shoemaker (2004) 'Streets of Shame?', pp. 236–7.
58 (1820) *Odes to the Pillory: Supposed to have been Written by a K——T and his Lady: To Which is Added 'The Pillory's Prayer'* (London: J. Johnston) [BL: G. 18981.(15)].
59 See particularly D. Wahrman (1995) *Imagining the Middle Class: The Political Representation of Class in Britain*, c. 1780–1840 (Cambridge: Cambridge University Press).
60 (1820) *Odes to the Pillory: Supposed to have been Written by a K——T and his Lady*.
61 H. Bradlaugh-Bonner (1934) *Penalties Upon Opinion* (London: Watts and Company), p. 37.
62 See particularly R. Shoemaker (2004) 'Streets of Shame?', p. 245.
63 J. Keane (1995) *Tom Paine: A Political Life* (London: Bloomsbury).
64 R. Shoemaker (2004) 'Streets of Shame?', p. 245.

65　Ibid. p. 251.

66　For more material on the Carlile prosecutions see J. Weiner (1983) *Radicalism and Freethought in Nineteenth-Century Britain: The Life of Richard Carlile* (Santa Barbara: Greenwood Press) and Levy, *Blasphemy* pp. 339–67.

Chapter 5

1　The Society for the Suppression of Vice (1807) *The Constable's Assistant, Being a Compendium of the Duties and Powers of Constables* (London) [Bodleian Library (BOD): Vet. A6 e. 561].

2　Baron De Montesquieu (1748) *The Spirit of Laws* [translated by Thomas Nugent] (London: J. Nourse and P. Valliant) p. 66 and p. 99 [BOD: Vet. A5. e.2168].

3　Ibid, pp. 101–2.

4　Ibid, p. 486.

5　Cesare Beccaria (1767) *An Essay on Crimes and Punishments, translated from the Italian; With A Commentary, Attributed To Monsieur Voltaire translated from the French* (London: J. Almon), p. 2 [BOD: Godw. 8° 454].

6　Ibid, p. 6.

7　Ibid, p. 16 and p. 23.

8　Ibid, pp. 26–7.

9　Ibid, p. 31.

10　Ibid, p. 42.

11　Ibid, p. 17.

12　Ibid, p. 36.

13　Ibid, p. 9.

14　Ibid, p. 36.

15　Ibid, pp. 19–20.

16　Ibid, p. 132.

17　Ibid, p. 82.

18　Ibid, p. 85.

19　Ibid, p. 86.

20　Voltaire, *A Commentary Upon the Book of Crimes and Punishments*, pp. i–iv in the appendix to Beccaria, *Essay on Crimes and Punishment*, see note 5 above.

21　Benjamin Rush (1787) *An Enquiry into the Effects of Public Punishments upon Criminals and upon Society: Read in the Society for Promoting Political Enquiries, March 9ᵗʰ 1787* (Philadelphia: Joseph James), p. 4 [Bodleian Law Library (BLL): Crim. 640 P415 (4)].

22　Ibid, p. 4.

23　Ibid, p. 14.

24　Ibid, pp. 10–11.

25　Ibid, p. 14.

26　Ibid, pp. 14–15.

27　Ibid, pp. 17–18.

28　Ibid, p. 18.

29　Ibid, pp. 21–2.

30　Ibid, p. 36.

31 Ibid, p. 37.
32 Sir George Mackenzie of Rosehaugh (1678) *The Laws and Customs of Scotland in Matters Criminal* (Edinburgh: Andrew Anderson), Title XXX, p. 279 [National Library of Scotland (NLS): Adv. MS. 25.3.15].
33 Baron D. Hume (1797, 1986 reprint) *Commentaries on the Laws of Scotland Respecting Crimes* (Edinburgh: The Law Society of Scotland), Volume I, Introduction, p. 10 [NLS: ILS: (16-0 RL) Vol. 1].
34 Ibid, p. 10.
35 Baron D. Hume (1797, 1986 reprint) *Commentaries on the Laws of Scotland Respecting Crimes* (Edinburgh: The Law Society of Scotland), Volume II, Chapter XVII: Of Sentence and Execution, p. 472 [NLS: ILS: (16-0 RL) Vol. 2].
36 Ibid, p. 473.
37 Ibid, p. 474.
38 Ibid, p. 472.
39 Ibid, p. 473.
40 Ibid, p. 488.
41 Ibid, p. 488.
42 Ibid, p. 489.
43 Ibid, p. 489.
44 Ibid, p. 490.
45 Ibid, p. 490. Our definitional addition is in parenthesis.
46 Jeremy Bentham (1830) *The Rationale of Punishment* (London: R. Heward), p. 6 [BLL: Crim. 600 B476a].
47 Ibid, p. 18.
48 Ibid, pp. 20–1.
49 It is worth noting that Bentham was nonetheless critical of how vague some of Beccaria's propositions could be when individuals tried to apply them practically. In part his *Rationale of Punishment* should be read as building on Beccaria's work through the application of more stringent utilitarian principles. See ibid, p. 54.
50 Ibid, p. 25.
51 Ibid, p. 30.
52 Ibid, p. 32, p. 34, pp. 36–7, pp. 39–40, p. 44 and p. 46.
53 Ibid, pp. 91–2.
54 Ibid, p. 94.
55 Ibid, pp. 115–16.
56 Ibid, p. 121.
57 Ibid, p. 407.
58 Ibid, p. 124.
59 Ibid, p. 130.
60 Ibid, p. 208.
61 Ibid, p. 220.
62 Ibid, p. 248.
63 Ibid, p. 353.
64 T.F. Buxton (1818) *An Appeal to the Friends of Humanity on behalf of English Prisoners'* (Stockton), p. 6 [BLL: Crim. 620 A646].
65 Ibid, p. 6.
66 Ibid, p. 6.

67 William Roscoe (1823) *Additional Observations on Penal Jurisprudence, and the Reformation of Criminals* (London: T. Cadell), pp. 83–4 [BOD: 8° W. 165 BS (part two) and Dunston C. 23 (part three)].

68 Ibid, p. 11.

69 William Smith (1778) *Mild Punishments Sound Policy: Or Observations on the Law Relative to Debtors and Felons* (London: J. Bew), p. 6 [BOD: ESTCN 4480].

70 Ibid, p. 11.

71 Ibid, p. 27.

72 Ibid, p. 27.

73 Ibid, p. 29 and p. 40.

74 Ibid, p. 31.

75 Ibid, p. 46.

76 George Onesiphorus Paul (1789) *An Address to the Magistrates of the County of Gloucester assembled at their Michaelmas Quarter Sessions* (Gloucester: R. Raikes), p. 5 [BOD: ESTCT 72000].

77 However this perhaps fits with policies which limited the execution of women to those who were penitent or in some other sense valuable examples to the populace.

78 Although other legal theorists published on the criminal law in Scotland at this time, they paid little attention to the process of punishment. See for example J. Burnett (1811) *A Treatise on Various Branches of the Criminal Law of Scotland* (Edinburgh: Archibald Constable and Co.) [NLS: BCL. D2766].

79 A. Alison (1833) *Practice of the Criminal Law of Scotland* (Edinburgh: William Blackwood), Chapter XVII, p. 671 [NLS: MS. 9161].

80 Ibid, pp. 671–2. For further discussion of the crime wave in early nineteenth century Scotland see A. Alison (1832) *Principles of the Criminal Law of Scotland* (Edinburgh: William Blackwood), Preface, p. v [NLS: MS. 9160].

81 A. Alison (1833) *Practice of the Criminal Law of Scotland*, Chapter XVII, p. 672.

Chapter 6

1 (1830) *A Full and Accurate Report of the Entire Proceedings in a Trial In the Cause of the Office v Rev. W.M. Hughes in the Consistorial Court, Dublin: Before his Grace the Archbishop of Dublin &c. &c. for several charges.... of, By him Committed* (Dublin) [British Library: 5155. b. 35] (Hereafter: *Full and Accurate Report*).

2 See Robert Darnton (1984) *The Great Cat Massacre: And Other Episodes in French Cultural History* (London: Allen Lane), Introduction.

3 *Full and Accurate Report*, p. 6. For other details on Hughes's career see Rev. James B. Leslie (1936) *Ferns Clergy and Parishes: Being an Account of the Clergy of the Church of Ireland in the Diocese of Ferns from the Earliest Period, with Historical Notices of the Several Parishes, Churches, etc.* (Dublin: Church of Ireland Printing and Publishing Co. Ltd.), p. 188 [BOD: G.A. Wexford 4° 8].

4 *Full and Accurate Report*, frontispiece.

5 Ibid, p. 3.

6 Ibid, p. 4.

7 Ibid, p. 21.

8 Ibid, p. 4.
9 See E.P. Thompson (1991) *Customs in Common* (London: Penguin), see chapters 3, 4, 5 and 8.
10 *Full and Accurate Report*, p. 4 and p. 80.
11 Ibid, p. 5
12 Ibid, p. 7.
13 Ibid, p. 7.
14 Ibid, pp. 6–7.
15 Ibid, p. 8.
16 Ibid, p. 8.
17 Ibid, p. 8.
18 Ibid, p. 9.
19 This mixture is believed to act as an aid to settling the stomach. I am grateful to Russell Trotman for this observation.
20 *Full and Accurate Report*, pp. 9–10.
21 Ibid, pp. 9–11.
22 Ibid, p. 11.
23 Ibid, p. 11.
24 Ibid, p. 29.
25 This version of the song comes from J. Catnach (1820) *Collection of Eighty Street Ballads on Forty Sheets* (London) [University of Minnesota Libraries: Wilson Rare Books Quarto 820.1 C683 found at http://mh.cla.umn.edu/catnach. html]. Kate Kearney is recorded as a tantalisingly buxom beauty whose appeal was enhanced by the considerable strength of the poitin (illegally distilled spirit) she dispensed. Hence inhaling her 'warm sigh' would most likely lead to an advanced stage of inebriation.
26 *Full and Accurate Report*, p. 12.
27 Ibid, p. 13 and p. 70.
28 Ibid, p. 13.
29 Ibid, p. 13 and p. 26.
30 Ibid, p. 30.
31 Ibid, p. 31.
32 Ibid, p. 18.
33 Ibid, p. 32.
34 Ibid, p. 34.
35 Ibid, p. 35 and p. 63.
36 Ibid, p. 33.
37 Ibid, p. 16.
38 Ibid, p. 35
39 Ibid, p. 36.
40 Ibid, p. 38.
41 Ibid, p. 40.
42 Ibid, pp. 40–1.
43 Ibid, p. 85.
44 Ibid, p. 39.
45 Ibid, p. 42.
46 Ibid, p. 44.
47 Ibid, p. 44.
48 Ibid, p. 70.

49 Ibid, p. 46.
50 Ibid, p. 52.
51 Ibid, p. 54.
52 Ibid, p. 53.
53 Ibid, p. 52.
54 Ibid, p. 52.
55 Ibid, p. 50.
56 Ibid, p. 67.
57 Ibid, p. 55
58 Ibid, p. 62.
59 Ibid, pp. 73–4.
60 Ibid, p. 74.
61 Ibid, p. 75.
62 Ibid, p. 77.
63 Ibid, p. 78.
64 Ibid, p. 79.
65 Ibid, p. 81.
66 Ibid, p. 83.
67 Ibid, p. 84.
68 Ibid, p. 85.
69 Ibid, p. 87.
70 Ibid, p. 89.
71 Ibid, p. 90.
72 Ibid, p. 94.
73 Ibid, p. 67.

Chapter 7

1 For an extended discussion of domesticity, the lower middle class and social expectations see A.J. Hammerton (1999) 'Pooterism of Partnership? Marriage and Masculine Identity in the Lower Middle Class, 1870–1920', *Journal of British Studies*, 38, pp. 291–321.
2 Anthony Trollope (1869) *He Knew He was Right* (London: Strahan and Co.). We are grateful to Professor Gail Savage for drawing this to our attention.
3 See A.J. Hammerton (1990) 'Victorian Marriage and the Law of Matrimonial Cruelty', *Victorian Studies*, 33, pp. 269–92.
4 *Reynolds's Newspaper*, 6th February 1870, p. 1.
5 One of the salient features of the Kelly case had been the husband's strict confinement of his wife to the marital home. See A.J. Hammerton (1990), 'Victorian Marriage', pp. 287–8.
6 Hammerton has noted that in divorce proceedings during this period, any admission of fault by the wife could result in 'legal complications', since this could be construed as condoning the husband's behaviour in a manner analogous to provocation. See ibid, p. 276.
7 Judicial separation was certainly rare in England and Wales at this time, constituting approximately 25 cases compared to approximately 200 divorces and approximately 825 protection orders. It was also dwarfed by the numbers of private separations. Although what transpired in this case is unclear, it is sug-

gested that mid-Victorian couples regularly separated with the aid of a solicitor, whilst a compliant magistrate secured financial provision for the wife. This would suit most readings of the Le Roi case and indeed Olive Anderson asserts: 'A summons for assault could thus pressurize a husband into agreeing to a private separation. This was not a species of full divorce but represented "Victorian semi-detached marriage"'. See O. Anderson (1999) 'State, Civil Society and Separation in Victorian Marriage', *Past and Present*, 163, pp. 161–201. This has also been referred to as separation from bed and board (divorce *a mensa et thoro*) which did not allow for the remarriage of either party, see A.J. Hammerton (1990) 'Victorian Marriage', p. 271.

8 See J. Carter-Wood (2004) *Violence and Crime in Nineteenth-Century England: The Shadow of Our Refinement* (London: Routledge).

9 A.J. Hammerton (1990) 'Victorian Marriage', p. 287.

10 See for example G. Savage (1998) 'Erotic Stories and Public Decency: Newspaper Reporting of Divorce Proceedings in England', *Historical Journal*, 41, pp. 511–28 and K. Ottesen Garrigan (1992) *Victorian Scandals: Repressions of Gender and Class* (Columbus, Ohio: Ohio University Press).

11 *Reynolds's Newspaper*, 6th February 1870, p. 1; *Birmingham Daily Post*, 3rd February 1870; *Liverpool Mercury*, 3rd February 1870; *Lloyds Weekly Newspaper*, 6th February 1870; *Illustrated Police News*, 12th February 1870 and *Pall Mall Gazette*, 2nd February 1870.

12 *Reynolds's* Newspaper, 6th February 1870, p. 1.

13 Ibid.

14 Ibid.

15 Ibid.

16 Ibid.

17 *Illustrated Police News*, 12th February 1870.

18 *The Times*, 3rd February 1870.

19 Ibid.

20 Interestingly the only other newspaper to cover *The Times* version of the story was the Welsh *Western Mail* (4th February 1870). This perhaps was a recognition of how *Reynolds's* and other newspapers treated stories from all areas of the Celtic fringe.

21 *Jersey Express*, 1st February 1870.

22 The court deposition in the case is disappointingly uninformative and the only fact of interest which emerges from this is that Mrs Le Roi's maiden name had been Ann Robinson. When juxtaposed with the assertion of John Le Roi's 'French' identity, this potentially introduces nationality and its attendant communal expectations as another possible dynamic driving the case. See The Jersey Archive, reference D/V/N4/3.

23 *Jersey Express*, 1st February 1870.

24 Ibid.

25 Ibid.

26 Ibid.

27 Ibid.

28 Ibid

29 *British Press and Jersey Times*, 31st January 1870.

30 Ibid.

31 Ibid.

32   Ibid.
33   T.N. Brushfield (1864) 'On Obsolete Punishments, with Particular Reference to those of Cheshire: Part I – The Brank, or Scold's Bridle', *Journal of the Archaeological Society of Chester*, 2, pp. 31–48.
34   See ibid, p. 42 for a bridle at Congleton (Cheshire) kept in the town hall for its use; see p. 44 for one used within the parish of Walton-on-Thames, and p. 45 for bridles belonging to the municipality of Chester, the Chester Board of Guardians and the Stockport Workhouse.
35   Ibid, p. 36.
36   See also the chapter on 'Rough Music', in E.P. Thompson (1991) *Customs in Common* (London: Penguin), pp. 501–2 for a discussion of other nineteenth century remnants of the Scold's Bridle.

Chapter 8

1   For histories of republicanism see A. Taylor (1999) *'Down with the Crown': British Anti-monarchism and Debates about Royalty since 1790* (London: Reaktion Books) and D.S. Nash and A. Taylor (2000) (eds) *Republicanism in Victorian Society* (Stroud: Sutton).
2   E.P. Thompson (1991) 'Class Struggle without Class' in *Customs in Common* (London: Penguin), pp. 16–96.
3   Ibid.
4   M. McKeon (2002) 'The Secret History of Domesticity: Private, Public, and the Division of Knowledge', in C. Jones and D. Wahrman (eds) *The Age of Cultural Revolutions: Britain and France, 1750–1820* (London: University of California Press), pp. 171–89.
5   See J. Plunkett (2003) *Queen Victoria: First Media Monarch* (Oxford: Oxford University Press), pp. 31–5.
6   See ibid and A. Munich (1996) *Queen Victoria's Secrets* (New York: Columbia University Press).
7   F. Prochaska (2001) *The Republic of Britain 1760–2000* (London: Penguin).
8   This is ostensibly the argument offered in the original, agenda setting piece by N.J. Gossman (1962) 'Republicanism in Nineteenth-Century England', *International Review of Social History*, 7, pp. 47–60.
9   See M. Taylor (2000) 'Republics versus Empires: Charles Dilke's Republicanism Reconsidered', in D.S. Nash and A. Taylor (2000) (eds) *Republicanism in Victorian Society*, pp. 25–34.
10   C. Bradlaugh (1877) *The Impeachment of the House of Brunswick* (London: Freethought Publishing Company) [Bodleian Library: Johnson d.2991].
11   A. Taylor (1995) 'Reynolds's Newspaper, Opposition to Monarchy and the Radical Anti-jubilee: Britain's Anti-monarchist Tradition Reconsidered', *Bulletin of the Institute of Historical Research*, 68, 167, pp. 319–37.
12   A. Taylor (2003) *Lords of Misrule* (Basingstoke: Palgrave Macmillan), pp. 14–15.
13   See B. Worden (2001) *Roundhead Reputations: The English Civil Wars and the Passions of Posterity* (London: Allen Lane), p. 210.
14   See E.F. Biagini (2003) 'Neo-roman Liberalism: "Republican" Values and British Liberalism, ca. 1860–1875', *History of European Ideas*, 29, 1, pp. 55–72.

15 See the discussion in D. Cannadine (2001) *History in Our Time* (Harmonds-worth: Penguin).

16 A. Munich (1996) *Queen Victoria's Secrets*, passim.

17 See the section on Goffman in the introduction to this volume.

18 Ibid, pp. 109–26. Munich argues that the permanent corps of bridesmaid's and the mental destabilisation of central female characters in the Gilbert and Sullivan Savoy operas were profoundly indicative of widespread concern about gender relations in flux throughout wider society.

19 Ibid.

20 A. Taylor (1999) '*Down with the Crown*', pp. 80–2.

21 L. Davidoff and C. Hall (1987) *Family Fortunes: Men and Women of the English Middle Class 1780–1850* (London: Hutchison).

22 Ibid, p. 21.

23 Historians have also noted that the Victorian rehabilitation of Oliver Crom-well as a benign and even heroic figure parallels the growth of mainstream Victorian Non-conformity. Similarly, an association of royalism with high church Puseyism was later to reinforce this bond. Cromwell also appeared in the radical anti-aristocratic and monarchical pantheon of the Norman Yoke. Allusions to the blamelessness of his private life and moral earnestness 'spoke well beyond Nonconformity to the wider seriousness of the Victorian Age', see B. Worden (2001) *Roundhead Reputations*, pp. 252–4.

24 Anna Clark has noted that sex scandals in this period mark an important demarcation line between public and private and often trigger political mobil-isation, see A. Clark (2004) *Scandal: The Sexual Politics of the British Constitution* (Princeton, N.J. and Oxford: Princeton University Press). See also I. McCalman (1993) *Radical Underworld: Prophets, Revolutionaries and Pornographers in London, 1795–1840* (Oxford: Clarendon Press) and J. Epstein (1994) *Radical Expression: Political Language, Ritual and Symbol in England, 1790–1850* (Oxford: Oxford University Press).

25 D. Wahrman (1995) *Imagining the Middle Class: The Political Representation of Class in Britain, c. 1780–1840* (Cambridge: Cambridge University Press), pp. 380–400.

26 See M. Homans (1993) '"To the Queen's Private Apartments": Royal Family Portraiture and the Construction of Victoria's Sovereign Obedience', *Victorian Studies*, 37, 3, pp. 1–41.

27 Ibid.

28 There is also a growing historiography which dwells on the upbringing of Victoria as steeped in an appreciation of the commercial wealth and poten-tial of the kingdom. See for example L. Valone (2001) *Becoming Victoria* (New Haven, C.T. and London: Yale University Press), p. 129.

29 F. Prochaska (1995) *Royal Bounty: The Making of a Welfare Monarchy* (New Haven, C.T. and London: Yale University Press), p. 28, p. 76, p. 81, p. 85 and p. 98.

30 We are particularly indebted to Detlev Mares (Institut für Geschicte, TU Darmstadt) for sharing his views on this area with us.

31 It is certainly possible to suggest that republicanism had a range of earlier meritocratic ideas to work with and formed a central core of the ideological writings and speeches of the ex-chartist veteran Christopher Charles 'Cockbill'

Cattell, see C. Rumsey (2000) *The Rise and Fall of British Republican Clubs 1871–1874* (Oswestry: Quinta Press), p. 10.

32 Here it is worth reminding ourselves that the early nineteenth century radicals were strangely suspicious of conventional readings and narratives of the construction of English liberties. These could be seen as having been the product of aristocratic endeavour with the sole intention of benefiting this same group. See B. Worden (2001) *Roundhead Reputations*, p. 209.

33 Bright was considered by some republicans to possess the ideal credentials for an English republic's first president, yet he declined to embrace such suggestions, see W. Thompson (1912) *The Life and Times of John Bright* (London: Allen and Unwin), p. 299. We are grateful to Tony Taylor for drawing this to our attention.

34 See J.P.D. Dunbabin (1975) 'Oliver Cromwell's Popular Image in Nineteenth Century England', *Britain and the Netherlands: Papers Delivered to the Fifth Anglo-Dutch Historical Conference* (The Hague: Martinus Hijhof), pp. 141–63, p. 143. Cromwell could function as a crossover point for eighteenth and nineteenth century radical identifications. Bradford politics of the 1840s cited both Cromwell and Richard Cobden as both providing evidence of 'genuine Saxon liberty' whilst being responsible for ushering in periods of enhanced material prosperity.

35 See the *Republican Herald*, 11th April 1874 for a description of the danger of 'privilege' constituting the true basis of local government power. This was responsible for making England, in the paper's words 'the land of mongrel institutions'. This belief in local autonomy had also been capable of taking on an anti-statist/anti-socialist stance in the hands of W.J. Linton and Isaac Ironside, see G. Claeys (1989) 'Mazzini, Kossuth, and British Radicalism, 1848–54', *Journal of British Studies*, 28, 3, pp. 225–61 at p. 256.

36 See R. Williams (1997) *The Contentious Crown: Public Discussion of the British Monarchy in the Reign of Queen Victoria* (Aldershot: Ashgate), p. 40 and also R. Sindall (1987) 'The London Garrotting Panics of 1856 and 1862', *Social History*, 12, 3, pp. 351–9. Sindall quotes the work of Stanley Cohen who notes that a moral panic's ability to catch the public eye, what he terms the 'inventory', determined expectations of deviance and the likelihood of its re-occurrence; in other words, a heightened level of sensitivity.

37 See A. Taylor (1999) *'Down with the Crown'*, pp. 80–7 for a discussion of the various dimensions of the 'absence' of monarchy.

38 See D.S. Nash (2000) 'Charles Bradlaugh, India and the Many Chameleon Destinations of Republicanism', in D.S. Nash and A. Taylor (eds) *Republicanism in Victorian Society* (Stroud: Sutton), pp. 106–24.

39 C. Bradlaugh (1877) *The Impeachment of the House of Brunswick*, p. 3.

40 *National Reformer*, I, 42, 2nd March 1861.

41 Ibid. The writer praises the ability amongst women to play the piano or the guitar, to sing and to 'use the needle for ornament as well as use'.

42 Ibid.

43 *National Reformer*, I, 43, 9th March 1861.

44 Ibid.

45 Ibid.

46 Ibid.

47 See *also* J. Plunkett (2003) *Queen Victoria: First Media Monarch* (Oxford: Oxford University Press), pp. 30–5.

48   *National Reformer*, IX, 24, 16th June 1867.

49   Ibid, X, 16, 20th October 1867.

50   Ibid, XIV, 7, 15th August 1869.

51   Ibid, XV, 23, 5th June 1870.

52   Ibid.

53   See for example C. Bradlaugh (1870) *George Prince of Wales With Recent Contrasts and Coincidences* (London: Johnson's Court) [Bodleian Library (BOD): Vet. A7 e.297] and T. Milton Kemnitz (1975) 'Matt Morgan of "Tomahawk" and English Cartooning, 1867–70', *Victorian Studies*, XIX, p. 20, for cartoons in which 'Bertie' is impelled to follow the poor example furnished him by the ghost of the Prince Regent.

54   *National Reformer*, XV, 10, 18th March 1870.

55   Ibid.

56   Ibid.

57   Ibid, XIII, 24, 13th June 1869.

58   Ibid, XXIV, 5, 2nd August 1874.

59   Ibid, XXV, 25th July 1875.

60   See J. Davis (1991) 'Slums and the Vote, 1867–90', *Historical Research*, 64, pp. 375–88. This article alludes to fears that local government had been financially hamstrung by the disappearance of compounding rates which had resulted in the 1869 Poor Rate Assessment and Collection Act. Alongside this parliamentary reform legislation set in motion by Disraeli was, by 1870, eroding the 'three major barriers to the enfranchisement of tenement occupiers'. This raised important questions about the possession of local governmental administration, see pp. 383–4 in particular.

61   Thomas Wright (1873) *Our New Masters* (London) [BOD: Nuneham (OC) 232 f.144].

62   See the chapter entitled 'The Press and the People' in ibid, p. 323.

63   See J. Tosh (2002) 'Gentlemanly Politeness and Manly Simplicity in Victorian England', *Transactions of the Royal Historical Society*, 12, pp. 455–72.

64   *Reynolds's Newspaper*, 27th February 1870.

65   *Reynolds's Newspaper*, 6th March 1870.

66   Ibid.

67   *National Reformer*, XXVII, 15, 9th April 1876.

68   See ibid. and the *National Reformer*, XXVII, 18, 30th April 1876.

69   See G. Standring (1879) *Court Flunkeys, their 'Work' and Wages* (London: Freethought Publications Company) [BOD: 2276 e.4 [8]). Standring finishes this pamphlet with the words 'Would any public institution be conducted in a similar manner without incurring speedy censure and sure retribution?' '…Until public opinion is aroused on the matter, there is little hope of any reform being accomplished', p. 12.

70   E.P. Thompson, 'The Moral Economy of the English Crowd' in *Customs in Common*, pp. 185–258.

71   A. Heller (1985) *The Power of Shame: A Rational Perspective* (London: Routledge Keegan Paul), pp. 15–17.

72   Ibid, p. 24.

73   The fear of the new significance of public opinion could manifest itself even in the reconstruction of English Revolution historiography. J.S.A. Adamson has emphasised how such concerns motivated S.R. Gardiner's influential reading of seventeenth century history. Gardiner was fearful of mass democracy's

power to nullify the beneficial influence of educated and committed minority interests. Whilst the monarchy's dissolution in 1649 had been 'an object lesson in political morality', Gardiner's desire to place the English Revolution in the hands of those who possessed 'character' and unfettered purpose, also made Puritanism heroic and made an older ideology of duty and parsimony seem once again fashionable. For further discussion see J.S.A. Adamson (1990) 'Eminent Victorians: S.R. Gardiner and the Liberal as Hero', *Historical Journal*, 33, 3, pp. 641–57 and also B. Worden (2000) 'The Victorians and Oliver Cromwell', in S. Collini, R. Whatmore and B. Young (eds) *History, Religion and Culture: British Intellectual History 1750–1950* (Cambridge: Cambridge University Press), pp. 112–35.

74 Margot Finn has suggested that the third quarter of the nineteenth century witnessed a radicalisation of the middle classes which makes this period a more plausible candidate for the widespread acceptance of principles of social democracy. See M. Finn (1993) *After Chartism: Class and Nation in English Radical Politics, 1848–1874* (Cambridge: Cambridge University Press), p. 260.

75 See *Strand Magazine*, July 1891.

Chapter 9

1 See D. Fellman (1957) 'Cruel and Unusual Punishments', *The Journal of Politics*, 19, 1, pp. 34–45 and S.P. Garvey (1998) 'Can Shaming Punishments Educate?', *The University of Chicago Law Review*, 65, 3, pp. 733–94 for two different perspectives on this issue separated by roughly 50 years.

2 E.P. Thompson's chapter entitled 'Time, Work-Discipline and Industrial Capitalism', in (1991) *Customs in Common* (London: Penguin), pp. 352–466.

3 D.S. Nagin (1993) 'Enduring Individual Differences and Rational Choice: Theories of Crime', *Law and Society Review*, 27, 3, p. 490.

4 This is the central argument of John Carter-Wood's (2004) *Violence and Crime in Nineteenth-Century England: The Shadow of Our Refinement* (London: Routledge).

5 T. Hardy (1994 edition, originally published 1886) *The Mayor of Casterbridge* (London and New York: Penguin).

6 This was a peculiarly charged display that demonstrated an openly ribald statement about the couple's sexual practices; see M. Ingram (1984) 'Ridings, Rough Music and the Reform of Popular Culture in Early Modern England', *Past and Present*, 105, p. 86. See also A.J. Nigro (2000) *The Net of Nemesis: Studies in Tragic Bondage* (Sellinsgrove, Pennsylvania: Susquehanna University Press), p. 101, for an analysis which reinforces this view.

7 See E.P. Thompson's chapter entitled 'Sale of Wives', in (1991) *Customs in Common* (London: Penguin). See also S.P. Menefee (1981) *Wives for Sale: An Ethnographical Study of British Popular Divorce* (Oxford: Blackwell).

8 E.P. Thompson (1999) 'Sale of Wives', pp. 447–9.

9 Ibid, pp. 404–6.

10 See M. Ingram (1984) 'Ridings, Rough Music', passim. Ingram notes that the meaning of skimmington only stabilised around wife and husband beating in the nineteenth century and that before this they were a more flexible method of expressing communal disapproval. Ingram is also sceptical that such behaviour was uniformly cast aside by the middle sort and gentry. If he is to be believed, then Hardy produced an ahistorical hybrid incident. This, in particular, located the impetus behind the skimmington with the populace – a wholly nineteenth century reading of custom and community.

11 S.P. Menefee (1981) *Wives for Sale*, passim.

12 See E.P. Thompson (1991) 'Patricians and Plebs', pp. 16–96 and 'Customs, Law and Common Right', in *Customs in Common*, pp. 97–184.

13 Here Thompson cites P.H. Ditchfield (1896) *Old English Customs extant at the Present Time: An Account of Local Observances, Festival Customs and Ancient Ceremonies Yet Surviving in Great Britain* (London: G. Redway), Preface.

14 E.P. Thompson (1991) 'Custom and Culture', in *Customs in Common*, p. 2.

15 E.P. Thompson (1991) 'Rough Music', in *Customs in Common*, p. 513.

16 See M. Ingram (1984) 'Ridings, Rough Music', p. 79, p. 81 and p. 112.

17 Ibid, p. 93, pp. 96–8 and p. 111.

18 See notes 13 and 14 above.

19 R.B. Shoemaker (2000) 'The Decline of Public Insult in London 1660–1800', *Past and Present*, 169, pp. 97–131.

20 Ibid, p. 125 and p. 128.

21 Ibid, p. 130.

22 R. Shoemaker (2004) 'Streets of Shame? The Crowd and Public Punishments in London, 1700–1820', in S. Devereux and P. Griffiths (eds) *Penal Practice and Culture, 1500–1900* (Basingstoke: Palgrave Macmillan), pp. 256–7.

23 R.P. Dobash and R.E. Dobash (1981) 'Charivari, Abstract Justice and Patriarchy', *Social Problems*, 28, 5, pp. 563–81.

24 Ibid.

25 V. Alford (1959) 'Rough Music or Charivari', *Folklore*, 70, 4, p. 505.

26 Ibid, p. 506.

27 Ibid, pp. 517–18.

28 A.W. Smith (1967) 'Some Folklore Elements in Movements of Social Protest', *Folklore*, 77, pp. 241–52.

29 A. Lang (1904 edition) *Custom and Myth* (London: Longmans Green), p. 21 [Bodleian Library (BOD): 93 e.294].

30 A.H. Krappe (1930) *The Science of Folklore* (London: Methuen), pp. xvii–xviii.

31 See N. Elias (1978) *The History of Manners: The Civilizing Process: Volume I* (New York: Pantheon Books) and N. Elias (1982) *Power and Civility: The Civilizing Process: Volume II* (New York: Pantheon Books).

32 C.S. Burne (1914 edition) *The Handbook of Folklore* (London: Folklore Society and Sidgwick and Jackson Ltd.), pp. 1–2 [BOD: Soc. 93 e.52 (73)].

33 Ibid, p. 7.

34 See typology listed in ibid, p. 4.

35 T. Brown (1979) 'A Further Note on the "Stag Hunt" Devon', *Folklore*, 90, 1, p. 109.

36 For an interesting extended commentary on this latter phenomenon see W.I. Miller (1993) *Humiliation and Other Essays on Honor, Social Discomfort, and Violence* (Ithaca and London: Cornell University Press), pp. 131–3.

37 S. Mennell and J. Goudsblom (1997) 'Civilizing Processes – Myth or Reality? A Comment on Duerr's Critique of Elias', *Comparative Studies in Society and History*, 39, 4, pp. 729–33.

38 See J.S. Levenson and L.P. Cotter (2005) 'The Effect of Megan's Law on Sex Offender Reintegration', *Journal of Contemporary Criminal Justice*, 21, 1, pp. 49–66.

39 For an introduction to perspectives upon restorative justice (some of them critical) see A.W. Dzur (2003) 'Civic Implications of Restorative Justice Theory: Citizen Participation and Criminal Justice Policy', *Policy Sciences*, 36, 3/4, pp. 279–306; J.P. Sterba (1977) 'Retributive Justice', *Political Theory*, 5, 3, pp. 349–62; C. Villa-Vicencio (1999–2000) 'The Reek of Cruelty and the Quest for Healing: Where Retributive and Restorative Justice Meet', *Journal of Law and Religion*, 14, 1 pp. 165–87 and S.M. Olson and A.W. Dzur (2004) 'Revisiting Informal Justice: Restorative Justice and Democratic Professionalism', *Law and Society Review*, 38, 1, pp. 139–76.

40 See J.Q. Whitman (1998) 'What is Wrong with Inflicting Shame Sanctions?', *The Yale Law Journal*, 107, 4 (1998), pp. 1055–92.

41 Ibid, p. 1081.

42 See S.P. Garvey (1998) 'Can Shaming Punishments Educate?', *University of Chicago Law Review*, 65, p. 738 and D.M. Kahan and E.A. Posner (1999) 'Shaming White-Collar Criminals: A Proposal for Reform of the Federal Sentencing Guidelines', *Journal of Law and Economics*, 42, 1, pp. 365–91.

43 See E.W. Sauer (2003) The Archaeology of Religious Hatred in the Roman and Medieval World (Stroud: Tempus), pp. 16–17.

Bibliography

Primary Sources

Unpublished Primary Sources
Jersey Archive (St Helier)
Court Record Files D/V/N4/3.

Mitchell Library (Glasgow)
Burgh Records of Glasgow G 941.435 REN.

National Archives of Scotland (Edinburgh)
Justiciary Court Records (JC):
JC 3/12/115-174.
JC 7/12/62-64.
JC 7/12/68-69.
JC 11/11.
JC 11/12.
JC 12/9.
JC 13/15.
JC 26/108/1263/4-5.
JC 26/108/1263/7b.
JC 26/108/1264/2.
JC 26/108/1266/7-12.
JC 26/143-145/2601-2721.
JC 26/1037-1041.

Kirk Session Records (CH):
CH 2/122/3.

Sheriff Court Records (SC):
SC 20/5/1.
SC 62/10/13-14.

National Library of Scotland (Edinburgh)
(1724) *A Warning to the Wicked, or Margaret Dickson's Welcome to the Gibbet.*
(1728) *Margaret Dickson's Penitential Confession.*
(1724) *News from Musselburgh: Giving a Faithful Narrative of the Wonderful Restoration of Margaret Dickson to Life, Who Was Execute in the Grass-Market of Edinburgh, the 2ᵈ of September, 1724.*
(1727) *The Last Speech and Dying Words of John Dalgleish, Hangman of Edinburgh.*
(1724) *The Last Speech, Confession and Warning of Margaret Dickson, who was Execute in the Grass-Mercat of Edinburgh, for the Unnatural Murder of her Own Child, on Wednesday the 2ᵈ of September 1724.*
(Undated) *Particulars of the Life, Trial, Character, and Behaviour of Margaret Dickson.*

225

Published Primary Sources

Official Documents and Publications (in chronological order)

(1820) *Odes to the Pillory: Supposed to have been Written by a K——T and his Lady: To Which is Added 'The Pillory's Prayer'* (London: J. Johnston).

(1830) *A Full and Accurate Report of the Entire Proceedings in a Trial In the Cause of the Office v Rev. W.M. Hughes in the Consistorial Court, Dublin: Before his Grace the Archbishop of Dublin &c. &c. for several charges.... of, By him Committed* (Dublin).

(1834) *Miscellany of the Maitland Club Consisting of Original Papers and Other Documents Illustrative of the History and Literature of Scotland Volume I* (Edinburgh: H. & J. Pillans).

(1861) *Notes and Queries: A Medium of Inter-Communication for Literary Men, Artists, Antiquaries, Genealogists, Etc.* (London: Bell and Daldy), Second Series, XI.

(1866) *Calendar of State Papers, Domestic Series, of the Reign of Charles II* (London: Longman Green).

(1868) *The Life of Calcraft: An Account of the Executions in Scotland for the Past 200 Years.*

(1877) *Calendar of State Papers, Relating to Ireland, of the Reigns of Henry VIII, Edward VI, Mary and Elizabeth* (London: Longman Green).

(1885) *Calendar of State Papers, Relating to Ireland, of the Reigns of Henry VIII, Edward VI, Mary and Elizabeth* (London: Longman Green).

(1888) *Middlesex County Records: Volume 3: 1625–67* (London) [Accessed at British History On-line].

(1892) *Middlesex County Records: Volume 4: 1667–88* (London) [Accessed at British History On-line.]

(1895) *Calendar of State Papers, Domestic Series of the Reign of William and Mary* (London: HMSO).

(1900) *Calendar of State Papers, Domestic Series of the Reign of William and Mary* (London: HMSO).

(1905) *Middlesex County Records: Calendar of Sessions Books 1689–1709* (London), [Accessed at British History On-line].

(1913) *Calendar of State Papers, Domestic Series of the Reign of William and Mary* (London: HMSO).

(1915) *Calendar of State Papers, Domestic Series, of the Reign of Charles II* (London: Longman Green).

(1933) *Calendar of State Papers, Domestic Series, of the Reign of Charles II* (London: Longman Green).

(1933) *Calendar of State Papers, Domestic Series of the Reign of William and Mary* (London: HMSO).

(1937) *Calendar of State Papers, Domestic Series of the Reign of William and Mary* (London: HMSO).

(1937) *County of Middlesex: Calendar to the Sessions Records: New Series, Volume 3: 1615–16* (London) [Accessed at British History On-line].

(1938) *Calendar of State Papers, Domestic Series, of the Reign of Charles II* (London: Longman Green).

(1941) *County of Middlesex: Calendar to the Sessions Records: New Series, Volume 4: 1616–18* (London) [Accessed at British History On-line].

(1960) *Calendar of State Papers, Domestic Series of the Reign of William and Mary* (London: HMSO).

(1964) *Calendar of State Papers, Domestic Series, James II* (London: HMSO).

Newspapers and Periodicals

Birmingham Daily Post, 3rd February 1870.

British Press and Jersey Times, 31st January 1870.

Illustrated Police News, 12th February 1870.

Jersey Express, 1st February 1870.

Liverpool Mercury, 3rd February 1870.

Lloyds Weekly Newspaper, 6th February 1870.

National Reformer, March 1861–April 1876.

Pall Mall Gazette, 2nd February 1870.

Republican Herald, 11th April 1874.

Reynolds's Newspaper, February–March 1870.

The Caledonian Mercury, September 1724–July 1725.

The Carmarthen Journal, 6th April 1838.

The Times, 3rd February 1870.

Western Mail, 4th February 1870.

Contemporary Books and Articles

Alison, A. (1833) *Practice of the Criminal Law of Scotland* (Edinburgh: William Blackwood).

Alison, A. (1832) *Principles of the Criminal Law of Scotland* (Edinburgh: William Blackwood).

Beccaria, C. (1767) *An Essay on Crimes and Punishments, translated from the Italian; With A Commentary, Attributed To Monsieur Voltaire translated from the French* (London: J. Almon).

Bentham, J. (1830) *The Rationale of Punishment* (London: R. Heward).

Bradlaugh, C. (1877) *The Impeachment of the House of Brunswick* (London: Freethought Publishing Company).

Burnett, J. (1811) *A Treatise on Various Branches of the Criminal Law of Scotland* (Edinburgh: Archibald Constable and Co.).

Buxton, T.F. (1818) *An Appeal to the Friends of Humanity on behalf of English Prisoners* (Stockton).

Carter Hall, S. (1860) *Tenby: Its History, Antiquities, Scenery, Traditions and Customs* (Tenby: Mason).

Chambers, R. (1861) *Domestic Annals of Scotland: From the Revolution to the Rebellion of 1745* (Edinburgh and London: W. and R. Chambers), Volume III.

Chambers, R. (ed.) (1879) *The Book of Days: A Miscellany of Popular Antiquities in Association with the Calendar* (Philadelphia: J.B. Lippincott and Co.), Volume I.

Chambers, R. (1828) *The Picture of Scotland* (Edinburgh: William Tait Publisher), Volumes I and II.

De Bruce Trotter, R. (1901) *Galloway Gossip or the Southern Albanich: 80 Years Ago* (Dumfries: Courier and Herald).

Defoe, D. (1703) *A Hymn to the Pillory* (London: H. Hills).

Defoe, D. (1703) *The Shortest-Way with the Dissenters; Or, Proposals for the Establishment of the Church* (London).

De Montesquieu, Baron (1748) *The Spirit of Laws* [translated by Thomas Nugent] (London: J. Nourse and P. Valliant).

Ditchfield, P.H. (1896) *Old English Customs extant at the Present Time: An Account of Local Observances, Festival Customs and Ancient Ceremonies Yet Surviving in Great Britain* (London: G. Redway).

Grant, J. (1890) *Old and New Edinburgh: Its History, Its People and Its Places* (London: Cassell and Co.), Volume IV.

Hardy, T. (1886) *The Mayor of Casterbridge* (London: Edward Arnold).

Hume, D. (1797, 1844 edition, 1986 reprint) *Commentaries on the Laws of Scotland, Respecting Crimes* (Edinburgh: The Law Society of Scotland), Volumes I and II.

Jackson, W. (1795) *The New and Complete Newgate Calendar* (London: Alexander Hogg Publisher), Volumes I–VI.

Mackenzie of Rosehaugh, Sir George (1678) *The Laws and Customs of Scotland in Matters Criminal* (Edinburgh: Andrew Anderson), Title XXX.

MacLaurin, M. (1774) *Arguments and Decision in Remarkable Cases Before the High Court of Justiciary and other Supreme Courts in Scotland* (Edinburgh: J. Bell).

Onesiphorus Paul, G. (1789) *An Address to the Magistrates of the County of Gloucester assembled at their Michaelmas Quarter Sessions* (Gloucester: R. Raikes).

Pennecuik, A. (1787) 'The Merry Wives of Musselburgh's Welcome to Meg Dickson', in A. Pennecuik (ed.) *A Collection of Scots Poems on Several Occasions by Alexander Pennecuik, Gentleman and Others* (Glasgow: Alexander Buchanan, Publisher).

Roscoe, W. (1823) *Additional Observations on Penal Jurisprudence, and the Reformation of Criminals* (London: T. Cadell).

Rush, B. (1787) *An Enquiry into the Effects of Public Punishments upon Criminals and upon Society: Read in the Society for Promoting Political Enquiries, March 9th 1787* (Philadelphia: Joseph James).

Rutt, J.T. (1828) (ed.) *Diary of Thomas Burton Esquire, Volume 1: July 1653–April 1657* (London: Colburn).

Scott, Sir Walter (1818) *The Heart of Mid-Lothian* (London: Macmillan).

Smith, W. (1778) *Mild Punishments Sound Policy: Or Observations on the Law Relative to Debtors and Felons* (London: J. Bew).

Standring, G. (1879) *Court Flunkeys, their 'Work' and Wages* (London: Freethought Publications Company).

The Society for the Suppression of Vice (1807) *The Constable's Assistant, Being a Compendium of the Duties and Powers of Constables* (London).

Wright, T. (1873) *Our New Masters* (London).

Secondary Sources

Adams, N. (1993) *Hangman's Brae: Crime and Punishment in and around Bygone Aberdeen* (Banchory, Kincardineshire: Tolbooth).

Adams, N. (1996) *Scotland's Chronicles of Blood: Torture and Execution in Bygone Times* (London: Robert Hale).

Adamson, J.S.A. (1990) 'Eminent Victorians: S.R. Gardiner and the Liberal as Hero', *Historical Journal*, 33, 3, pp. 641–57.

Alford, V. (1959) 'Rough Music or Charivari', *Folklore*, 70, pp. 505–18.

Allan, D.G.C. (1952) 'The Rising in the West, 1628–1631', *The Economic History Review*, 5, 1, pp. 76–85.

Anderson, O. (1999) 'State, Civil Society and Separation in Victorian Marriage', *Past and Present*, 163, pp. 161–201.

Andrews, W. (1991) *Old Time Punishments* (New York: Dorset Press), pp. 42–50.

Arch, J. (1986) *From Plough Tail to Parliament: An Autobiography* (London: Cresset Library).

Baelde, M.R. (1935) *Studiën over Godslastering* (Den Haag: Nijhof).

Bailey, A.C. (2005) *African Voices of the Atlantic Slave Trade: Beyond the Silence and the Shame* (Boston, Mass.: Beacon Press).

Bailey, J. (2010) 'Cruelty and Adultery: Offences against the Institution of Marriage', in A.M. Kilday and D.S. Nash (eds) *Histories of Crime: Britain 1600–2000* (Basingstoke: Palgrave Macmillan), pp. 39–59.

Bailey, J. (2003) *Unquiet Lives: Marriage and Marriage Breakdown in England, 1660–1800* (Cambridge: Cambridge University Press).

Berry, H. (2001) 'Rethinking Politeness in Eighteenth-Century England: Moll King's Coffee House and the Significance of "Flash Talk", *Royal Historical Society Transactions*, XI, pp. 65–81.

Biagini, E.F. (2003) 'Neo-roman Liberalism: "Republican" Values and British Liberalism, ca. 1860–1875', *History of European Ideas*, 29, 1, pp. 55–72.

Bland, J. (1984) *The Common Hangman: English and Scottish Hangmen Before the Abolition of Public Executions* (Essex: I. Henry Publications).

Boose, L.E. (1991) 'Scolding Brides and Bridling Scolds: Taming the Woman's Unruly Member', *Shakespeare Quarterly*, 42, 4, pp. 179–213.

Bosco, R.A. (1978) 'Lectures at the Pillory: The Early American Execution Sermon', *American Quarterly Review*, XXX, pp. 156–76.

Bourke, J. (2008) *Rape: A History from 1860 to the Present Day* (London: Virago).

Boyd, K.M. (1980) *Scottish Church Attitudes to Sex, Marriage and the Family, 1850–1914* (Edinburgh: Donald).

Bradlaugh, C. (1870) *George Prince of Wales With Recent Contrasts and Coincidences* (London: Johnson's Court).

Bradlaugh-Bonner, H. (1934) *Penalties Upon Opinion* (London: Watts and Company).

Brown, T. (1979) 'A Further Note on the "Stag Hunt" Devon', *Folklore*, 90, 1, pp. 104–9.

Brushfield, T.N. (1864) 'On Obsolete Punishments, with Particular Reference to those of Cheshire: Part I – The Brank or Scold's Bridle', *Journal of the Archaeological Society of Chester*, 2, pp. 30–48.

Brushfield, T.N. (1864) 'On Obsolete Punishments, with Particular Reference to those of Cheshire: Part II – The Cucking-Stool and Allied Punishments', *Journal of the Archaeological Society of Chester*, 2, pp. 203–34.

Burg, B.R. (2007) *Boys at Sea: Sodomy, Indecency and the Courts Martial in Nelson's Navy* (Basingstoke: Palgrave Macmillan).

Burne, C.S. (1914 edition) *The Handbook of Folklore* (London: Folklore Society and Sidgwick and Jackson Ltd.).

Butler, S.M. (2007) 'A Case of Indifference? Child Murder in Late Medieval England', *Journal of Women's History*, XIX, pp. 59–82.

Carter-Wood, J. (2004) *Violence and Crime in Nineteenth-Century England: The Shadow of Our Refinement* (London: Routledge).

Cawte, E.C. (1963) 'Parsons Who Rode the Stang', *Folklore*, 74, 2, pp. 399–401.

Claeys, G. (1989) 'Mazzini, Kossuth, and British Radicalism, 1848–54', *Journal of British Studies*, 28, 3, pp. 225–61.

Clark, A. (1987) *Women's Silence, Men's Violence: Sexual Assault in England, 1770–1845* (London and New York: Pandora).

Clark, A. (2004) *Scandal: The Sexual Politics of the British Constitution* (Princeton, N.J. and Oxford: Princeton University Press).

Collinson, P. (1967) *The Elizabethan Puritan Movement* (Oxford: Clarendon Press).

Cunnington, B.H. (1930) '"A Skimmington" in 1618', *Folklore*, 41, 3, pp. 287–90.

Darnton, R. (1984) *The Great Cat Massacre: And Other Episodes in French Cultural History* (London: Allen Lane).

Davidoff, L. and C. Hall (1987) *Family Fortunes: Men and Women of the English Middle Class 1780–1850* (London: Hutchison).

Davis, J. (1991) 'Slums and the Vote, 1867–90', *Historical Research*, 64, pp. 375–88.

D'Cruze, S. (1998) *Crimes of Outrage: Sex, Violence and Victorian Working Women* (DeKalb: Northern Illinois University Press).

D'Cruze, S. (2000) *Everyday Violence in Britain, 1850–1950: Gender and Class* (Harlow: Longman).

Delumeau, J. (1990) *Sin and Fear: The Emergence of Western Guilt Culture: 13th–18th Centuries* [translated by Eric Nicholson] (New York: St. Martin's Press).

Dobash, R.P. and R.E. Dobash (1981) 'Charivari, Abstract Justice and Patriarchy', *Social Problems*, 28, 5, pp. 563–81.

Dickinson, J.R. and J.A. Sharpe (2002) 'Infanticide in Early Modern England: The Court of Great Sessions at Chester, 1650–1800', in M. Jackson (ed.) *Infanticide*, pp. 35–51.

Donajgrodski, A.P. (1977) (ed.) *Social Control in Nineteenth Century Britain* (London: Croom Helm).

Dunbabin, J.P.D. (1975) 'Oliver Cromwell's Popular Image in Nineteenth Century England', *Britain and the Netherlands: Papers Delivered to the Fifth Anglo-Dutch Historical Conference* (The Hague: Martinus Hijhof).

Dzur, A.W. (2003) 'Civic Implications of Restorative Justice Theory: Citizen Participation and Criminal Justice Policy', *Policy Sciences*, 36, 3/4, pp. 279–306.

Elias, N. (2000) *The Civilizing Process* [translated by E. Jephcott] (Oxford: Wiley Blackwell).

Emsley, E. (1996, second edition) *Crime and Society in England 1750–1900* (London: Longman).

Epstein, J. (1994) *Radical Expression: Political Language, Ritual and Symbol in England, 1790–1850* (Oxford: Oxford University Press).

Faller, L.B. (1976) 'In Contrast to Defoe: The Rev. Paul Lorrain, Historian of Crime', *The Huntington Library Quarterly*, XL, pp. 59–78.

Faller, L.B. (1987) *Turned to Account: The Forms and Functions of Criminal Biography in Late Seventeenth- and Early Eighteenth-Century England* (Cambridge: Cambridge University Press).

Fellman, D. (1957) 'Cruel and Unusual Punishments', *The Journal of Politics*, 19, 1, pp. 34–45.

Finn, M. (1993) *After Chartism: Class and Nation in English Radical Politics, 1848–1874* (Cambridge: Cambridge University Press).

Fitts, J.L. (1973) 'Newcastle's Mob', *Albion*, V, 1, pp. 41–9.

Fletcher, A. (1994) 'Men's Dilemma: The Future of Patriarchy in England 1560–1660', *Transactions of the Royal Historical Society*, Sixth Series, 4, pp. 77–8.

Flynn, M. (1995) 'Blasphemy and the Play of Anger in Sixteenth Century Spain', *Past and Present*, 149, 1, pp. 29–56.

Forsdkye, S. (2008) 'Street Theatre and Popular Justice in Ancient Greece: Shaming, Stoning and Starving Offenders Inside and Outside the Courts', *Past and Present*, 201, pp. 3–50.

Foucault, M. (1991, third edition) *Discipline and Punish: The Birth of the Prison* (translated from the French by Alan Sheridan) (Harmondsworth: Penguin).

Foyster, E. 'Creating a Veil of Silence? Politeness and Marital Violence in the English Household', *Royal Historical Society Transactions*, XII, pp. 395–415.

Francus, M. (1997) 'Monstrous Mothers, Monstrous Societies: Infanticide and the Rule of Law in Restoration and Eighteenth-century England', *Eighteenth-Century Life*, XXI, pp. 133–56.

Frank, S.P. (1987) 'Popular Justice and Culture among the Russian Peasantry, 1870–1900', *Russian Review*, 46, 3, pp. 239–65.

Garland, D. (1985) *Punishment and Welfare: A History of Penal Strategies* (Aldershot: Gower).

Garvey, S.P. (1988) 'Can Shaming Punishments Educate?', *University of Chicago Law Review*, 65, 4, pp. 733–94.

Gatrell, V.A.C. (1994) *The Hanging Tree: Execution and the English People, 1770–1868* (Oxford: Oxford University Press).

Gibson, I. (1978) *The English Vice: Beating, Sex and Shame in Victorian England and After* (London: Duckworth).

Goffman, E. (1963) *Behaviour in Public Places: Notes on the Social Organisation of Gatherings* (New York: Free Press).

Goffman, E. (1967) *Interaction Ritual: Essays on Face-to Face Behaviour* (Princeton, N.J. and Oxford: Princeton University Press).

Goffman, E. (1971) *Relations in Public: Micro-studies of the Public Order* (Harmondsworth: Penguin).

Goffman, E. (1963) *Stigma: Notes on the Management of Spoiled Identity* (Harmondsworth: Penguin).

Goffman, E. (1959) *The Presentation of Self in Everyday Life* (Harmondsworth: Penguin).

Gorsky, M. (1994) 'James Tuckfield's "Ride": Combination and Social Drama in Early Nineteenth-Century Bristol', *Social History*, 19, 3, pp. 319–38.

Gowing, L. (1997) 'Secret Births and Infanticide in Seventeenth-Century England', *Past and Present*, CLVI, pp. 87–115.

Gossman, N.J. (1962) 'Republicanism in Nineteenth-Century England', *International Review of Social History*, 7, pp. 47–60.

Guthrie, E.J. (1994) *Old Scottish Customs: Local and General* (London and Glasgow: Llanerch Publishers).

Habermas, J. (1962) [trans. 1989] *The Structural Transformation of the Public Sphere: An Inquiry into a Category of Bourgeois Society* (Cambridge: Polity).

Hammerton, A.J. (1999) 'Pooterism of Partnership? Marriage and Masculine Identity in the Lower Middle Class, 1870–1920', *Journal of British Studies*, 38, pp. 291–321.

Hammerton, A.J. (1990) 'Victorian Marriage and the Law of Matrimonial Cruelty', *Victorian Studies*, 33, pp. 269–92.

Hardy, T. (2007, new edition) *The Mayor of Casterbridge* (London: Penguin).

Harrison, J.G. (1998) 'Women and the Branks in Stirling c.1600 to 1730', *Scottish Economic and Social History*, 18, pp. 114–31.

Heimannsberg, B. and C.J. Schmidt (1993) (eds) *The Collective Silence: German Identity and the Legacy of Shame* (San Francisco: Jossey-Bass).

Heller, A. (1995) *The Power of Shame: A Rational Perspective* (London: Routledge Keegan Paul).

Helmholz, R.H. (1987) 'Infanticide in the Province of Canterbury during the Fifteenth Century', in R.H. Helmholz (ed.) *Canon Law and the Law of England* (London: Hambledon), pp. 157–68.

Hoffer, P.C. and N.E.C. Hull (1984) *Murdering Mothers: Infanticide in England and New England, 1558–1803* (New York: New York University Press).

Homans, M. (1993) '"To the Queen's Private Apartments": Royal Family Portraiture and the Construction of Victoria's Sovereign Obedience', *Victorian Studies*, 37, 3, pp. 1–41.

Ingram, M. (1984) 'Ridings, Rough Music and the "Reform of Popular Culture"', pp. 79–113.

Ingram, M. (1995) '"Scolding Women Cucked or Washed": A Crisis in Gender Relations in Early Modern England', in J. Kermode and G. Walker (eds) *Women, Crime and the Courts in Early Modern England* (Chapel Hill, North Carolina and London: The University of North Carolina Press), pp. 48–80.

Jackson, M. (1996) *New-Born Child Murder: Women, Illegitimacy and the Courts in Eighteenth-Century England* (Manchester: Manchester University Press).

Johnson, L.T. (1990) 'Charivari/Shivaree: A European Folk Ritual on American Plains', *Journal of Interdisciplinary History*, 20, 3, pp. 371–87.

Jones, R.A.N. (1991) 'Women, Community and Collective Action: The 'Ceffyl Pren' Tradition', in A.V. John (ed.) *Our Mother's Land: Chapters in Welsh Women's History, 1830–1939* (Cardiff: University of Wales Press), pp. 17–41.

Kahan, D.M. and E.A. Posner (1999) 'Shaming White-Collar Criminals: A Proposal for Reform of the Federal Sentencing Guidelines', *Journal of Law and Economics*, 42, 1, pp. 365–91.

Karant-Nunn, S.C. (1994) 'Neoclericalism and Anticlericalism in Saxony 1555–1675', *Journal of Interdisciplinary History*, XXIV, 4, pp. 615–37.

Keane, J. (1995) *Tom Paine: A Political Life* (London: Bloomsbury).

Kelly, J. (2001) *Gallows Speeches from Eighteenth-Century Ireland* (Dublin: Four Courts Press).

Kelly, J. (1992) 'Infanticide in Eighteenth-Century Ireland', *Irish Economic and Social History*, XIX, pp. 5–26.

Kenneally, J. (2007) *The Honour and the Shame* (London: Headline Review).

Kent, J.R. (1983) '"Folk Justice" and Royal Justice in Early Seventeenth-Century England: A "Charivari" in the Midlands', *Midland History*, 8, pp. 70–85.

Kilday, A-M. (2010) 'Desperate Measures or Cruel Intentions: Infanticide in Britain since 1600', in A-M. Kilday and D.S. Nash (eds) *Histories of Crime: Britain 1600–2000* (Basingstoke: Palgrave Macmillan), pp. 60–79.

Kilday, A-M. (2008) '"Monsters of the Vilest Kind": Infanticidal Women and Attitudes towards their Criminality in Eighteenth-Century Scotland', *Family and Community History*, 11, 2, pp. 100–15.

Kilday, A-M. (2007) *Women and Violent Crime in Enlightenment Scotland* (Woodbridge, Suffolk: Boydell Press).

Kilday, A-M. and K.D. Watson, 'Infanticide, Religion and Community in the British Isles, 1720–1920: Introduction', *Family and Community History*, 11, 2, pp. 88–91.

Krappe, A.H. (1930) *The Science of Folklore* (London: Methuen).

Lake, P. (1994) 'Deeds Against Nature: Cheap Print, Protestantism and Murder in Early Seventeenth-Century England', in K. Sharpe and P. Lake (eds) *Culture and Politics in Early Stuart England* (Basingstoke: Macmillan), pp. 257–83.

Lake, P. and M. Questier (1996) 'Agency, Appropriation and Rhetoric Under the Gallows: Puritans, Romanists and the State in Early Modern England', *Past and Present*, CLIII, pp. 64–107.

Lang, A. (1904 edition) *Custom and Myth* (London: Longmans Green).

Langford, P. (2002) 'The Uses of Eighteenth Century Politeness', *Royal Historical Society Transactions*, XII, pp. 311–31.

Laqueur, T. (1989) 'Crowds, Carnivals and the State in English Executions, 1604–1868', in A. Beier, D. Cannadine and J. Rosenheim (eds) *The First Modern Society: Essays in English History in Honour of Lawrence Stone* (Cambridge: Cambridge University Press), pp. 305–55.

Larner, C. (1984) *Witchcraft and Religion: The Politics of Popular Belief* (Oxford: Blackwell).

Lawton, D. (1993) *Blasphemy* (London: Harvester).

Leslie, Rev. J.B. (1936) *Ferns Clergy and Parishes: Being an Account of the Clergy of the Church of Ireland in the Diocese of Ferns from the Earliest Period, with Historical Notices of the Several Parishes, Churches, Etc.* (Dublin: Church of Ireland Printing and Publishing Co. Ltd.).

Levenson, J.S. and L.P. Cotter (2005) 'The Effect of Megan's Law on Sex Offender Reintegration', *Journal of Contemporary Criminal Justice*, 21, 1, pp. 49–66.

Levy, L. (1993) *Blasphemy, Verbal Offense Against the Sacred from Moses to Salman Rushdie* (New York: Knopf).

Leys, R. (2007) *From Guilt to Shame: Auschwitz and After* (Princeton, N.J. and Woodstock: Princeton University Press).

MacAloon, J.J. (1984) *Rite, Drama, Festival, Spectacle: Rehearsals Toward a Theory of Cultural Performance* (Philadelphia, Pennsylvania: Institute for the Study of Human Issues).

Malcolmson, R.W. (1977) 'Infanticide in the Eighteenth Century', in J.S. Cockburn (ed.) *Crime in England, 1550–1800* (London: Methuen), pp. 187–209.

Manning, D. (2008) 'Anti Providentialism in Late Stuart England: A Case Study of the "Stage Debate"', *Journal of Religious History*, 32, 4, pp. 422–38.

Marland, H. (2004) *Dangerous Motherhood: Insanity and Childbirth in Victorian Britain* (Basingstoke: Palgrave Macmillan).

Marland, H. (2002) 'Getting Away With Murder? Puerperal Insanity, Infanticide and the Defence Plea', in M. Jackson (ed.) *Infanticide: Historical Perspectives on Child Murder and Concealment, 1550–2000* (Aldershot: Ashgate), pp. 168–92.

McCalman, I. (1993) *Radical Underworld: Prophets, Revolutionaries and Pornographers in London, 1795–1840* (Oxford: Clarendon Press).

McGowen, R. (1986) 'A Powerful Sympathy: Terror, The Prison, and Humanitarian Reform in Early Nineteenth Century Britain', *Journal of British Studies*, 25, 3, pp. 312–34.

McGowen, R. (1999) 'From Pillory to Gallows: The Punishment of Forgery in the Age of the Financial Revolution', *Past and Present*, 165, pp. 107–40.

McGowen, R. (1987) 'The Body and Punishment in Eighteenth-Century England', *Journal of Modern History*, 59, pp. 651–79.

McKeon, M. (2002) 'The Secret History of Domesticity: Private, Public, and the Division of Knowledge', in C. Jones and D. Wahrman (eds) *The Age of Cultural*

Revolutions: Britain and France, 1750–1820 (London: University of California Press), pp. 171–89.

McKnight, M. (2005) 'Charivaris, Cowbellions and Sheet Iron Bands: Nineteenth-Century Rough Music in New Orleans', *American Music*, 23, 4, pp. 407–25.

McLynn, F. (1989) *Crime and Punishment in Eighteenth-Century England* (London: Routledge).

Mellinkoff, R. (1973) 'Riding Backwards: Theme of Humiliation and Symbol of Evil', *Viator: Medieval and Renaissance Studies*, 4, pp. 153–76.

Menefee, S.P. (1981) *Wives for Sale: An Ethnographical Study of British Popular Divorce* (Oxford: Blackwell).

Mennell, S. and J. Goudsblom (1997) 'Civilizing Processes – Myth or Reality? A Comment on Duerr's Critique of Elias', *Comparative Studies in Society and History*, 39, 4, pp. 729–33.

Merback, M.B. (1999) *The Thief, The Cross and The Wheel: Pain and the Spectacle of Punishment in Medieval and Renaissance Europe* (London: Reaktion Books).

Miller, W.I. (1993) *Humiliation and Other Essays on Honor, Social Discomfort, and Violence* (Ithaca and London: Cornell University Press).

Milton Kemnitz, T. (1975) 'Matt Morgan of "Tomahawk" and English Cartooning, 1867–70', *Victorian Studies*, XIX, pp. 5–34.

Mitchison, R. and L. Leneman (1989) *Sexuality and Social Control: Scotland, 1660–1780* (Oxford: Basil Blackwell).

Moore, J.R. (1939) *Defoe in the Pillory: A New Interpretation* [Humanities Series No. 1] (Bloomington, Indiana: Indiana University Publications).

Moore, P. (2005) *Beyond Shame: Reclaiming the Abandoned History of Radical Gay Sexuality* (Boston, Mass.: Beacon Press).

Munich, A. (1996) *Queen Victoria's Secrets* (New York: Columbia University Press).

Nagin, D.S. (1993) 'Enduring Individual Differences and Rational Choice: Theories of Crime', *Law and Society Review*, 27, 3, pp. 467–96.

Nash, D.S. (2007) *Blasphemy in the Christian World: A History* (Oxford: Oxford University Press).

Nash, D.S. (2000) 'Charles Bradlaugh, India and the Many Chameleon Destinations of Republicanism', in D.S. Nash and A. Taylor (eds) *Republicanism in Victorian Society* (Stroud: Sutton), pp. 106–24.

Nash, D.S. (2008) '"To Prostitute Morality, Libel Religion and Undermine Government": Blasphemy and the Strange Persistence of Providence in Britain since the Seventeenth Century', *Journal of Religious History*, 32, 4, pp. 439–56.

Nash, D.S. and A. Taylor (2000) (eds) *Republicanism in Victorian Society* (Stroud: Sutton).

Newburn, T. and E.A. Stanko (1994) *Just Boys Doing Business? Men, Masculinities and Crime* (London: Routledge).

Nigro, A.J. (2000) *The Net of Nemesis: Studies in Tragic Bond/age* (Sellinsgrove, Pennsylvania: Susquehanna University Press).

Olli, S-M. (2008) 'Blasphemy in Early Modern Sweden – An Untold Story', *Journal of Religious History*, 32, 4, pp. 457–70.

Olson, S.M. and A.W. Dzur (2004) 'Revisiting Informal Justice: Restorative Justice and Democratic Professionalism', *Law and Society Review*, 38, 1, pp. 139–76.

Oppenheimer, P. (1997) *An Intelligent Person's Guide to Modern Guilt* (London: Duckworth).

Ottesen Garrigan, K. (1992) *Victorian Scandals: Repressions of Gender and Class* (Columbus, Ohio: Ohio University Press).

Parker, C. (1997) 'The Moral Agency and Moral Autonomy of Church Folk in the Dutch Reformed Church of Delft 1580–1620', *Journal of Ecclesiastical History*, 48, 1, pp. 44–70.

Paster, G.K. (1993) *The Body Embarrassed: Drama and the Disciplines of Shame in Early Modern England* (Ithaca: Cornell University Press).

Pettifer, E.W. (1992 reprint) *Punishments of Former Days* (Winchester: Waterside Press).

Plunkett, J. (2003) *Queen Victoria: First Media Monarch* (Oxford: Oxford University Press).

Pollak, O. (1950) *The Criminality of Women* (Philadelphia: University of Pennsylvania Press).

Postles, D. (2003) 'Penance and the Market Place: A Reformation Dialogue with the Medieval Church (c. 1250–1600)', *Journal of Ecclesiastical History*, 54, 3, pp. 441–68.

Prochaska, F. (1995) *Royal Bounty: The Making of a Welfare Monarchy* (New Haven, C.T. and London: Yale University Press).

Prochaska, F. (2001) *The Republic of Britain 1760–2000* (London: Penguin).

Quinn, C. (2002) 'Images and Impulses: Representations of Puerperal Insanity and Infanticide in Late Victorian England', in M. Jackson (ed.) *Infanticide: Historical Perspectives on Child Murder and Concealment, 1550–2000* (Aldershot: Ashgate), pp. 193–215.

Rabin, D. (2002) 'Bodies of Evidence, States of Mind: Infanticide, Emotion and Sensibility in Eighteenth-Century England', in M. Jackson (ed.) *Infanticide: Historical Perspectives on Child Murder and Concealment, 1550–2000* (Aldershot: Ashgate) pp. 73–92.

Radbill, S.X. (1968) 'A History of Child Abuse and Infanticide', in R.E. Helfer and C.H. Kempe (eds) *The Battered Child* (Chicago: University of Chicago Press), pp. 3–17.

Rasmussen, S.J. (2007) 'Continuing Commentary – Revitalizing Shame: Some Reflections on Changing Idioms of Shame – Expressions of Disgrace and Dishonour in the Narratives of Turkish Women Living in Denmark', *Culture and Psychology*, 13, pp. 231–42.

Renwick, R., Sir J. Lindsay and G. Eyre-Todd (1931) *History of Glasgow: Volume II – From the Reformation to the Revolution* (Glasgow: Jackson, Wylie and Co.).

Riezler, K. (1943) 'Comment on the Social Psychology of Shame', *The American Journal of Sociology*, 48, 4, pp. 457–65.

Robinson, M. (1985) (ed.) *The Concise Scots Dictionary* (Aberdeen: Aberdeen University Press).

Rollinson, D. (1981) 'Property, Ideology and Popular Culture in a Gloucestershire Village, 1660–1740', *Past and Present*, 93, pp. 70–97.

Rogers, Rev. C. (1884) *Social Life in Scotland From Early to Recent Times*, Volume II (Edinburgh: William Paterson).

Rose, L. (1986) *The Massacre of the Innocents: Infanticide in Britain 1800–1939* (London: Routledge and Kegan Paul).

Rose, R.B. (1960) 'The Priestley Riots of 1791', *Past and Present*, 18, pp. 68–88.

Rublack, U. (1999) *The Crimes of Women in Early Modern Germany* (Oxford: Clarendon Press).

Rudé, G. (1959) 'The London "Mob" of the Eighteenth Century', *Historical Journal*, II, 1, pp. 1–18.

Ruff, J.R. (1984) *Crime, Justice and the Public Order in Old Regime France: The Sènèchaussèes of Libourne and Bazas, 1696–1789* (London and Dover, N.H.: Croom Helm).

Ruff, J.R. (2001) *Violence in Early Modern Europe* (Cambridge: Cambridge University Press).

Rumsey, C. (2000) *The Rise and Fall of British Republican Clubs 1871–1874* (Oswestry: Quinta Press).

Ryley Scott, G. (1968) *Flagellation: A History of Corporal Punishment in Its Historical, Anthropological and Sociological Aspects* (London: Tallis P.).

Savage, G. (1998) 'Erotic Stories and Public Decency: Newspaper Reporting of Divorce Proceedings in England', *Historical Journal*, 41, pp. 511–28.

Sauer, E.W. (2003) *The Archaeology of Religious Hatred in the Roman and Medieval World* (Stroud: Tempus).

Scheff, T.J. (1988) 'Shame and Conformity: The Deference-Emotion System', *American Sociological Review*, 53, 3, pp. 395–406.

Scheff, T.J. (2000) 'Shame and the Social Bond: A Sociological Theory', *Sociological Theory*, 18, 1, pp. 84–99.

Schwerhoff, G. (2005) *Zungen wie Schwerter, Blasphemie in alteuropäischen Gesellschaften 1200–1650* (Konstanz Verlag: UvK).

Sharpe, J.A. (1983) *Crime in Seventeenth Century England – A County Study* (Cambridge: Cambridge University Press).

Sharpe, J.A. (1985) '"Last Dying Speeches": Religion, Ideology and Public Execution in Seventeenth Century England', *Past and Present*, CVII, pp. 144–67.

Sharpe, J.A. (1986) 'Plebeian Marriage in Stuart England: Some Evidence from Popular Literature', *Transactions of the Royal Historical Society*, 36, pp. 69–90.

Shoemaker, R. (2004) 'Streets of Shame? The Crowd and Public Punishments in London, 1700–1820', in S. Devereux and P. Griffiths (eds) *Penal Practice and Culture, 1500–1900* (Basingstoke: Palgrave Macmillan), pp. 232–57.

Shoemaker, R. (2004) *The London Mob: Violence and Order in Eighteenth Century London* (London: Hambledon and London).

Shoemaker, R.B. (2000) 'The Decline of Public Insult in London 1660–1800', *Past and Present*, 169, pp. 97–131.

Sinclair, Sir J. (ed.) (1975) *The Statistical Account of Scotland, 1791–1799: Volume II – The Lothians* (Wakefield: EP Publishing).

Sindall, R. (1987) 'The London Garrotting Panics of 1856 and 1862', *Social History*, 12, 3, pp. 351–9.

Smith, A.W. (1967) 'Some Folklore Elements in Movements of Social Protest', *Folklore*, 77, pp. 241–52.

Smith, R. (1982) 'Defining Murder and Madness: An Introduction to Medicolegal Belief in the Case of Mary Ann Brough, 1854', in R.A. Jones and H. Kuklich (eds) *Knowledge and Society: Studies in the Sociology of Culture Past and Present*, vol. 4 (Greenwich, CN and London: JAI Press Inc), pp. 173–225.

Soman, A. (1976) 'Press, Pulpit and Censorship in France before Richelieu', *Proceedings of the American Philosophical Society*, 120, 6, pp. 439–63.

Spierenburg, P. (1984) *The Spectacle of Suffering – Executions and the Evolution of Repression: From a Pre-Industrial Metropolis to the European Experience* (Cambridge: Cambridge University Press).

Stanko, E.A. (1990) *Everyday Violence: How Women and Men Experience Sexual and Physical Danger* (London: Pandora).

Sterba, J.P. (1977) 'Retributive Justice', *Political Theory*, 5, 3, pp. 349–62.

Stevenson, K. (2010) '"Most Intimate Violations": Contextualising the Crime of Rape', in A.M. Kilday and D.S. Nash (eds) *Histories of Crime: Britain 1600–2000* (Basingstoke: Palgrave Macmillan), pp. 80–99.

Symonds, D.A. (1997) *Weep Not For Me: Women, Ballads and Infanticide in Early Modern Scotland* (University Park, PA: Pennsylvania State University Press).

Taylor, A. (1999) *'Down with the Crown': British Anti-monarchism and Debates about Royalty since 1790* (London: Reaktion Books).

Taylor, A. (2003) *Lords of Misrule* (Basingstoke: Palgrave Macmillan).

Taylor, A. (1995) 'Reynolds's Newspaper, Opposition to Monarchy and the Radical Anti-jubilee: Britain's Anti-monarchist Tradition Reconsidered', *Bulletin of the Institute of Historical Research*, 68, 167, pp. 319–37.

Taylor, M. (2000) 'Republics versus Empires: Charles Dilke's Republicanism Reconsidered', in D.S. Nash and A. Taylor (2000) (eds) *Republicanism in Victorian Society*, pp. 25–34.

Thompson, E.P. (1991) *Customs in Common* (London: Penguin).

Thompson, E.P. (1992) 'Rough Music Reconsidered', *Folklore*, 103, 1, pp. 3–26.

Thompson, W. (1912) *The Life and Times of John Bright* (London: Allen and Unwin).

Tod, T.M. [with additional material by W. Nelson] (1985) *Scottish Crime and Punishment: Scots Black Kalendar – 100 Years of Murder and Execution* (Newtongrange: Lang Syne Publishing).

Todd, M. (2002) *The Culture of Protestantism in Early Modern Scotland* (New Haven, Connecticut and London: Yale University Press).

Tosh, J. (2002) 'Gentlemanly Politeness and Manly Simplicity in Victorian England', *Transactions of the Royal Historical Society*, 12, pp. 455–72.

Trollope, A. (1869) *He Knew He was Right* (London: Strahan and Co.).

Underdown, D.E. (1985) 'The Taming of the Scold: The Enforcement of Patriarchal Authority in Early Modern England', in A. Fletcher and J. Stevenson (eds) *Order and Disorder in Early Modern England* (Cambridge: Cambridge University Press), pp. 116–36.

Valone, L. (2001) *Becoming Victoria* (New Haven, C.T. and London: Yale University Press).

Van Dülmen, R. (1990) *Theatre of Horror: Crime and Punishment in Early Modern Germany* [translated by Elisabeth Neu] (Oxford: Polity Press).

Villa-Vicencio, C. (1999–2000) 'The Reek of Cruelty and the Quest for Healing: Where Retributive and Restorative Justice Meet', *Journal of Law and Religion*, 14, 1 pp. 165–87.

Ward, T. (1999) 'The Sad Subject of Infanticide: Law, Medicine and Child Murder', *Social and Legal Studies*, VIII, pp. 163–80.

Wahrman, D. (1995) *Imagining the Middle Class: The Political Representation of Class in Britain, c. 1780–1840* (Cambridge: Cambridge University Press).

Watt, J.R. (1989) 'The Reception of the Reformation in Valangin, Switzerland, 1547–1588', *Sixteenth Century Journal*, 20, 1, pp. 98–104.

Webster, J. (2009, new edition) *The Duchess of Malfi* (Oxford: Oxford Paperbacks).

Whitman, J.Q. (1998) 'What is Wrong with Inflicting Shame Sanctions?', *The Yale Law Journal*, 107, 4 (1998), pp. 1055–92.

Weiner, J. (1983) *Radicalism and Freethought in Nineteenth-Century Britain, The Life of Richard Carlile* (Santa Barbara: Greenwood Press).

Williams, R. (1997) *The Contentious Crown: Public Discussion of the British Monarchy in the Reign of Queen Victoria* (Aldershot: Ashgate).

Wilson, D. (1863) *Prehistoric Annals of Scotland* (London and Cambridge: Macmillan and Co.).

Wilson, D. (1851) *The Archaeology and Prehistoric Annals of Scotland* (Edinburgh: Sutherland and Knox).

Worden, B. (2001) *Roundhead Reputations: The English Civil Wars and the Passions of Posterity* (London: Allen Lane).

Worden, B. (2000) 'The Victorians and Oliver Cromwell', in S. Collini, R. Whatmore and B. Young (eds) *History, Religion and Culture: British Intellectual History 1750–1950* (Cambridge: Cambridge University Press), pp. 112–35.

Wrightson, K. (1975) 'Infanticide in Earlier Seventeenth-Century England', *Local Population Studies*, XV, pp. 10–22.

Wrightson, K. (1982) 'Infanticide in European History', *Criminal Justice History*, III, pp. 1–20.

Zemon Davis, N. (1971) 'The Reasons of Misrule: Youth Groups and Charivaris in Sixteenth-Century France', *Past and Present*, 50, pp. 41–75.

Unpublished Dissertations

Kilday, A-M. (1998) 'Women and Crime in South-west Scotland: A Study of the Justiciary Records, 1750–1815' (Unpublished PhD thesis, University of Strathclyde).

Web-Sites

http://www.britsh-history.ac.uk
http://mh.cla.umn.edu/catnach.html
http://www.oldbaileyonline.org

Index